CRITICAL ANALYSIS OF ANAÏS NIN IN JAPAN

CRITICAL ANALYSIS OF ANAÏS NIN IN JAPAN

Edited by Paul Herron

A special edition of
A Café in Space: The Anaïs Nin Literary Journal

Sky Blue Press

State College, PA

COPYRIGHT INFORMATION

Library of Congress Cataloging-in-Publication Data

Names: Herron, Paul (Paul S.) editor.
Title: Critical analysis of Anaïs Nin in Japan / edited by Paul Herron.
Description: State College, PA : Sky Blue Press, 2023. | "A special edition
  of A Café in Space: The Anaïs Nin Literary Journal" --T.p. | Includes
  bibliographical references. | Summary: "Since 1966 when Anais Nin
  visited Japan after the US publication of her Diary, Japanese scholars
  have been studying, translating and publishing her work. Little known
  abroad, Japanese Nin studies have been one of the most astute and
  consistent in the world. This English-language collection features works
  by Japanese scholars, writers and translators over the past several
  decades up to the present time and offers the reader a unique view of
  Anais Nin, the writer and the person. Seventeen essays, with
  illustrations, make for an important addition to global Nin studies"--
  Provided by publisher.
Identifiers: LCCN 2023006407 (print) | LCCN 2023006408 (ebook) | ISBN
  9798985524031 (paperback) | ISBN 9798985524048 (Kindle edition)
Subjects: LCSH: Nin, Anaïs, 1903-1977--Criticism and interpretation. |
  Nin, Anaïs, 1903-1977--Translations into Japanese--History and
  criticism. | Criticism--Japan. | American literature--Women
  authors--History and criticism. | American literature--20th
  century--History and criticism.
Classification: LCC PS3527.I865 Z593 2023 (print) | LCC PS3527.I865
  (ebook) | DDC 818/.5209--dc23/eng/20230411
LC record available at https://lccn.loc.gov/2023006407
LC ebook record available at https://lccn.loc.gov/2023006408

INTRODUCTION

Reception of Anaïs Nin in Japan

I t was probably when Henry Miller's *Tropic of Cancer* was translated into Japanese in 1953 that Japanese readers discovered the name of Anaïs Nin in its Preface. *Black Spring*, which was also translated into Japanese the same year, is dedicated to Anaïs Nin. In short, she was introduced to Japanese readers as an intermediary with and a close friend of Henry Miller, one of the representative writers of twentieth-century America, yet she herself was an enigma, like a woman with a veil over her face. (Brassaï, a mutual friend of Nin's and Miller's, took a photograph of her exactly in that manner.) There are two points of notice here. First, Nin not only wrote a strong preface to *Tropic of Cancer* but also to the biography of Lou Andreas Salomé and the autobiography of Judy Chicago, *Through the Flower*. That is, Nin served as a medium, midwife, and communicator for art and artists. Second, Nin has been recognized as a woman standing beside "a big man," such as Miller, Artaud, and Rank, even in the twenty-first century, which poses a significant problem.

As an author, Anaïs Nin stripped herself of the veil in 1966 when *A Spy in the House of Love* was translated into Japanese by Koji Nakata as a volume in the "Human Literature" series, which collects experimental foreign literature by Kawade Shobo Publishing. This coincided with the publication of *The Diary of Anaïs Nin* in America, and world recognition of her as a writer. In the translator's note titled "On Anaïs Nin," Nakata defines her *Diary* as part of her "I-novel," a Japanese counterpart of auto-fiction with a long-established tradition. He also describes Nin's relationship with her father as "narcissism with libidinal quality," an insight equal to that of readers of the unexpurgated series. Nin, on the publication of her novel in Japan, was invited to the country and had a chance to talk with critic Jun Eto and novelist Kenzaburō Ōe for a literary magazine. However, what captured her heart more than a tête-à-tête with the future Nobel Prize winner was the delicate respect of the Japanese people. Nin writes in her *Diary*, volume 7: "In Japan I had a weeping fit. The sweetness, kindness, consideration touched me. For once in my life I felt I was treated as I always treated people" (11).

The first volume of *The Diary of Anaïs Nin* was published in Japan in 1974, with Masako Meio (née Hara) as translator, and the reception of Nin, supposedly the greatest diarist of the twentieth century, entered a new phase in Japan. The translator was in her mid-thirties, roughly the same age as the *Diary*'s protagonist. She was striving to give her ego and talent shape and also struggling with the female gender precisely in the same manner as the diarist was, as a human, woman, and writer. That is why her translation, in addition to its fine literary quality, embraced a certain poignancy with intelligently and emotionally deep sympathy for the author. Meio, who wrote an essay entitled "Anaïs Nin's Daughters," was without a doubt Nin's eldest "daughter" in Japan. Her dream of translating and publishing Nin's seven (edited) *Diaries* did not come to fruition, but, in 2017, more than forty years after the publication of Meio's translation and on the fortieth anniversary of Nin's death, excerpts from the *Early Diaries* (volumes 2-4) and the edited *Diaries* (7 vols.) were published with my translation.

As mentioned earlier, Nin has been considered to be "a woman standing beside a man," and her definition of herself as "a man's woman" has been controversial and misleading. However, even before the gender/sexuality critique in the 1990s, which shed light on overlooked issues including woman-to-woman relationships, clear-sighted people acknowledged that her relationships with women such as June Miller and her own mother must have played an equally important role for Nin as her relationships with men. Meio's aforementioned essay is one example; Hidekatsu Nojima, in *The Women of the Labyrinth* (1981), in which he discusses femme fatales in English and American literature extensively, devotes chapters to Anaïs Nin and June Miller, respectively; Jungian psychoanalyst Satoko Akiyama also pays attention to the two women in *Meta-Sexuality* (1985), a volume in "The Weekly Book" series. (The Weekly Book was a paperback series written by popular writers of the day, aiming to be something between a magazine and a book). Reading guidebooks for young people was also popular at that time. Postmodern philosopher Akira Asada selects *The Diary of Anaïs Nin* in *The Pleasure of Reading—Best 100 Books* (1985); scholar/translator Motoyuki Shibata, who once called himself "a shadow of Haruki Murakami" (he serves as a proofreader when Murakami translates American literature into Japanese), addresses *Henry and June* in *The Pleasure of Love Stories—Best 600* (1990). Nin may have found a niche in the hemline of the intellectual world of 1980s Japan, an era called New Academism.

Henry and June, the first volume of the Unexpurgated Diary, was published in the U. S. in 1986 and marked a major turning point for Nin reception. Philip Kaufman's film adaptation had a great impact on the field of popular culture. Kazuko Sugisaki, close to Nin both officially and privately and a trustee of the Anaïs Nin Trust, translated it into Japanese in 1990, and it became a bestseller. Nin once wrote, "I enjoy carrying this diary like dynamite" (*Fire* 394), and "My evil will be posthumous" (*Incest* 203).

The Unexpurgated Diary of Anaïs Nin must have seemed like dynamite that she flung at us from the other world. First of all, this iconoclastic book destroyed the icon named Anaïs Nin. Some frowned at the new face of Nin emerging from the smashed persona, feeling betrayed. Others—new and young readers—took interest in her, which was a global phenomenon. Along with the publication of the Unexpurgated Diary, in regard to Nin's reception in Japan, we should refer to the fact that Sumiko Yagawa, as if taking over Meio's work, began introducing Nin energetically. It is significant that Yagawa, widely known as a writer of fantastic literature and a translator of English, French, and German, published two books on Nin—*Father's Daughters: Mari Mori and Anaïs Nin* (1997) and *Anaïs Nin as a Young Girl* (2002)—as well as a posthumous publication of her translation of Nin's erotica, *Little Birds* (2003). If, for Meio, one of the keywords for reading Nin was "maturity," another for Yagawa was "girl." Yagawa, who called herself "immortal girl" and "anti-girl," translated a small portion of *Linotte* in *Anaïs Nin as a Young Girl*. (Excerpts from *Linotte* were later published with Sugisaki's translation [2014].)

Apart from being a diarist, Anaïs Nin was a novelist, an essayist, and a critic. To understand Nin as a whole, *The Anaïs Nin Collection* (6 vols, 1993-97), translated by Junko Kimura (with the exception of one volume by Toyoko Yamamoto), played a major role among the Japanese readership; it spans from Nin's first book, *D. H. Lawrence: An Unprofessional Study* and her first book of fiction, *House of Incest*, to her last book of fiction, *Collages*, and a collection of essays related to gender issues, *In Favor of the Sensitive Man*. Three works in the continuous novel *Cities of the Interior*, a missing link in *The Anaïs Nin Collection*, have recently been translated: *Seduction of the Minotaur* by Asako Ono (2010), *Children of the Albatross* by Toyoko Yamamoto (2017), and *Ladders to Fire* by Atsuko Miyake (2019).

The second volume of the Unexpurgated Diary, *Incest,* was translated by Sugisaki and resonated with Japanese readers (2008). It coincided with the publication of *My Man* by Kazuki Sakuraba, depicting a sexual relationship between a daughter and a father-in-law, which received the prominent Naoki Award. Even more iconoclastic than *Henry and June*, however, *Incest* has not been critically discussed enough in Japan or elsewhere. There is a possibility that the Japanese, not restricted by the Christian taboo consciousness, could stand in the Anaïs Nin vanguard with respect to sexuality. (Shigeru Kashima, a renowned critic of French literature, points out in the review of *The Diary of Anaïs Nin* [my translation] that as a written record of sexuality penned by a female author, nothing so far has come close to Nin's Unexpurgated Diary.)

The Anaïs Nin Study Group, founded by Sugisaki in 2011 and succeeded by Yamamoto, published *Anaïs Nin: A Guidebook* (2018), the first critical guidebook on Nin in Japan. A collection of essays on Nin, written by the members of the Study Group, will follow suit. I am planning to publish a monograph on Nin, also the first in Japan, this year, which I hope to translate into English. With this special issue of *A Café in Space* as a marvelous gift, we will celebrate the one hundred and twentieth anniversary of Anaïs Nin's birth in a new dimension in Japan.

—*Yuko Yaguchi, Niigata University*

TABLE OF CONTENTS

Rupert Pole and Anaïs Nin, Tokyo, Japan, 1966

The women of Japan are at once the most present and the most elusive inhabitant of any country I have seen. They are everywhere, in restaurants, streets, shops, museums, subways, trains, fields, hotels and inns, and yet achieve a self-effacement that is striking to foreign women. In the hotels and inns they are solicitous, thoughtful, helpful to a degree never dreamed of except by men, but this care and tender lavishness is equally given to women visitors. It was as if one's dream of an ever-attentive, ever-protective mother were fulfilled on a collective scale, only the mother is forever young and daintily dressed. They were laborious and yet quiet, efficient and yet not intrusive or cumbersome.

—*Anaïs Nin, 1966, from "A Joyous Transformation"*

Catherine Vreeland (Broderick)

Anaïs Nin's *Diary* and the Japanese Literary Diary Tradition

One of the oldest, most fertile and revealing literary traditions against which to measure the nature and extent of Anaïs Nin's achievement as a diarist is that of the Japanese. Nin, who long felt a close affinity with Japanese literature, was delighted to be translated into this language and formed a close relationship with Masako Hara-Karatani, her foremost translator and critic in Japan.[1] Nin's reception in Japan,[2] however, has been very different from the enthusiasm with which her *Diary* was greeted in America, and an analysis of the reasons for this difference goes far to illuminate the originality of her contribution to American literature as well as the respective orientations of the two cultures.

To briefly survey first the history and development of the Japanese diary tradition, the diary originated as a documentary written by men of noble birth to record their official and ceremonial life at Court, and was passed on from father to son as an education about Court life. These formal records served as texts, in a sense, and were preserved as a monument to the success of a particular family.[3]

Japanese literary diaries, however, began with the *Tosa Diary* (936), a "travel diary" written by a man, Ki no Tsurayuki. Tsurayuki departed from the traditional journal-documents of court nobles in two pioneering ways: first he explored and expressed personal experience and included poems in his diary; second, he abandoned the "masculine" Chinese ideograph deemed too rigid for such personal expression and used instead the "feminine" Japanese cursive syllabary, *hiragana*.[4] Considering both of these innovations as unmanly, however, he adopted the persona of a woman: "Diaries are things written by men, I am told. Nevertheless I am writing one, to see what a woman can do."[5]

The genre was quickly exploited by the gifted women of the Heian period (794-1186), women from the aristocratic and semi-aristocratic classes who found themselves in a unique socio-political as well as literary situation. Wealthy, leisured, and well-educated, the Heian woman was also independent. Having left parental authority as women of marriageable age, they lived in service at Court, often as tutors to daughters of the Emperor and the nobles closest to him, or as wife or mistress to noblemen who did not live with them but only visited at will. In this halfway state of relative freedom yet virtual imprisonment with ladies-in-waiting and attendants in her apartments, the Heian woman blossomed within herself and took seriously her ultimate responsibility for herself as well as for the prosperity of her family. A fall from favor with a man, or men, she rarely saw could bring ruin upon her family, and her simultaneous preoccupation with and separation from the world of men led her to cultivate her inner strength which appeared as a refined emotionalism in her writing.

The Heian woman of letters was also the product of a rich and sophisticated poetic tradition, and she had long been respected as a poet. The irony of literary respect and social ambivalence was that this dual system freed women from conformity to the Chinese classics and language which were inflexible models for men writers. Women could reveal their learning and skill in the popular custom of writing poems in the Chinese tradition, but they could link these poems with prose written in Japanese in their diaries. Having "a room of their own, and money," as Virginia Woolf would say, along with this literary freedom led to their creation of the original genre of the feminine literary diary.

The earliest of the Heian women's diaries was *The Gossamer Years* (954-74), written by a woman known only as the mother of Michitsuna. Composed toward the end of her life, it is a sort of memoir which marks the pivotal antithesis to the poetic tradition from which it emerged. Melancholy, bitter, intensely personal, this diary is, however, clearly a literary creation rather than mere recording: "Early the next morning he left. He had work to do, he said, but he would come again in a day or two. I did not really believe him. Still I thought he might have had a change of heart— and then in the back of my mind was always a fear that he might not come again."[6]

The Gossamer Years was followed by *The Pillow Book of Sei Shonagon* (1002), perhaps the most down-to-earth of these diaries. A typical entry, for example, reads: "A preacher ought to be good-looking. For, if we are properly to understand his worthy sentiments, we must keep our eyes on him while he speaks; should we look away, we may forget to listen. Accordingly, an ugly preacher may well be the source of sin..."[7] Possibly the most "fictional" of the Heian diaries is that by Izumi Shikibu (1003-04); her *Diary* is the saga of an unhappy love affair, and is typical of the Heian diary in its inclusion of short poems:

But there was none to know of my despondency. Even the grass grew pale before my eyes, and though the winter rains should still be far off, it bent in seeming pain before the wind. As I looked upon this scene I compared myself, apt to vanish at any moment like the dew, to the frail leaves of grass, and in my sadness simply lay down near the veranda without making the effort to go into the inner room. But I was quite unable to sleep, though everyone else lay in a profound slumber. There was no specific reason for my wakefulness; still I lay there through the listless hours, completely unable to drop off and utterly out of sorts. And then there came the faint cry of a wild goose. Others may not be much affected by such things, but I was moved almost beyond my power to endure:

> Untouched by drowsiness,
> How many are the nights, alas,
> That I have lain,
> Nothing for me to do but hear
> The calling of wild geese?[8]

Other significant examples from the Heian period are the brilliant literary *Diary* (1007-10) by Murasaki Shikibu,[9] the author of the *Tale of Genji,* and Lady Sarashina's *Diary,* the only Heian diary to cover an entire life, written as a memoir preceding the author's death in ?1059.[10] Less well known are diaries from the Kamakura period (1195-1392), notably Lady Nijo's *Diary* which adheres closely to Heian models.[11]

When the social system in Japan changed in the Muromachi period (1392-1568) and the feudal or samurai society began, women were taken into their husbands' homes upon marriage, and this stabilizing of their position in society together with the concomitant loss of personal freedom and leisure hours caused the flowering of the literary diary genre to wither. Diaries have continued, as always, to occupy a place in Japanese life and writing, of course, but the subject matter and style have never again reached the heights of Heian achievement. Indeed, the feminine diary in Japan gradually degenerated into amateurish writing, characterized by sensationalism and bathos—thereby becoming immensely popular in today's marketplace, particularly if the author had committed suicide at a tender age, as in the case of Nobuko Nagasawa and Etsuko Takano.[12]

Only two diaries of literary value have been written by Japanese woman in modern times. The first is the Meija era diary of Ichiyo Higuchi (1872-96), whom M. H. Shima describes as "Japan's first professional woman writer"[13]; in entries such as the following she seems to reflect her self-consciousness in the face of the situation: "I should be ashamed of myself. To think of supporting my family by writing novels which is a very difficult subject even in literature, when I know perfectly well that I do not have much learning or education. Should I call it boldness or recklessness. Nobody knows it, but just to think of it makes me wet with sweat when I awaken during the night."[14] The other work of quality is the diary of Itsue Takamure (1894-1964), also author of a monumental history of Japanese women; her diary begins with the following explanation: "I was welcomed when I was born into this world. And there was an interesting story about my birth. However, before I am going to tell that story, I think it necessary to talk about my roots, that means about my ancestors and the marriage of my parents."[15]

It is, however, the *shi-shosetsu,* the extremely personal "I-novel" of Japan, which is the real descendant of the Heian diaries, and it is in such autobiographical fiction that the modern Japanese woman writer expresses herself most often.[16]

In the West, the socio-political as well as the literary history of women has been quite the opposite of that of the Orient. Long the chattels of the men they married, women have only recently begun psychologically to leave their so-called security and to venture forth to live and write on their own as Japanese women lived and wrote a thousand years ago. Exploring her new independence, the American woman has responded as her Japanese sisters did, by writing diaries. The difference is that as American women have sought more and more self-determination, the search for personal and sexual identity[17] has become central for them in a way it has never been for Japanese women. This intense search for the true self and for a means of self-expression has found many voices in the recent flowering of intimate literary forms in America, and Nin's *Diary* is among them "the most extraordinary contemporary document about the human psyche and the birth of a personality."[18]

If the search for a personal and sexual identity is relatively alien to the Japanese female writer, however, the revelation of personal experience—the diary mode—together with a concomitant recognition of the validity of inner or psychological experience has long been a natural and integral part of the Japanese literary and cultural tradition —as it has not been for Americans. As a still young country, America has typically produced writers whose primary concern was to record the "Americanness" of experience; only secondarily, or only very recently, has the intimate revelation of personal and psychological experience become acceptable in the mainstream of American literature. This sort of split, between the expression of a "native" or nationalistic consciousness and the expression of psychological experience, is not found in Japanese literature.

Hence the peculiar, ironic—and to her, painful—nature of Nin's reception in these two countries. In the initial stages of her career, the literary qualities which she embodied were foreign to American literary standards, and consequently she was denied recognition; what Americans today regard and champion as the new and revolutionary nature of her literary expression, the Japanese, as old practitioners, find singularly unimpressive. What is, for Americans, the explosive impact of the assertion of the validity of inner psychological experience in Nin's writing is but a natural and commonplace mode of expression in Japanese literature. Japanese literary readers (a group distinct from ordinary or "non-literary" readers, a distinction Americans do not make) do not become enthused about the content of personal revelation or psychological probing; they are rather eager for fresh style, perfected literary form, and beautiful use of language. What the success of Nin's *Diary* represented in terms of a cachet of acceptability for the expression of the personal and the psychological in American literature is simply of no great moment in the Japanese literary climate.

Furthermore, to write out of the self and at the same time to write in search of the self, as Kate Chopin attempted and Anaïs Nin succeeded in making artistically valid in American literature, is a concept foreign to the Japanese. At the heart of the Japanese literary impulse is the question of what life is and how to integrate personal experience into the whole of common existence and experience—quite the opposite from the Western search for personal, individual selfhood. The question "Who am I?" was unthinkable for the Heian woman; she knew who she was and accepted all the limits and hopelessness her knowledge implied. Her diary looked back, attempted to understand the bitterness of her memories, tried to find the points of integration into common experience. Nin's *Diary* looks ever forward, shows the struggles for an integration of the self, questions, rebels, progresses.

Another factor which may be involved in the differing reactions of the Americans and Japanese to Nin's *Diary* has to do with the respective attitudes of the two cultures toward the nature and degree of "truthfulness" to be found in autobiographical works. As Nin herself describes her journal, "The diary is like life itself—*une oeuvre inachevée,* ever incomplete. Sometimes I would like to live long enough to terminate it in every detail, make of it a Proustian work. But to follow the life line is always of greater concern to me than the perfection of detail. I put enough perfection in the novels" (*Diary V* 219). Masako Hara-Karatani calls this the "naïve concept of immediacy in diary and autobiography," with "naïve" meaning the opposite of "sophisticated" in a literary sense. That is, as she has explained to me, Japanese literary people have long since abandoned the concept that the diary or autobiography tells the truth. These are not literary forms in themselves and thus cannot express the self or true feeling. Since they appear through the medium of language it is naïve to say they are immediate. The Japanese are more sophisticated in that they recognize these facts and thus use strict literary forms such as the *shi-shosetsu* (I-novel) rather than naïve direct expression in a simple diary.[19]

This rationale also explains the use, in the title of my study, of the term "Literary Diary." The Japanese make a distinction between *jun-bungaku* (pure literature) and *tai-shu-bungaku* (popular literature). The concept of "pure literature" is derived from the *Nikki Bungaku* (diary literature of the Heian Period) and the term is used nowadays to talk about the *shi-shosetsu* (I-novel) or private novel. The Nagasawa or Takano diaries, in contrast, are regarded as mere "popular literature." Ken Akiyama apparently systematized what the Japanese have taken for granted from the first—i.e., that the Heian diaries are not diaries in our, Western, sense of the word, but rather are works of literature, "pure literature" at that.[20]

Anaïs Nin is far too rooted in the actual and immediate to appear to the Japanese reader as "pure literature"—of course she is not "popular literature" either, which presents a problem of labeling her for the Japanese. Her method of writing at café tables, en route, always at the moment, is not "literary" for the Japanese. They demand a formal principle in the literary diary and a strict attention to the use of language. There is neither in the Western diary, they think.

More important, however, than the differing attitudes on the part of the Japanese and Americans toward the nature of autobiography and diary are the underlying cultural/philosophical premises which such literary conventions reflect, and it is in emphasizing this organic relationship between the artist's ethos and his mode of expression, in the context of the difference between masculine and feminine expression, that Nin makes an important contribution to American literature at the same time that she indirectly helps to explain the nature of her reception in Japan, and possibly the difficulties of Americans in understanding it.

As Joanna Russ has observed, in America "Culture is male,"[21] and the Western idea of creativity has long been founded on an essentially male concept of the inorganic nature of the relationship between the artist and his creation. Accordingly, until very recently, literature written by women was treated as if it had been written by men; the same things expected of a male artist—specifically, the distance from his creation—were expected of the female artist. What is now beginning to be recognized, as a result of deliberate attempts to separate literature written by women in order to study it independently of the culturally induced terms of male creation, is that when a woman writes as a woman—that is, out of the fullness of her own sexual identity—she writes organically: there is a direct relationship between her voice and the voice expressed in her work. This does not mean, however, that we must radically revise the concept of the difference between the author and the characters or speakers which appear in the fiction, drama, or poetry by that author; as much as Nin, for example, emphasized the organic nature of her writing, so much did she also insist upon the absolute separation of her voice and the voices in her fiction. The issue that is at hand here is the nature of artistic creativity, and the point is that male culture, male experience of the world, promoted a false notion of the tie between the artist and his or her work—false for both men and women—which studies of women's writing together with the work of women writers such as Anaïs Nin have gone far to correct. There is an organic tie between any writer, male or female, and his or her writing, just as—to return to our initial point—there is an organic tie between an artist's ethos and his art. For a Westerner to achieve a formal about-face in line with Japanese writing would be much more than a matter of the appropriate literary conventions.

Another major contribution made by women's writing in America, and in particular by Nin's work, is an understanding of the relationship between respective modes of literary expression and what we might, in these days of women's studies, call the dichotomy of masculine and feminine conflict. Conflict seen as a person's clash with the outside world, between a person and his honor, his obligation to society, his oppression by others, for example, and the active or attempted resolution thereof can be called masculine conflict. This masculine conflict is most dramatically illustrated by the samurai in Japanese history and literature, but women also experience masculine conflict—witness the *Joshi-do,* for example, which was the feminine counterpart to the *Bushi-do,* The Way of the Samurai.

Feminine conflict, on the other hand, is interior; it is the struggle between one's many selves and their incompatible needs, desires, and demands. In feminine conflict a person must do his or her best vis-à-vis each and every one of the conflicting selves. The *context* of Japanese women's diaries may well be the struggle in a comfortless and demanding world, but the *expression,* as Tsurayuki's decision to masquerade as a woman demonstrated, is that of feminine conflict. Masculine conflict touches us more immediately, but feminine conflict, being more psychologically complex, remains with us in all its significance much longer. Certainly Nin's pioneering novel, *A Spy in the House of Love,* or the short story, "Under a Glass Bell," to take only two examples, found acceptance difficult at first because they did not fit the category determined by this phenomenon of the dominance of masculine conflict in American literature.

In a sense, Japanese literature has reflected the same dual conflict value system, although the experience of inner, psychological "feminine" conflict has always been acceptable for men or women as it has not been in America. The more rigid Japanese social structure, did, of course, result in a predominance of expression of masculine conflict, and the need to express the experience of feminine conflict may be another reason for the flowering of the literary diary genre in Heian Japan and its descendent, the I-novel in modern Japan. Certainly Nin's case in America shows that feminine conflict is more acceptable in the "feminine" genre of the diary, the intimate work, than in the traditionally male-defined novel.

The Japanese literary diary, however, treats feminine conflict in a descriptive manner. Perceptions, feelings, and emotions are presented objectively, as reflections of struggles with the outside world rather than as expressions of inner turmoil to be explored as such. The Heian woman always connected her feeling with something in nature, and the actual description of a natural phenomenon was a sort of metaphor for her feelings as well as being the thing which brought those feelings to the surface for expression. Thus Murasaki Shikibu writes of "snow" in her diary: "I longed for snow while we were staying there, but just then I had to go home to my parents. Two days after retiring from Court a great snow came. The old familiar trees of my home reminded me of those melancholy years when I used to gaze upon them musing when the colors of flowers, the voices of birds, the skies of spring and autumn, moon shadows, frost and snow, told me nothing but that time was revolving, and that I was menaced with a dreary future."[22] The expression of conflict is of the same order as a description of nature —a declaration of something one takes for granted in life—no resolution, no hope for change, no rebellion; she describes her conflict with an attitude of acceptance, and stops with that. The Japanese diarist perishes in her experience, much as Kate Chopin's "Edna Pontellier" drowns in hers.

The Japanese diary is not a touchstone for the self nor is it a record of the search for individual wholeness. It is a gathering of fragments, and at the same time it is a way of letting go of one's life, and so there is the remarkable absence of the flow we find in Nin's *Diary*. Perhaps this is partly because of the difference in the concept of change in the Orient and the West. The Japanese does not feel threatened by what Westerners call change, fragmentation, the unfinished business of life. The cyclical nature of his experience of the universe posits wholeness beyond his fragmented life. For Westerners, on the other hand, change is ominous for its connotation of deterioration, and we are therefore obsessed with making sense, unity, and whole meaning out of the fragments of change which make up one individual life. Thus Nin's *Diary*, with its personal revelation of inner dreams, fears, desires, with its frank explorations of feelings about fragmentary experience, with its flow towards the hoped-for wholeness of self is entirely alien to the concern of the Japanese diary.

Another difference is highlighted by Nin's comment in Volume I of her *Diary*: "I think I have an immediate awareness in living which is far more terrible and more painful... What is remembered later does not seem as true to me. I have such need of truth! It must be that need of immediate recording which incites me to write almost while I am living, before it is altered, changed by distance or time" (*Diary I* 65). Japanese literary diaries, on the contrary, were written as recollections of memories. The mother of Michitsuna opens her diary, *The Gossamer Years,* in the following retrospective way:

> These times have passed, and there was one who drifted uncertainly through them, scarcely knowing where she was. It was perhaps natural that such should be her fate. She was less handsome than most, and not remarkably gifted. Yet, as the days went by in monotonous succession, she had occasion to look at the old romances, and found them masses of the rankest fabrication. Perhaps, she said to herself, even the story of her own dreary life, set down in a journal, might be of interest; and it might also answer a question: had that life been one befitting a well-born lady? But they must all be recounted, events of long ago, events of but yesterday. She was by no means certain that she could bring them to order.[23]

This seems to be the same motivation for the twentieth-century diary of Itsue Takamure. During the year before she died in 1964, knowing she was mortally ill, she completed the composition of her diary as a memoir from the ages of ten to forty-seven, having used her father's diary to record her life up to the age of ten. Her husband completed the diary, recounting her life from the ages of forty-eight to seventy, after his wife's death. This attitude to the diary as an "officially private" document is quite different from Nin's concept of the diary as an intimate and personal search. Nin's *Diary* is thus hard for the Japanese to read because the reader is allowed to see her front the "inside out," and also because the Japanese do not have this same concept of "self."

A final way of illustrating the difference between Nin's work and that of the Japanese is, paradoxically, to examine what look like similarities. "One thing is very clear," Nin wrote in *The Novel of the Future*, "—that both diary and fiction tended towards the same goal: intimacy with people, with experience, with life itself (155). In this respect, though with a significant difference, Nin would seem to have some affinities with Murasaki Shikibu. Nin enriched her life through relationships with many people, whereas, as a widow, Shikibu lived a very isolated life. But in her creation of *The Tale of Genji*, Shikibu peopled her inner world with friends and acquaintances who replaced those she could not know in actual life. Similarly, though the artistry of her novel secured for Lady Murasaki a position at Court, she felt out of place and lonely; but she confronts herself in her *Diary,* and though she does so in the framework of a fragmented recitation of the rituals and daily life at Court, as a woman as well as an artist she was able to express her feelings about these things in her writing. Most to the point of her resemblance to Nin, however, is the "immediate" character of her writing:

> Having no excellence within myself, I have passed my days without making any special impression on any one. Especially the fact that I have no man who will look out for my future makes me comfortless. I do not wish to bury myself in dreariness. Is it because of my worldly mind that I feel lonely? On moonlight nights in autumn, when I am hopelessly sad, I often go out on the balcony and gaze dreamily at the moon. It makes me think of days gone by. People say that it is dangerous to look at the moon in solitude, but something impels me, and sitting a little withdrawn I muse there. In the wind-cooled evening I play on the koto, though others may not care to hear it. I fear that my playing betrays the sorrow which becomes more intense, and I become disgusted with myself—so foolish and miserable am I.[24]

Ken Akiyama is of the opinion that what Murasaki Shikibu wrote in her *Diary* came to her *while* she wrote, and that her sentences have the power to express her inner world, her inner psychology.[25] In the immediate act of writing she could realize what she thought and felt.

This possible exception aside, however, Japanese women's diaries, in contrast to Nin's, are melancholy and dark, with greater or lesser rations of bitterness, loneliness, and despair. The exploration of relationships is absent, as is the desire to discover and define the self. The Heian women diarists were trying to see what life was, particularly under the influence of the Buddhist concept of mutability. They were sophisticated and highly philosophical women who transferred the notion of mutability into the aesthetic realm and refined it in the literary expression of their dilemma between present thinking versus final reality. This was not an ongoing search, however, but the result of a realization of the impossibility of ever finally resolving the dilemma. Nin was doing something entirely different in her *Diary:* "The diary, then, was where I checked my realities and illusions, made my experiments, noted progress or its opposite. It was the laboratory! I could venture into the novel with a sense of psychological authenticity and fictionalize only externals, situations, places" (*Novel* 157). Both the purpose and the very concept of a diary, then, were quite different for the Japanese women diarists of old than they were for Nin.

Nor does the case appear to be very different if we compare Nin's work with that of a more modern Japanese woman diarist, Ichiyo Higuchi (1872-96), who upon first the impoverishment and later the death of her father (and brother) attempted to support her family by writing. Her objectivity in fiction and her silent, introverted personality in the world were both belied in her short diary which she kept from the age of twenty until her death of tuberculosis. Perhaps begun to practice composition and penmanship, as she began to write more and more short stories, her diary became deeper and showed more of her inner life: "In an old saying, they say that not to say what you think irritates the stomach. So, I will write whatever I feel, either happy or sad. However, since this is not a thing for other people to see, the words will not be so beautiful."[26] If intimate and honest, however, her *Diary* never was a laboratory like Nin's was.

One similarity between Higuchi's diary and both those of Nin and the Heian diarists is the concept of the diary as a cage for what Nin called one's "demons." Japanese women diarists have always used their diaries for this purpose of taming the demons of "anger, jealousy, envy, revengefulness, vanity" by locking them "up in a diary" (*Diary III* 164). Conversely, Higuchi's diary like Nin's was also a source of consolation and later a private forum for her to deal with the misunderstanding of her writing because it was not in the fashion of the times:

This time a love suicide; the elegancy of a poet; too many tears don't please the readers; delicate writing is not fashionable now; the public does not understand mysteriousness; something with history in it would not be good; a title with politics in it would be good; detective stories are exceptionally good... To be asked to write within these barriers by unselfish bookkeepers is a thing I have not experienced too much, but I will put a stop to these annoyances now. I would like to be outside of these limits and at least, in the literary world, to be a free mind.[27]

Although Nin's *Diary* shows the longer wait for acceptance—Higuchi was soon recognized as a major talent and hailed as a modern Murasaki Shikibu—both women thus used their diaries to mull their relationship with literary criticism and the critics themselves. In Higuchi's case, the diary was the place in which she tried to stabilize herself so that she would not fall into the easy trap of facile praise. We cannot know how much she really said, however, as her diary was subsequently edited by the literary men mentioned in it, who surely deleted anything which did not show them in the best possible light. But while, therefore, the affinity between the *Diary* of the young Anaïs and that of Ichiyo Higuchi is certainly far greater than that between Nin's *Diary* and the literary diaries of the Heian period, even this similarity is slight.

While indicating that the purpose and achievement of Nin's *Diary* and the diaries of Japanese women are fundamentally different, making Nin's *Diary* difficult for Japanese to appreciate fully, it has certainly not been my purpose to suggest that Japanese women's diaries are in any way inferior to Western ones. It is as much a matter of cultural values as anything else—"fragmented" connotes a defect to Westerners, for example, which it does not to Japanese; in the same way the search for "self" on Nin's part is not *rejected* by the Japanese, it simply does not have the same meaning. In a culture like that of the Japanese, where assimilation—to society, to nature, to one's ancestors and future generations—is the norm, awareness or understanding of an individual self is not an obsession. The Westerner goes inward, searching, exploring, examining a self; the Japanese reveals what he is inside himself as it is, without glosses. The Western concern seems romantic, if not immature, to the literary-minded Japanese. The "thereness" of a moment as a moment in its final reality for the Japanese is as much a value as the search for meaning or for self for the American. The Western wish to fill a diary, a mind, a life, is far from the Japanese concern with how much can be left out, can be let go, while retaining the essence. And this minimum which is to be expressed must be presented in appropriate form and literary language; the diary as form, as a sort of personal, psychological prose poem, is perhaps more important than its actual content. To the Japanese, the range of human emotion and human insight is to be expressed sparely and for itself, not for the author's self. The Westerner admires this but cannot imitate it.

Thus, despite the fact that Nin's *Diary* can be placed into the broad category the Japanese call diary literature, as Tristine Rainer does when she says that "like the great Japanese poetic diaries of the tenth and eleventh centuries, [Nin's journals] go far beyond the mere recording of daily events, and like those diaries of the Heian court ladies, they transcend the artificial Western categories of fact and fiction, life and art, in order to discover the power of truth combined with the poetry of fiction,"[28] there is really very little basis for comparison between Nin's *Diary* and the Heian women's diaries, or between Nin and the modern Japanese *shi-shosetsu* (I-novel) writers. The radical differences between them, however, serve to illuminate the achievement of each. The diary form, after all, is the most intimate in literature, and it is by speaking each in her own way that both the Japanese and the Western woman writer enrich our experience and prove significant.

Notes

[1] See Catherine Broderick and Masako Karatani, "The Reception of Anaïs Nin in Japan," *Under the Sign of Pisces*, 5 (*Winter*, 1974), 5-11 for translations of Anaïs Nin into Japanese in 1973. Subsequent publications in Japan are: *Anaïs Nin no Nikki*, Volume I, 1931-1934, trans. Masako Hara (Tokyo, 1974); *Under a Glass Bell & Other Stories*, ed. with notes in Japanese by Catherine Broderick and Masako Karatani (Tokyo, 1975); *Collages*, ed. with notes in Japanese by Kaoru Tan and Kazuko Sugisaki (Tokyo, 1977).

[2] Nin is known generally in Japan as a mysterious "shadow" who wrote the "Preface" to Miller's *Tropic of Cancer* and influenced him together with other male writers; her literary theories, as expressed in *The Novel of the Future*, have been criticized as being "obsolete." In a memorial article, Kenzaburo Ohashi of Tokyo University stressed the universality of her "search for the very root of being" in her *Diary*, while Koji Nakata, whose translation of *A Spy in the House of Love* was published in an Erotic Literature Series, tended to mystify her work and observed that her "novels (they are almost like poetry) assume an aspect of a sort of holy stigma" (see "Anaïs Nin," *Eureka*, 9 [April, 1977], 238). As a representative of female response to Nin's work, Karatani's reaction is ambivalent: though skeptical about the literary value of Nin's theories, she has consistently emphasized the psychological and feminine aspects of her work;

similarly though she sees Nin as one of those Lolitas who chooses to remain a daughter forever, she has tried to evaluate her as a woman who has added a new "feminine" quality to American literature at the same time that her work also reflects peculiarly American traits. See her "Anaïs Nin's Daughters," *Boku-shin* (Pan), 9 (May-June, 1977), 8-12.

[3] A typical entry is the following:

> February 10, 1008. Sadaiben sent Sachuben to me with a letter. He asked whether we have Rekken ceremony tomorrow. I could not decide by myself so I asked the Emperor to give his advice.

See Fujiwara Michinaga, *Mido Kanaku-ki* (*The Diary of the Honorable Prime Minister*) 14 vols. (998-1020), in *Nihon no Rekishi* (A History of Japan), by Naosumi Tsuchida, trans. Keiko Tamura (Tokyo, 1965), p. 245.

[4] See Shigeru Matsumoto, *Motoori Norinaga: 1730-1801* (Cambridge, Mass, 1970), pp. 50-51.

[5] Ki no Tsurayuki, *Tosa Nikki* (*The Tosa Diary*), in *Anthology of Japanese Literature from the earliest era to the mid-nineteenth century*, comp. and ed. Donald Keene (Rutland, 1956), p. 82 (first entry of diary).

[6] See *The Gossamer Years (Kagero Nikki): The Diary of a Noblewoman of Heian Japan*, trans. Edward Seidensticker (Tokyo & Rutland, 1973), p. 86.

[7] See Sei Shonagon, *The Pillow Book of Sei Shonagon*, 2 vols., trans. and ed. Ivan Morris (New York, 1967), p. 33

[8] Izumi Shikibu, *The Izumi Shikibu Diary: A Romance of the Heian Court*, trans. and intro. Edwin A. Cranston (Cambridge, Mass., 1969), p. 158.

[9] See *Diaries of Court Ladies of Old Japan*, trans. Annie Shepley Omori and Kochi Doi (Tokyo, 1935).

[10] See *As I Crossed a Bridge of Dreams: Recollections of a Woman in Eleventh-Century Japan*, trans. Ivan Morris (New York, 1971).

[11] *Lady Nijo's Own Story: Towazu-gatari: The Candid Diary of a Thirteenth Century Japanese Imperial Concubine*, trans. Wilfrid Whitehouse and Eizo Yanagisawa (Tokyo & Rutland, 1974).

[12] Nagasawa committed suicide in 1949, the year she graduated from high school, and her diary—entitled *Tomoyo watashi ga shinda kara to te* (Friend, even though I die)—contains such reflections and verse as the following:

I have always wanted to kill myself. I have solved my problems by the pain of this wound—ever since I was a little child... I have no emotions or dreams whatsoever concerning my departure from this world...

Departure

Friend,

Please do not visit my grave though I die,

Do not disturb my deep slumber

By bringing flowers and tears.

See *Seishun no Kiroku* (Records of Adolescence), ed. Yasumo Hisayama, trans. Kyoko Mori (Tokyo, 1974), pp. 273-76.

Similarly, four days before her suicide under the wheels of a train (1969), Etsuko Takano wrote in her "notebook": "Until now, as I thought this notebook is only myself, I thought sometimes to get ease by showing it to someone. But I thought of burning it as I sat dreaming today. I tried to forget everything... It's true that this notebook is myself. The truth of this notebook lies in the words I write on the paper which tell about myself with intensity." See *Ni jyu sai no genten* (*Reflections at Twenty*), trans. Yuri Nakamura (Tokyo, 1969), pp. 169-70.

[13] See M. H. Shima, "Introduction" to Ichiyo Higuchi, *Crossroads,* trans. Yoko Chiba (Osaka, 1975), n.p.

[14] See *Higuchi Ichiyo no Nikki* (*The Diary of Ichiyo Higuchi*). ed. Yoshie Wada, trans. Chiho Adachi (Tokyo, 1943), p. 246.

[15] See *Hi no Kuni Onna no Nikki* (*The Diary of a Woman in the Land of Fire*), trans. Keiko Tamura (Tokyo, 1966), p. 13.

[16] A good example of the genre is the novel by Yoko Hagiwara, *Irakusa no Ie* (*House of Nettles*), trans. Mariko Hayashi (Tokyo, 1977). Daughter of the poet, Sakutaro Hagiwara, who appears in the novel under the name of Yonosuke, Yoko herself takes the name of Futaba. In the following excerpt, Futaba asks her father to meet her lover: "Yonosuke spat out the words: 'No, it's no good!' His eyes, opened wide and staring at me with fear, suggested that he would creep backwards to run away from the evil spirits. It was the first time I saw such a frightened father. It was also the first time to see his face fixed on me with blame" (p. 134).

[17] Signe Hammer, *Daughters and Mothers: Mothers and Daughters* (New York, 1975), pp. 134-35, 164-65.

[18] Jean Normand, "Anaïs Nin ou Le Labyrinthe Radieu," *Deux Cents ans de littérateur américaine, Etudes Anglaises*, 29 (Juillet-Septembre, 1976), 478. (Translation mine)

[19] See, for example, the diary by Barbara Kraft, *The Restless Spirit: Journal of a Gemini* (Millbrae, 1976).

[20] See Ken Akiyama, *Ocho Joryu Bungaku no Sekai* (The World of Literature by Court Ladies) (Tokyo, 1972), p. 189.

[21] Joanna Russ, "Why Women Can't Write," in *Images of Women in Fiction: Feminist Perspectives*, ed. Susan Koppelman Cornillon (Bowling Green, 1972), p. 4.

[22] Murasaki Shikihu, pp. 110-11.

[23] *The Gossamer Years*, p. 33

[24] Murasaki Shikibu, p. 135.

[25] Akiyama, p. 189.

[26] See *Ichiyo Zenshu* (*The Collected Works of Ichiyo*), ed. Ryohei Shioda and Yoshie Wada. vol. 3, trans. Chiho Adachi (Tokyo, 1955), p. 10.

[27] *Ichiyo Zenshu,* III, p. 362

[28] Tristine Rainer, "Anaïs Nin's *Diary I*: The Birth of the Young Woman as an Artist," in *A Casebook on Anaïs Nin*, ed. Robert Zaller (New York, 1974), p. 167.

Yuko Yaguchi

Twittering Machine of Paradise
Glimpses of two of Anaïs Nin's Japanese daughters

On May 29, 2002, a well-known Japanese woman of letters, Sumiko Yagawa, committed suicide at the age of seventy-one. The next day, on May 30, her new book entitled *Anaïs Nin as a Young Girl*, in which she introduces excerpts of *Linotte* in excellent translation and offers her unique view on "being a girl," was published, seemingly in accordance with her last will and testament.

It was also in the spring seven years before, on April 21, 1995, that another Japanese woman writer who played an inerasable role in Nin's reception in Japan passed away from a ruptured artery at the age of fifty-six. Masako Meio was then studying at the Steiner College in Fair Oaks, California. Though her death was natural, it was so sudden and shocking that some felt it was almost like a suicide.[1]

The two women had more than a few things in common. Apart from being two of the best Japanese translators of Anaïs Nin and themselves writers of unique talents, at least one from each set of parents was a teacher, both were exceptionally proficient in foreign language(s) for Japanese of their generation, and they were both married to men of letters, name, and authority. On the other hand, there were marked contrasts between them, most notably their differing viewpoints on Anaïs Nin, which create a multi-faceted portrait of Nin when read as a palimpsest.

Since Yagawa often mentions that Anaïs was born in the same year as her mother, and Meio once wrote an essay titled "The Daughters of Anaïs Nin,"[2] they may be rightfully considered two of Nin's Japanese daughters. How did Anaïs Nin influence and inspire these two daughters from the Far East who were to die such tragic deaths?

Masako Meio—A woman with four names

I was introduced to the world of Anaïs Nin through Masako Hara's Japanese translation of *The Diary of Anaïs Nin Volume 1*. Not only is the translation written as if Anaïs herself is speaking directly to us, the "Translator's Afterword" is, in my opinion, one of the best essays ever written on Anaïs Nin, not only in Japanese but also in English. Hara's insight stands apart from the stereotypical worship/accusatory responses to Nin and is filled with critical sympathy of a woman sharing the same intellectual/artistic/life stage with the author (the translator was then in her early thirties, about the same age as the diarist in the volume).

As early as 1974, Hara declared Anaïs Nin's *Diary* a grand fiction, that Nin's obsessive search for "true self" itself betrays its absence—to Anaïs Nin womanhood is more of an "idea" than "nature," which sounds too postmodern to have been said in the seventies.

Though I came to know her as Masako Hara, she later wrote novels by the name of Masako Meio. In 1979 Meio made a literary debut with *A Glimpse of a Woman*, which earned her the prominent Bungei Literary Award. She also used the name Masako Karatani after marriage, as a critic/translator. When the Japanese translation of *Diary 1* was published as a paperback edition in 1991, the translator procured herself a fourth name, Akie Hara. While Anaïs Nin declared possession of a "thousand faces," Meio literally lived her life with four names, suggesting multiplicity/fragmentation of identity, a familiar theme to Nin readers.

Judith Butler, in discussing Willa Cather's crossing of gender/ sexuality, makes a noteworthy point which could explain Meio's obsession with names as well as indicate her literary theme:

> For women, then, propriety is achieved through having a changeable name through the exchange of names, which means that the name is never permanent, and that the identity secured through the name is always dependent on the social exigencies of paternity and marriage. Expropriation is thus the condition of identity for women. Identity is secured precisely in and through the transfer of the name, the name as a site of transfer or substitution, the name, then, as precisely what is always impermanent, different from itself, more than itself, the non-self-identical.[3]

Here Butler counterplots a social code which is supposed to interfere with women's independence/identity in the name of propriety and transfers it in the postmodern context. Yet as it is manifest in Butler's discussion, woman's changeable name works as a revolving door of the modern/postmodern; while it restricts women's identity within the bounds of paternity and marriage, it paradoxically enables women to escape the clutching hands of the Father.

Meio's female character is driven by a double-edged fear of, and desire for, multiple identity. Yukiko, in Meio's autobiographical novel *A Glimpse of a Woman*, confesses that she gets bored with herself before anyone gets bored with her and lives a "self which is scarcely born before ruptured like an unfinished book."[4] She always dreams of another self she could have lived if she hadn't chosen this life. She is obsessed with a Puerto Rican "Dark Lady," Dolores, a femme fatale who torments her husband Leonard, an Anglo-Saxon Shakespearean. Yukiko-Leonard-Dolores form a triangle in the manner of Anaïs-Henry-June. Yukiko identifies herself sometimes with Dolores, sometimes with Leonard, and has an ambivalent desire to tear up and make up their relationship.

The difference lies outside the triangle: while Anaïs was married to the "generous" Hugo, Yukiko's husband, a visiting scholar to a university in New Haven, serves as a criterion for Yukiko to assume value (O paternity!). Her father was also the indignant God, the "rigid law rather than a human father"[5] (the law of the Father!). When the severe, often violent father softens once in a while, she feels so nervous it almost takes on an erotic air. Yukiko is afraid she might be taking her revenge on her children when she scolds or beats them hard. Later it is revealed that the exotic Dark Lady Dolores is also under control and subjected to the violence of her scholar husband, a "big man" from the United States, the symbol of power and authority.

Noriko Mizuta, a pioneering feminist critic in Japan, insightfully points out that Yukiko and Dolores, who are seemingly in direct contrast with one another, are actually two domestic women, both within the domain of patriarchy, and that the narrative of modern women cannot escape the modern family which produced the women themselves.

Alongside the father-daughter narrative in the modern family romance is romantic love ideology, or what another prominent Japanese feminist, Chizuko Ueno, calls the "couple illusion,"[6] which is definitely detectable in Meio's novels.

In the "Translator's Afterword" in the paperback edition of *Diary 1*, Meio recollects that women of her generation looked up to Sartre and Beauvoir as the ideal couple and were busy looking for *their* Sartre. She adds, to her regret, that after Beauvoir's death, it was revealed that instead of being the supposed role model who sought gender equality to the hilt, she was actually subjugated to her great partner ideologically and sexually, serving as mother in order not to lose him.

This could be read as the self-criticism that put an end to Meio's twenty-year marriage to Kojin Karatani, "arguably the most influential critic in Japan in the past twenty years,"[7] presumably when she was writing her last novel, *The Son of the Southern Cross*. In the posthumously published novel—the last of her autobiographical family narratives and most likely a metaphorical "will"—we find harsh criticism of Japanese marriage, in which a woman is doomed to play the role of mother to her husband, who is under the spell and control of his birth mother. Meio's character Mioko laments falling into the trap that is Japan, entrapping herself in marriage. Her architect husband Iwao serves on one hand as a tyrant-father who captures Mioko's soul by fear and is incapable of loving his sons, on the other as a spoiled child who declares that his doing housework is a national waste (!)

The feminist historian Etsuko Yamashita reports that she received through an editor Meio's unpublished English essay "Glimpses of the Present-Day Japanese Women" in 1992, in which Meio refers to *Southern Cross* as the epitome of her forty-six years as a woman deeply influenced by the West.[8] Meio, as Yamashita tells us, calls the behavior pattern of her generation for Japanese women trapped in the role of the Great Mother archetype a "general hushing,"[9] and points to Anaïs Nin, who declared she would "write as a woman," as a role model of the future generation. Meio's prediction may come true if we remember that Anaïs Nin continued "shedding yesterday's woman to pursue a new vision,"[10] and that the word "woman" itself, according to Butler, is a "term in process, a becoming, a construction that cannot rightfully be said to originate or to end."[11]

Masako Meio

Meio defines Anaïs Nin as "a winner, a strong woman and a woman with celestial wings."[12] It is true that Anaïs refused to be dominated by one man, that she was determined not to be like her mother, as is often the case with modern woman writers. She didn't deny motherhood totally but rather chose to be a symbolic one. Kate Millet once called Anaïs a "Mother to Us All"[13]—she was a mother not only to men and art, as is sometimes (mis)understood, but also to women who welcomed the publication of the *Diary*, saying Anaïs wrote *their* diary. It is to transgress or subvert women's dual stereotypes if the pleasure-seeking woman is also a "Mother to Us All," creating another woman, Dona Juana-Mary-Anaïs.

Nevertheless and imaginably, it requires a woman with idiosyncratic ability and ambition to achieve that state, who is free from a "fear of flying" and is determined to devote her life to an aerial effort. In *Children of the Albatross* Anaïs Nin has a research scientist explain with how much intensity birds live their lives:

> Their body temperatures are regularly as high as 105 to 110 degrees, and anyone who has watched a bird at close range must have seen how its whole body vibrates with the furious pounding of its pulse... The bird's indrawn breath not only fills its lungs, but also passes on through myriads of tiny tubules into air sacs that fill every space in the bird's body not occupied by vital organs. Furthermore the air sacs connect with many of the birds' bones, which are not filled with marrow as animals' bones are, but are hollow. These reserve air tanks provide fuel for the bird's intensive life, and at the same time add to its buoyancy in flight.[14]

For a human being to realize the state of a bird would mean strenuous, perhaps almost inhuman will and energy. The extent of freedom Anaïs Nin acquired herself was equal to the depth of her inner darkness and secrecy. This inaccessibility to Nin's core of truth more than a quarter of a century after her death and a century after her birth might partially explain why she remains in the ambiguous or peripheral realm as a writer. Anaïs Nin's greatest secret, in any case, is how she could escape insanity (unlike Zelda Fitzgerald or Chieko Takamura[15]), or suicide (unlike Sylvia Plath or Sumiko Yagawa), and transform herself into a "woman with celestial wings."

Meio's female character, however energetic, talented and ambitious, often stumbles before her husband's judgmental statements and suffers in silence. But the writer refused to be a hushed wife by representing herself in the novels, in a way simultaneously playing the roles of Anaïs Nin and Nancy Durrell as described in *Diary 2*: "'Shut up,' says Larry to Nancy. She looks at me strangely, as if expecting me to defend her, explain her. Nancy, I won't shut up. I have a great deal to say, for June, for you, for other women."[16]

One feels at a loss whether to call it tragic or inspirational, but Meio, as a writer, survived the wife who may have sacrificed her life in the "trap that is Japan," and left her works to younger daughters of Anaïs Nin and of Masako Meio herself.

Sumiko Yagawa: The immortal anti-girl

While Meio's interest in Anaïs Nin is focused on Nin as woman/ writer, her desire for maturity, and all the difficulties she experiences, Sumiko Yagawa makes it clear that her fascination with Nin comes mostly from the unexpurgated diary of her younger days, *Linotte*. In *Anaïs Nin as a Young Girl*, Yagawa introduces in superb translation the young Anaïs or "Linotte" ("little bird," a nickname given by her mother) who seems charming and lovable to Japanese readers, while accurately indicating that the volume of *Linotte* lacks description between January 8, 1918 and March 1919 and that the young Anaïs restrains herself from writing anything physical or sexual so that we don't even know when she had her first menstruation.

Yagawa names Anaïs Nin and Anne Frank as the two true authors of literature written by and for children. The young Anaïs is referred to as the "eldest daughter in a fatherless family" or the "unpopular immigrant girl," quite different from the image of Anaïs as a young woman rich in love and talent, but akin to Yagawa's definition of the "anti-girl." She expounds that the anti-girl is a girl who cannot get along with herself and the world, someone like Anaïs/Sumiko who believes she is ugly and escapes into the "wordland."[17] She also adds that in order to immortalize a girl, which is only a phase in process (interestingly in accordance with Butler's interpretation of woman), one should crown her with a word of negation such as "anti," "no," "non," and that a girl who doesn't say *no* is no girl.

In other words, Yagawa's anti-girl, which in her definition has nothing to do with age, is someone who cannot be content with female gender. Any woman writer will keep this anti-girl in an inner room of her own, as Yagawa herself (again self-mockingly?) labels a woman writer an unhappy outcome of the anti-girl. In the same context, Noriko

Mizuta says that the girl as archetype/double plays a crucial role for modern woman writers.[18] The archetypal girl, such as Alice or Princess Kaguya in a Japanese fairytale, belongs nowhere in this world and therefore functions as a messenger, just as a woman writer occupying a peripheral place in society speaks as a medium.

Another important concept Yagawa adopts is that of a Jungian "father's daughter." In *Father's Daughters: Mari Mori and Anaïs Nin*, published five years before *Anaïs Nin as a Young Girl*, she takes up two woman writers, one from Japan and the other from America, as examples of a father's daughter who identifies more with father than mother. Yagawa assumes that any girl residing in the "wordland" whose best friend is a book or a father's daughter, which corresponds to the feminist idea that written words are basically male property and tradition, that the oral is female.

Sumiko Yagawa

She regards Anaïs Nin a proficient bilingual who speaks men's and women's languages, pointing to *Henry and June* in which Anaïs serves as a translator between the two. (We can trace the translator Anaïs in *Linotte*, in which she tries to reconcile the separated parents.) Yagawa herself remembers having two accents in her family: her father's accent from a southern part of Japan and her mother's Tokyo accent which is considered to be standard Japanese. Her father was a scholar of English literature whose books nourished her mind, and her mother was a "spoiled" housewife who was the anti-girl's anti-mentor, so to speak. Nevertheless, Yagawa later found her "mother tongue," a smooth Tokyo accent she inherited from her mother, a great help when she translated children's books. She became a professional translator (from English, French and German into Japanese) as a means of livelihood after divorce, and her rule was to translate books out of which she heard her own Japanese while reading them.

Yagawa portrays the "little bird" Anaïs as someone who loves her hard-working mother, respects her absent musician father, and is devoted to both, who gradually finds out she is not ugly as told by her father, and finally finds her true love in Hugo Guiler. The book ends rather abruptly in a naïve idealization of the Anaïs-Hugo marriage, concluding that Anaïs finally finds her lost father in young Hugo.

The ending feels not only abrupt, but also unfinished since we know that their marriage (including its sexuality, about which Yagawa admits Anaïs was self-repressive until her encounter with Henry Miller) strayed far from any happy conclusion. Yagawa's ending is almost like a fairytale ending in which a poor, young girl is rescued by a handsome prince. It is perhaps more intriguing than persuasive as to why she ended her book that way.

Yagawa admires the Anaïs-Hugo relationship ("This mutual trust!"[19]) and compares it to a pair of identical twins or a Platonic union of androgynous halves. We find the almost identical description in her autobiographical fantasy *A Woman Called Rabbit*, written "like automatic writing" six months after a divorce from Tatsuhiko Shibusawa, a cult critic of French literature, whose Japanese translations of Marquis de Sade resulted in obscenity charges. In Yagawa's *Rabbit*, dedicated "To Him," the narrator recollects her failed marriage: "We were an ideal couple, the 'one and only' match, as they said and we believed, for we were opposites. He had everything I lacked, and vice versa. We were one, yes, we were doubles." A listener replies, "It's Platonic. I envy you, having met your double."

In such an ideal marriage as the narrator describes it, "He was literally my master, for me to obey. If he was to be called 'husband,' I should be 'wife.'" Calling one's husband "master" may appear an anachronism in English, yet (believe it or not) it is a common practice in present-day Japan. Though some may say it is only nominal, in 1983 Yagawa wrote, in a form of autobiographical fiction, that it was literally the case in her marriage. More shockingly and/or metaphorically telling is the husband's remark, "Woman is not human," to which the wife responds, "You are right."

> If woman is not human, she is inhuman. God. A thing. A beast. Whatever… What am I? …
> If he is man, I am woman.
> If he is an animal, I am an angel.
> If he is human, am I a human figure? …
> However / If he is a child, I am his mother.[20]

We should remind ourselves that in English as well, we let "man" represent human beings until only several decades ago. Therefore, Shibusawa's and Yagawa's master-servant relationship, in which the servant testifies she was busy and content with being the master's wife-mother-secretary-housekeeper, cannot be regarded as a backward example in the Far East, but as portraying a universal phenomenon concerning gender.

The first chapter of *Rabbit* is titled "The Wing." The "wing" is a strange little bone-like thing in the shape of a "V." The narrator converses with a man about it as follows:

> "It's so delicate… I bet it must be the wing of an angel figure or something."
> "Yes, a figure, and an angel… By implanting this plastic wing inside my body, I could transform into an angel both in name and reality. Into a fake angel flying empty-heartedly upon the air, against nature, feet over the ground, with artificial wings."[21]

The wing that transfigures a woman into a fake angel is an intrauterine device, or IUD. The narrator discloses that in order to live up to her husband's principle to not seek everyone's happiness, she had to abort burgeoning lives that came to her as they did to everyone else, and that her husband gave her the "plastic wing" so he can monopolize her as mother. This is how she became, in the double meaning of the word, an "ideal" mother embracing a fake child-husband, who is inseparably embraced by his biological mother—exactly the same portrait of marriage as Meio depicted.

According to an essay Yagawa wrote three months before her death, she had to go through a series of abortions during the nearly two-decade marriage to Shibusawa: "Now I think about it, it was always the wife who had to bleed for the no-child principle. There was a time I almost uttered, 'Is it not unfair?' But it was never voiced in the end."[22] When she broke the silence, it was the end of their Platonic union and his paradise.

For Yagawa, the "plastic wing" was also the killer of possible lives. If we remember once again Anaïs Nin's vivid description of a bird's aerial mechanism which is fueled with its own will to fly, Yagawa's angel feels more like a kite or a puppet manipulated by her lord and master. Likewise, while Nin is a survivor of an abortion made of her own will, as detailed in *Incest*, Yagawa is rather a victim of the abortions, carried out according to her husband's phallo-egocentric principle, which may well be labeled another form of domestic violence.

To speak, or not to speak; that is Yagawa's question.

In *The Lost Garden*, which can be regarded as a retelling of *Rabbit*, the narrator FG analyzes the monstrosity she has directed at her ex-husband. She concludes that it does not lie in her final betrayal, but rather in the utmost obedience with which she never said *no* in a decade of marriage, something she regrets. Bearing in mind the "Author's Note" to *The Immortal Girl*, which concludes that a girl who says *no* is no girl, Yagawa's life passage was that of anti-bildungsroman, in which the anti-girl married to be an obedient wife, then divorced to be the immortal girl (again).

In the coda of *Garden*, FG explains the failure of her marriage to EH and feels frustrated:

> No. This man doesn't understand, either. Do you know what I really want to say? More. There's a lot more to it...
> Vain. All is vain without words.
> FG swallows all those unvoiced words and uttered instead:
> "All I want to say is—let me be silent. Period."[23]

The predictive passage makes us wonder if silence was Yagawa's last word. There is a claim that she was to meet an editor to work on a magazine's special edition featuring Nin[24] several days after her death, which tempts us to think her suicide was impulsive. On the other hand, some facts—a day's difference between her death and the publication of *Anaïs Nin as a Young Girl*, that she sent the book to many of her friends as if in time for her own death, and that her favorite music was playing by her body—speak otherwise.

In the previously mentioned essay written three months before her death, Yagawa acknowledges that her aim as a writer is to "speak out of experience written in my body as text."[25] Could we go a step further and hypothesize that she aimed to speak through her (dead) body, turning it into her final work of art, as suggested by the original title of *Rabbit*, "The Confession of a Beautiful (Dead) Body"? If that is the case, Yagawa transcends Nin's ambition of creating her life as art and reaches out to break the boundary between life and death, in the same manner as Gayatri Spivak interprets/translates an Indian woman's suicide: "Bhubaneswari attempted to 'speak' by turning her body into a text of woman/writing."[26]

Before concluding this article on two Japanese woman writers who may have been made scapegoats by the Japanese gender system, let us strike a positive note.

The fake angel, the figure with plastic wings, may transform into the "twittering machine" of paradise, as in a watercolor by Yagawa's favorite artist Paul Klee, who left a series of angel figures, most of which were created in his last years. The two Japanese daughters of Anaïs Nin will join their symbolic mother in a celestial chorus, just as Yagawa depicted a chorus of female voices in *Rabbit* ("Three women make a chorus!"), and sing/speak the "language of our mothers' land."[27]

In fact, they never stop speaking in this world as well, as long as we read their works (none of which is translated into English, unfortunately). The third and latest posthumous publication by Yagawa is a translation of Nin's *Little Birds*.[28] There is a project under way to publish Meio's collected essays on Anaïs Nin later this year, and hopefully there are many more voices to come.

Notes

[1] Noriko Mizuta writes: "The news of Ms. Masako Meio's abrupt death came as a great shock to me. Somehow it resembled a feeling of regret, an urge to stop her as soon as possible, if it had not been too late." (Translation mine, as all the other translations from Japanese to English are in this article.) "Fuyu e mukatte no Tabidachi (A Departure for Winter)" in Meio, *Yuki Mukae* (*Snow-Welcoming*). Tokyo: Kawade Shobo Shinsha, 1995. 261-65.

[2] Hara, Masako. "Anaïs Nin no Musume-tachi" ("The Daughters of Anaïs

Nin"), *Bokushin* 9, 1977. 8-21.

3 Butler, Judith. *Bodies That Matter*. NY: Routledge, 1993. 153.

4 Meio, Masako. *Aru Onna no Glimpse* (*A Glimpse of a Woman*). Tokyo: Kodan-sha, 1999. 42.

5 Ibid. 104.

6 Ueno, Chizuko. *Onna to iu Kairaku* (*The Pleasure That Is Woman*). Tokyo: Keisô Shobô, 1986. 16.

7 *http://web.princeton.edu/sites/sics/speakers.htm*

8 She studied a year in the US in 1957 as an exchange student for AFS, majored in English literature as an undergraduate and graduate student in Japan, and spent another year in the US when Kojin Karatani was a visiting scholar at Yale. This American/English experience had a great influence on the shaping of her sense of split/multiple identities.

9 Yamashita, Etsuko. "Josei no Jiritsu to Haha-teki Jubaku no Genkai" ("Women's Independence and the Limit of Maternal Bind"). *Tokyo Shinbun, 24 Apr. 1996, late ed.*

10 Nin, Anaïs. *The Diary of Anaïs Nin, Vol. 1*. Ed. Gunther Stuhlmann. San Diego: Harcourt, 1966. 204.

11 Butler. *Gender Trouble: Feminism and the Subversion of Identity*. NY: Routledge, 1990. 33.

12 Hara, Akie. "Yakusha Atogaki" ("Translator's Note"), *Anaïs Nin no Nikki* (1931-34). Tokyo: Chikuma-shobo, 1991. 643.

13 Millet, Kate. "Anaïs—A Mother to Us All," *ANAIS: An International Journal* vol. 9, 1991.

14 Nin. *Children of the Albatross, Cities of the Interior*. Chicago: Swallow Press, 1974. 160.

15 The wife of a famous Japanese sculptor/poet Kôtarô Takamura. She had an artistic talent and was one of the "new women" in modern Japan, but later suffered from a nervous breakdown. Kôtarô's most popular book of poems, *Chieko-shô*, is written about his mentally ill wife.

16 Nin. *The Diary of Anaïs Nin, Vol. 2*. Ed. Gunther Stuhlmann. New York: Harcourt/Swallow, 1967. 233.

17 Yagawa, Sumiko. *Alice in the Wordland,* in *Yagawa Sumiko Sakuhin Shûsei* (*The Collected Works of Yagawa Sumiko*). Tokyo: Shoshi Yamada,

1999. 133-192.

[18] Mizuta, Noriko. "Shôjo to iu Bunshin" ("The Girl as a Double"). Ed. Eiji Sikine, in *Uta no Hibikiki Monogatari no Yokubo.* Tokyo: Shinwa-sha, 1996. 132.

[19] Yagawa. *Anaïs Nin no Shôjo Jidai (Anaïs Nin As a Young Girl).* Tokyo: Kawade Shobô Shinsha, 2002. 19.

[20] Yagawa. *Usagi to Yobareta Onna (A Woman Called Rabbit)* in Sakuhin Shûsei. 267.

[21] *Ibid. 265.*

[22] Yagawa. "Itsumo Sobani Honga" ("Books Always by My Side"), *Asahi Shinbun*, 10 Feb. 2002.

[23] Yagawa. *Ushinawareta Niwa (The Lost Garden)* in *Sakuhin Shûsei.* 568, 570.

[24] *Bookish* 2 (2002): 49-55.

[25] Asahi Shinbun, *17 Feb. 2002.*

[26] Spivak, Gayatri Chakravorty. *A Critique of Postcolonial Reason.* Cambridge: Harvard UP. 308.

[27] Yagawa. *Usagi* in *Sakuhin Shusei.* 277.

[28] Nin. *Kotori-tachi.* Trans. Yagawa. Tokyo: Shinchô-sha, 2003.

Toyoko Yamamoto

Examining *Anaïs Nin no Shôjo Jidai*
Sumiko Yagawa's *"Anaïs Nin as a Young Girl"*

For those familiar with Anaïs Nin's writings, it is not difficult to picture her as a *Japonisante*. Nin often mentions her rereading Lady Murasaki's work as much she does that of Proust. Nin writes in her *Diary of Anaïs Nin*, Vol. 7: "…one of my most important childhood readings was a volume on Japan from a collection, *Voyage Autour du Monde*" (5). The publication of the Japanese version of *A Spy in the House of Love* translated by Koji Nakata gave Nin an opportunity to visit Japan in 1966, and her essay entitled "Women and Children of Japan" from *In Favor of the Sensitive Man*—excerpted from *Diary 7*—reflects Nin's respect for Japanese sensitivity and aesthetics. Despite her appreciation for Japanese values, she was not satisfied with the limited number of books written by Japanese women that had been translated into English by the 1960s and the early 1970s.

In *Collages*, Nin uses the traditional Japanese kimono as a metaphor to represent the people's isolation from liberation: "Nobuko was bound in her enveloping kimono, the wide sleeves like closed wings against her body, the feet in white cotton and sandals, seeking to shake off the ritualistic past, the thoughtful meditative forms, the contained stylizations, and she wondered whether she could emerge from centuries of confinement" (82). This also reminds me of the Japanese doll on the fireplace mantel in Nin's Los Angeles house that I saw when I visited Rupert Pole there in the early spring of 1983. The glass case that had previously surrounded the doll in real kimono fabric had been removed to save the doll from suffocation. The doll was placed in the foreground on the brick mantel as a symbolic feature of Anaïs's taste.

In reflecting on these impressions of Anaïs Nin as a *Japonisante*, I will examine one Japanese literary woman's accomplishment as a token of appreciation for Nin's centenary birthday on February 21, 2003. I am confident that Anaïs Nin would have been pleased to know that Sumiko Yagawa appreciated her writings and sought to bring them to a wider audience.

Just as Nin felt the need to remove her Japanese doll from its glass case so that it could "breathe" naturally, her description of Nobuko in *Collages* seeking her independence from "centuries of confinement" is symbolized by the doll's traditional Japanese costume. Nin clearly hoped to create a liberated Japanese woman, as her question in *In Favor of the Sensitive Man* gives evidence: "What kind of modern woman would emerge from the deep, masked, long-hidden Japanese woman of old?" (43) Nin also wanted to read more Japanese literature, much of which unfortunately had not been translated into English during her lifetime.

Tracing the genealogy of Anaïs Nin scholarship in Japan, a study such as *Anaïs Nin no Shôjo Jidai* (*Anaïs Nin as a Young Girl*) is rare. Yagawa, known chiefly as a translator of foreign literature for children[1] and as an essayist, wrote the book to help Japanese readers become familiar with Anaïs Nin. *Anaïs Nin as a Young Girl* was printed by a major Japanese publisher and was displayed by the most prestigious bookstores in Japan. The connection between Nin and Yagawa was rather unexpected for those who have read the works of one or the other, or for those in Japan who are familiar with the works of both. This essay will introduce *Anaïs Nin as a Young Girl* in terms of synthesizing Yagawa's exposition on the profiles of Nin's girlhood and will highlight one aspect of contemporary trends of Nin study in Japan.

In the beginning of *Anaïs Nin as a Young Girl*, Yagawa explains why she became a devoted reader of Anaïs Nin. She confesses that she did not find Nin a particularly exciting writer when she first read the Japanese version of *Diary 1 (Anaïs Nin no Nikki Dai Ikkan)* in the mid-1970s. Rather, Yagawa became an ardent reader of Nin after reading her unexpurgated diaries. After Yagawa read *Henry and June* and watched the movie of the same title, her curiosity about Nin's girlhood increased substantially. She began to wonder what extraordinary secrets might be hidden in Nin's youth and what her teenage years were like as well. What was it Nin had been yearning for since her adolescence? Yagawa states: "A nonprofessional judgment of investigating one's career accomplished after becoming an adult mostly offers clues to pin down what that particular woman 'wanted (missed)' in her teens." Yagawa reminds both herself and us that in the English language "want" means both *desire* and *deficiency*. From such double meanings, Yagawa refers to one of the common traits girls share: they tend to work hard to fulfill what they think they are "lacking (wanting)" when comparing themselves to other girls. Yagawa speculates, and feels she is not alone in her opinion, that the navigation of one's life is mostly determined by analyzing what is lacking (wanting) in one's individual existence after gaining consciousness to look at oneself and one's condition after the early teens.

As mentioned before, Yagawa did not write this book as a scholarly analysis, but rather to attract a more general Japanese readership. Yagawa presents a profile of Anaïs Nin as an adult before focusing on the essence of her book: what kind of young "girl" was Nin? Paralleling Yagawa's goals, Margot Beth Duxler indicates in *Seduction: A Portrait of Anaïs Nin*, "Rereading *Linotte* allowed me to work backward from the present to the past, picking up clues, evidence from the child about who the woman was to become" (15).

Amidst Yagawa's overall depiction of Nin's womanhood, what strikes her most is the relationship between Anaïs and Hugo (Hugh Guiler). Yagawa understands their matrimonial bond is only possible because of their utter sophistication and absolute confidence in each other's intellect and mind, otherwise there would have been no way to maintain their relationship. Yagawa sincerely admires such a reliable relationship. She speaks to us of her moments of admiration and her deep fascination with the couple as she viewed pictures of them performing a Flamenco dance in costume—a photo that appears in the fourth volume of *The Early Diary*. In fact, Yagawa thinks the book *Henry and June* actually should have been titled *Hugo and Anaïs*.

Here, of course, Yagawa indicates that the couple's encounter with Henry Miller seemed almost inevitable, and she sees the fatalistic meeting, if you will, and the subsequent relationship to be the seed of the personal rebirth that signifies both the awakening of Anaïs's sexuality and her craftsmanship as a writer. Yagawa points to Anaïs's life in the Paris of the 1930s as the period of her rebirth and calls *Diary 1* an extraordinary book in its novelty and inquisitiveness. Yagawa sees this volume as Anaïs's autobiography rather than a diary as seen from the perspective of current readers who have read the series of the expurgated volumes. She calls the first volume a book of self-inspection and discusses her ironic views towards Nin's literary skills after she had spent decades trying to fictionalize it. Yagawa, given her seventy-one years of life, expresses her own sympathy and understanding of one writer's impatience at remaining a minor author when she is over sixty.

In addition to this profile of Anaïs Nin's womanhood, Yagawa also introduces Japanese readers to details of Nin's relationships with Hugo Guiler, Rupert Pole and other men, some of those surrounding her in Paris. Since Yagawa considers this period a renaissance for Nin, it allows her to develop an understanding of Nin's introspective character as she matured from childhood to greater levels of intellectual liberation throughout her life. It is this liberation that Yagawa celebrates in *Anaïs*

Nin as a Young Girl. She sees Nin as a magnificent woman and whole-heartedly encourages new generations of girls to read her work. The preface helps Japanese readers understand some of Anaïs Nin's background as an adult and the social circles in which she moved as well as other influences in her life. Yagawa then focuses on developing a better understanding of Nin's childhood.

Yagawa's investigation spans Nin's youth from the time she was eleven years old until she was eighteen and met Hugo Guiler. She starts with excerpts from the first page of *Linotte,* dated July 25, 1914. She points to the hardship Nin experienced being exiled from Europe to the New World against the historical backdrop of the beginning of World War I as a life-shaping experience. She also praises the literary spirit demonstrated by young Anaïs's writing during the voyage to New York. Yagawa investigates her own motivation for exploring Nin's childhood and states that her image of Anaïs Nin was distinctively altered by reading *Linotte.* Her rising curiosity about the early years is spurred on by the fact that Anaïs kept a continuous diary from the age of eleven. By being able to enter the personal realm of her diary, *Linotte,* Yagawa became more fascinated with Nin. She shares a memory of walking by a secondhand bookstall where *The Diary of Anne Frank* in Japanese was piled up among the others, almost imploring her to write about Nin's childhood diary for the benefit of her readers.

As for Yagawa, who accomplished much with notable translations of children's foreign and juvenile literature into Japanese, Nin's story of exile offers an excellent opportunity to delve deeply into her childhood because her daily life during this time was recorded faithfully. Yagawa astutely notes the lack of any father figure among the group of exiles with whom Nin associates and is interested in learning how she copes with this absence. Yagawa reminds the readers of the dramatic irony in which we are aware of a father and a daughter's reunion and the incidents of incest twenty years later.[2] Here, she wonders how much Anaïs was told of the fundamental causes of the exile based on her parent's divorce and by whom.

Leaving this important question for the reader to ponder, Yagawa examines *Linotte* chronologically. She declares that any girl over ten years of age has her own "history" and uses this as a point of reference in analyzing Anaïs, now eleven years old and looking back on her "history" in France and on her diary writing experience originally carried out in her mother tongue of French. In the New World, Anaïs was not an exception to the adverse experiences common to immigrants. The girl talks tête-à-tête to her diary-confidante not only of her exciting new life in New York but also of her sense of alienation as an immigrant. Yagawa introduces excerpts that mirror the young Nin's frustration and embarrassment as a non-native speaker in the classroom. I agree with Yagawa's focus on Anaïs's ESL syndrome, even though it was not as bad as the girl's case in Maxine Hong Kingston's *The Woman Warrior, Memoirs of a Girlhood Among Ghosts*. Still, Anaïs's linguistic shift from French to American English to exhibit her "brain" and "personality" in her classes must have been a difficult part of her adjustment.

Citing a September 13, 1914 letter from Anaïs's father, Yagawa examines Nin's separation from her father as she expected it to be— simply a temporary situation: Anaïs clings to her hope of returning to her "fatherland" where he lives, a hope she never completely abandons. She also reflects on the girl's faith in Catholicism that was cultivated in the Old World and believes it is this Catholic piety that gives Nin a way to mentally reconcile the distance between her and her father. Yagawa sees that the girl cannot obtain God, father, or France, save through her dreams, envisioning and praying that her mortal father metamorphoses into God in his absence. Yagawa also refers to Nin's *Winter of Artifice* and the description of the heroine: "Her true God was her father. At communion it was her father she received, and not God. She closed her eyes and swallowed the white bread with blissful tremors. She embraced her father in holy communion" (44).

Yagawa cites a January 19, 1915 diary entry because here she can find her father's future second wife Maria Luisa called by her rightful name instead of Maruca, the name Nin used in the years to follow. Yagawa believes that the sensitive Anaïs can certainly guess there is a love affair between her father and Maria Luisa as Nin notes in *Linotte*: "The other day I received a picture postcard of Mouleau from Maria Luisa. I asked Papa to thank her for me, but I confess to my diary that I don't like her. Isn't it she who has stolen my Papa from me? Yes, it is she, for she keeps him from coming to hold me in his arms and I shall never forgive her" (44). Yagawa also touches upon the story of Nin's "Stella" in *Winter of Artifice* in which the twelve-year-old Stella, upon her first meeting with Lora, the daughter of a wealthy family and her father's lover, whispers to her father to buy her new stockings. The meeting inspiring the scene in "Stella" apparently occurred when Nin was still in Europe and was therefore not written about in *Linotte*, but

Yagawa highlights the obvious and unforgettable feelings of humiliation that resulted. Regarding the torn stockings, Yagawa reminds us of Anaïs's daily domestic chore to mend not only hers but also her younger brothers' socks when the family lived as immigrants in New York.

To her confidante, *Linotte*, Nin confesses that she still holds her "secrets" and that she cannot allow herself to tell all. Yagawa notes this tendency, especially in light of her parents' matrimonial discord, the loss of her father resulting in the "defeat" and exile of mother and daughter, and even worse, the women with whom her father consorts are not far removed in age from Anaïs herself. Yagawa understands Nin purposely staying away from unpleasant incidents and repressing any traumatic matters deep in her psyche. Nin does this so well that Yagawa believes that her perspective throughout *Linotte* is subjective. Yagawa even proffers that Nin's state of mind seems to almost mirror that of an autistic child.

It is only on November 7, 1919—five years after their immigration to New York—that Anaïs writes about the extent of her parents' marital problems in relating a conversation she had with her mother, recorded near the epilogue in *Linotte*. Yagawa's diction as a storyteller invites and entices Japanese readers to think about Anaïs's state of mind. To the girl's question, "Can Papa ever ask us to live with him?" her mother's reply is, "Oh, no, he has lost all his rights over you... Fifille, do you really think that one day Papa might come back and that we could be happy and all that? Those are romantic illusions, my daughter, which are good for nothing in life" (365). The sixteen-year-old Anaïs writes: "My childish illusions, the cherished dream of a reunion, the vision of a father in our home, the mysterious charm with which my imagination had surrounded the name 'Papa'—all that was in ruins, all that was dead. My romantic dream had become one of those real and terribly sad dramas such as we see all around us" (366). As one reads the diary, even with this shocking knowledge, Nin quickly tries to gather her self-resilience in face of this recognition of the end of her dream. Yagawa quotes many excerpts from this part of the girl's diary ending with Nin saying, "Oh! Let's not talk any more about the past. Only the future counts, and yet the Future is born of the Past... Courage! Courage!" (366).

Three years had passed since Nin's immigration to New York, and the spring of 1917 was literally a late spring's awakening for the indoor-orientated, fatherless fourteen-year-old girl whom Yagawa describes Nin to be. She points out two remarkable activities in Anaïs's pursuit of a career in arts: dancing in an amateur theatre group and modeling for a painter. Yagawa assumes that being a dancer and a model influenced Anaïs and her attempt to gain the self-confidence she needed to transcend her self-consciousness and to realize what it is like to have others pay attention to her.

Yagawa wonders why *Linotte* lacks any entries from January 1918 to March 1919 [an entire volume had been lost] and laments that this prevents her from tracing the fifteen-year-old girl's emotional and physical transformation that would have been revealed in her adolescent writing. Even so, given Anaïs's involvement in dance, Yagawa eagerly offers the belief that dancing was a bridge to early womanhood from childhood. Yagawa thinks Anaïs's Latin blood, rooted in her Cuban family heritage, allowed her to discover her talent in dancing. It is dancing that also brings the young Anaïs opportunities for courtship and ultimately leads to her engagement.

Along with her introduction of the sixteen-year-old girl's entries about her boyfriends and her growing social status, Yagawa could not help but digress to recall the dancing of Anaïs and Hugo after they had married. In 1921, Anaïs Nin met Hugh Parker Guiler and they married in 1923. According to Yagawa, both Anaïs and Hugo were the descendants of talented dancers and, as previously stated, she favors a particular picture of them dancing. She is struck not just by the couple as lovers, but also by the fact that they almost seem to relate to each other like psychological twins—a relationship that is described by Plato's theory of spherical bodies, at least according to her. The snapshot of the couple dancing inspires Yagawa to emphasize the significant impact dancing had on Anaïs's life. The book ends with an idealized image of the marriage.

As for Anaïs's modeling attempts, Yagawa displays frustration that there are no satisfactory descriptions regarding this experience in *Linotte*. She attributes this deletion to Nin's reluctance to "tell all," using Rupert Pole's preface in *Henry and June* as evidence: "The puritanical Catholic girl who could not bring herself to describe to her diary her salacious (to her innocent mind) experiences as a model was now faced with recording her awakening to passions" (vii). Interestingly enough, Yagawa discusses Nin's 1940 erotic short story "A Model," which appears in *Little Birds*, and her period as a "madam of a literary salon" financially helping out poor writers in New York. Yagawa translated "A Model" into Japanese herself and appends it with her exposition at the end of *Anaïs Nin as a Young Girl*. Yagawa warns readers not to confuse the story of "A Model" with what Anaïs could not confess to in the diary of her teens. She defends and praises Nin's lofty character as an artist and her woman's voice in her erotic writing and declares her endless respect for Nin's notion of sexuality: the heightened sensuous quality of relations is only enhanced by the tie of love and sex in its emotional bondage (and not merely sex itself).

So, much of Anaïs's being a dancer and model embodies her transition from childhood to early adulthood. The last incident during her childhood, in terms of Yagawa's definition of it, has to do with encountering her "knight," Hugo Guiler, and their marriage. She includes excerpts from February 7, 1921, two months before Anaïs met Hugo for the first time, one of which mentions Nin's acceptance to Columbia University. Yagawa points out the girl's desire for intellectual pursuit[3] as she writes in a letter to her cousin Eduardo: "Perhaps I do seem a featherhead and a 'fawn' whom it is a pity to startle and bewilder and bruise with cold philosophy. But I will show [the Columbia advisor] that the 'little French girl' (as she calls me) has gigantic ambitions, and that if people must smile at my *accent*, they will have to be serious when I write" (*Early Diary 2*, 146). Yagawa notes the Ariadne thread that winds through Anaïs and Hugo's encounter and inextricably intertwines them. It was fate that brought them together at the dance party where they first met and discovered their common interests. Hugo was a multi-talented man with a wonderful personality. He carried Emerson in his pocket and Stevenson was his favorite writer. He kept a diary, could recite Lamartine's poems, was a good dancer, and was financially mature enough to be employed at the National City Bank. He was also a student at Columbia University. Hugo was tall, trim, and five years older than Nin. With the amount of detail that Yagawa includes about him, it is evident that she thinks he is the perfect man for Anaïs to have married and that he filled the roles of both husband and father figure. She mentions Anaïs's concern for her mother's thoughts on her marriage and theorizes that her decision to marry Hugo could have been an attempt to finally find a surrogate father. Yagawa, of course, shows that Hugo would be influential in Anaïs's life and help facilitate her career as a woman writer.

Sumiko Yagawa captures the essence of Anaïs Nin, the life she led and the possible reasons for the choices that she made in her life, as Duxler describes: "Who Anaïs was in *Linotte* was who she became"

(104). Yagawa provides evidence for her assertion that Nin's life was shaped by her parents' divorce, her longing for her father, and her difficult immigration to New York. Nin worked through her experiences almost as if speaking a soliloquy publicly as she wrote in her journal on a consistent basis. As for some of her maturation processes, Yagawa takes educated guesses because even though Nin confided much in her journal, many significant aspects of her maturation are not recorded. Nonetheless, her genius comes through despite—and possibly because of—her childhood experiences. The end of her youth came when she met and married Hugo Guiler. This event also allowed Nin to overcome some of her early pain and gave her a basis from which she could excel in her creative endeavors as an adult.

In *Communion: The Female Search for Love,* bell hooks writes: "We wanted to be girls forever. As girls we felt we had power. We were strong and fierce and sure of ourselves. Somehow, as we made our entrance into the realm of young womanhood, we began to lose power. Research today confirms that young girls often feel strong, courageous, highly creative, and powerful until they begin to receive undermining sexist messages that encourages them to conform to conventional notions of femininity. To conform they have to give up power" (7). Some critics describe Sumiko Yagawa as a writer with a notion of being an eternal-girl. Although one may wonder whether Anaïs Nin wanted to be a girl forever, she was willing to become a woman, and moreover, she continuously searched to gain "power" throughout the stream of her life's-work of diary writing originating in her childhood

Notes

[1] Some of Sumiko Yagawa's (1931-2002) translations of foreign juvenile literature into Japanese are: *Little Women* by Louisa May Alcott, *Alice's Adventures in Wonderland and Through the Looking-Glass* by Lewis Caroll, *The Happy Prince* and *Lord Arthur Savile's Crime* by Oscar Wilde, *The Snow Goose* and *Snowflake* by Paul Gallico, and *Juggler's Tale* by Michael Ende.

[2] Sumiko Yagawa published *Chichi no Musumetachi—Mari Mori to Anaïs Nin* (*Father's daughter—Mari Mori and Anaïs Nin*) in 1997. Yagawa renders the comparisons between Ougai Mori (1863-1911), translator of Faust and a naval surgeon's daughter who was one of the notable Japanese writers in the Meiji period, Mari Mori (1903-1987), a Japanese woman

writer and essayist, and Anaïs Nin in terms of their father-daughter relationships. Yagawa thinks if Mari's father complex is a positive one, then that of Anaïs is a negative one. Yagawa believes one pattern of incest is namely a father's girl's first step in the process to her own self-establishment.

[3] Yagawa uses a metaphor of the Queen's mirror in *Snow White* for young Anaïs's diary. As for Anaïs, unlike the Queen's desire for the affirmation of beauty ("You are the fairest one of all"), she wants both beauty *and* intelligence and to be reassured that "You are the wisest one of all." Cf. *Chichi no Musumetachi—Mari Mori to Anaïs Nin* (*Father's daughter—Mari Mori and Anaïs Nin*), Shinchosh, 1997, p. 102. Duxler also refers to the metaphor of mirrors: "The themes of being understood that first appear in *Linotte* are sometimes expressed by the image of a mirror as a reflection of the self—a metaphor that fascinated Anaïs throughout her life" (141).

Masako Meio

Glimpses of Present-Day Japanese Women

In 1974, I translated and published Volume One of *The Diary of Anaïs Nin* with a hope that this brave woman's search for the self might help to add a new dimension to the consciousness of the Japanese woman, which seemed to have reached a new turning point as the high wave of America's feminist movement had begun to beat our shores. I was in my mid-thirties, a time to look back on my own growing years and reexamine my past motivations and their consequences. For a better understanding of the general situation I was in at that time, a quick review of the overall change in women's consciousness and social status during the previous three decades after the war may be needed.

I was born in 1939 and was five years old when the war ended. That is, I was fully imbued with the new concepts of democracy and equal rights from the outset of my education. Women were given suffrage without fighting for it. There seemed to be a momentary equality between men—smaller in number and posture—and women in the struggle for reconstruction of everyday life and society. I remember my parents arguing heatedly over food and politics above my head.

My parents were schoolteachers. My mother was happy because she was now paid as much as her male colleagues. Schoolteachers formed one of the most radical groups of the society, for they had to brainwash themselves quicker than anyone else. Traditional thinking was suppressed, and teaching of Japanese history was forbidden. There were plenty of opportunities for a totally new identity as an individual and as a nation. Communist teachers, lurking long and patient, were the most active of all, and socialists followed them in reorienting the confused minds. Teachers experimented with one method after another on what is called democratic education at the same time as they went on strikes and marched along the streets for betterment of their status as laborers. But all too soon there came the fatal Red Purge, the banishment of communists from society, which split the mind of the Japanese schizophrenic. My father, who had voted for the Socialist Party immediately after the war, converted himself to conservatism, pursuing his advancement as an educator and eventually became a rightist ideologue, confirming his belief in the supremacy of the Imperial system, while one of his closest friends, who was a feverish communist, went jobless and after long years of adversity became an alcoholic and ended up in a mental hospital.

As a girl, I was split between two opposing ideologies. Most of the intellectuals were duly on the leftist wing, drafting schemes for revolution or fighting for the lowest rungs of the society, but they had no time for women's issues. Women intellectuals were discouraged from pursuing their own interests in preference to the benefit of the lower class or of the masses in general. This retreat resulted, I think, in the gradual retrieval of conservative or almost reactionary mentality concerning women's status in the 1950s. I was later to find that leftist men were not at all believers of equality between men and women even though they professed themselves to be. Through my girlhood I fought against my father's rightist ideology, but, strangely, he was "progressive" and daring about his daughters' education. He encouraged me to receive the highest possible education for a girl and even supported my going to the U.S. to study when I was only seventeen. Married to a career woman himself, my father was a practicing advocate of equal rights. For better or for worse, I did not have to brood much on my being a female until years later when I married a most conservative leftist.

The postwar commotion was soon to be appeased as the single-winged nation, led by the victorious conservative party, took its course toward economic reconstruction on capitalist principles and the general cry for revolution calmed down to grumbling as men were organized into the monolithic system, which grew more secure. And women, who for a time after the war were deemed "as strong as stockings," as the saying goes, silenced themselves in taking up again the traditional role of housekeeping while their husbands were mustered for another war, this time an economic war, even at the sacrifice of family life. This new war was to reinforce the traditional agrarian mentality that characterizes the Japanese collectivism. By the time I was an adolescent in the early 1950s, the general trend of the society was reactionary in many areas of life. The Peace Treaty was concluded between the United States and Japan in 1952, and Japan became a full-fledged independent nation.

In the same year, Simone de Beauvoir's *The Second Sex* was introduced to the Japanese readers ironically by a male translator. It was an eye-opening thrill for some women who considered themselves "progressive," but a threat to most men. I remember one of my male teachers at high school commenting with a grin, "You will be done for if you ever get a kick out of Beauvoir." Under pressure of this kind, the majority of young women remained indifferent. Those "progressive" women were one generation older than I. They defied "old-fashioned" men and woman around them and at the same time they were eager to find their own "Jean-Paul Sartres" among intellectuals. But they were to be more disillusioned by men than the women of my generation. Some of the most productive contemporary female authors such as Teako Tomioka, Kazuko Saegusa and Minako Ohba belong to this Beauvoirean generation. They sound either more resentful or more resigned than, say, Yuko Tushima, two generations younger but with no less pains.

It was toward the end of the 1950s that Fumiko Enchi published *The Waiting Years* and became a celebrity. The setting of the novel was the Meiji Period when the patriarchal order had its way, but the spirit of the novel was distinctly contemporary. It is the story of a strong and intelligent woman persevering as a housewife and matron of a feudal family. Tomo, the heroine, endures all humiliations nobly, silencing herself to non-existence, utterly invisible to her husband. At the last moment of her life, Tomo asks her husband almost demandingly to throw her body into the sea as mercilessly as he has treated her. Tomo's silence is pregnant with madness, as Noriko Mizuta points out in her inspiring book of criticism, *Beyond Feminism*, published in early 1961. *The Waiting Years* is an expression of the maddening silence that Japanese women had to force themselves into within a decade after the war, and this is a big step backward in the history of modern Japanese women. Although we have those glorious women of the Blue Stocking Movement (1911-1916) as our predecessors, patience and silence again became women's code of conduct on which the nation's prosperity rested. Instead of asking for equal partnership with men, the postwar women chose the role of "mothering" men who restored their dignity only as hard workers. Japanese women became monstrously strong as mothers and only as mothers, the consequences of which we now suffer. It was an easy choice for them, because at the root of our culture there lies the ancient matriarchal layer which has helped to characterize the curiously feminine receptiveness of the Japanese with the Sun Goddess Amaterasu both as the most remote ancestor of the Emperor and as the supreme divine figure. In this climate some of the Buddhist divinities have been effeminized and rendered all the more divine because of their all-embracing motherliness. The virtue of patience and silence is likened to the very femininity of these divine figures, and men have to prostrate themselves before the Great Mother sublimities while abusing the feminine omnipotence and obscurity very much like tyrant babies.

Tomo's husband in *The Waiting Years*, too, was awestruck at Tomo's mystified dignity on her deathbed and cried out loud, "I'll give you a great funeral ceremony." It only reveals men's psychic bondage to the mother-figure, and women know it instinctively. Thus motherhood readily becomes the socially accredited perfection of femininity in our culture. Ours is a uniquely role-playing society, in which women compete with one another to embody the highest value the culture points to.

Beauvoir's influence could have triggered in young Japanese women an ardent quest for individuality in the late 1950s and early 1960s when I was a university student. We, the first generation of postwar Japan, could have freed ourselves of the past fetters our elders were still in. We started out as passionate pilgrims in search of broadened possibilities for women. There were far more women studying at universities than before, the rapid economic growth enabling the siblings even of the lower middle class to receive higher education. Our pilgrimage coincided with the rise and fall of the student movement over the renewal of the U.S.-Japan Security Pact, which culminated in 1960. For a time young women were oblivious of their own feminine issues in the midst of the nationwide upheaval. Ryumei Yoshimoto, one of the leading critics of the time, commented that the anti-Security Pact movement was basically an outburst of the nationalistic sentiment, which I believe is partly true. True in the light of the shift in the U.S.-Japan relationship accelerated by our growing economy. My own feelings are that it was an emotional anarchism, a disoriented search for a new mode of being colored with individualism. The Communist Party had lost the reins, unable to catch up with this new flow on the part of the students. At the height of the movement, Yumiko Kurahashi made a sensational debut with her short story, "Partei," which questioned the spiritual authority of the Communist Party. The battle was lost, mainly because of the split among the leftists. The masses, who preferred peaceful compromises and material comfort, ebbed away even before the battle was over and reoriented themselves in preparation for the Olympic Games of 1964. The intellectuals, too, retreated, "back to sobriety" being their acquiescence. Sobriety meant for us then that we had to submit ourselves to the upsurging popular will which constituted the realities. We found ourselves trapped between the ideal and the real, and the real meant conformity while the ideal meant anything else. The "idealistic" young women had no models for self-development except Simone de Beauvoir at that time after they had let go of Rosa Luxenburg and other revolutionary women, but, in retrospect, Beauvoir had already lost her grip on the stray souls in the quickly conforming society.

The short period in the early 1960s marked a shift in the consciousness of the Japanese. We witnessed the birth of a new middle class consciousness on a conformist basis. You might call it the "others-directed" mentality, but this new phase was in close touch with conventionalism. The royal wedding ceremony of 1959 had been another focus of national attention, and young women's eyes were riveted on the Cinderella of modern Japan. The Crown Princess of upper middle class origin seemed to exemplify the utmost feminine elegance a Japanese woman could attain, and she was someday to become the National Mother as we traditionally call the Empress. Women's weekly magazines that had just come into existence succeeded in setting up a model for the rising middle class women with photo after photo of the Crown Princess as well as detailed manuals for the ideal in homemaking. With success in our economy, for the first time in our history the better part of the population was now able to lead a fairly comfortable life. The successful Olympic Games, the highlight of the 1960s, brought to the Japanese a sense of fulfillment, an elevated feeling of nationalism. In this atmosphere women were affirmative in their feminine role, presiding over the domestic domain into which they poured all their frustrated energies.

This new middle class consciousness was yet to find its literary expression. Probably it was felt as too banal for literature, or it might have been too subtle for words. Established female authors were nauseatingly conventional and even regressive—Sawako Ariyoshi, the author of *Doctor's Wife*, for one. Perhaps those gifted writers were too unique and privileged to catch up with the general trend and too self-conscious to indulge in their own consciousness. Yumiko Kurahashi, once a mouthpiece for the existentialistic youth, turned sarcastic and even reactionary against those "stray" women who sought career and independence. Takako Takahashi seems to be the first to write about the solitude and isolation of the women of the age. On the whole, it was a fermenting period for the eminent female authors with new consciousness such as Minako Ohba, Yuko Tsushima, or Taeko Tomioka, who were to emerge in the 1970s and 1980s. It was a lulling period when currents were shifting, and a new current was gathering force as literary women with college educations focused their attention on the ordinary phases of life. It was in 1968 that Minako Ohba shook the literary circle with her prize-winning novel *The Three Crabs*. She seemed to give full expression of the ennui of a middle-class woman living in a foreign country with no sense of direction or fulfillment, and her sentiment was shared by not a few intellectuals.

It was in that environment that I ventured to translate Anaïs Nin's *Diary*. I had been married for eight years, had two children, and had taught in a women's college for five years. I was energetic but weary of the status quo of the stagnating society. Conformity and conventionalism had been the choice of middle class women, and the society was particularly inimical to married women or mothers who wanted some freedom of their own. A mother should stay at home and tend to her young ones; a mother should not have a full-time job unless necessitated by economic reasons; a mother should give up all her personal pleasures until her children are old enough to be left alone. And if the children should become ill or "eccentric" in behavior, all blames were placed on their "erratic" mothers. Psychologists prompted witch-hunting with jargon that frightened educated mothers. I was obliged to look inward in search of the root of my "erratic" drives. This was my motivation for psychoanalytical self-examination, and I had Anaïs Nin as my mentor.

Anaïs Nin, already a worldwide celebrity, counted on her success in Japan. She had visited Japan several years before and felt that she had much in common with the Japanese. And she was right in a way. With all her emphasis on sensitiveness, subtlety, delicateness, and intuitiveness as posed against what she considered masculine qualities, she might have felt far more at home with the Japanese than with the Americans, as she wrote in the preface to the Japanese version of the *Diary*. Above all, the diary form in which personal thoughts and feelings are most freely and directly expressed is the very literary form that the Japanese court-women of yore brought to perfection and that, in the course of time, determined the nature of the mainstream of Japanese literature, that is, the "I" novel. But there are vital differences between her *Diary* and the Japanese "I" novels—Anaïs Nin's *Diary* is an Odyssean search of the self, her eyes turned inward, while in the case of our literature, the author is a seer, an observer of the surrounding world and of the mood the author is in. The psyche is exposed in the "I" novel as if it were inside out, as one psychoanalyst put it. The self, the identity of an individual is never questioned. Divided as I was, my main concern had always been to question the validity of the imposed image of what a woman ought to be against the anguish of what she could not be. To be in close touch with suppressed emotions and drives might help a woman free herself from neurotic frustration and from an excessively guilty conscience, which indeed is a negation of the self, I thought, even if it did not give her a clear image of what a woman could be like.

But Anaïs Nin did not win popularity in Japan—the *Diary* sold less than 6,000 copies in five years and went out of print. I concluded bitterly that the majority of Japanese women were content with the historically endorsed definition of femininity, the silent Great Mother. Minako Ohba's short story titled "The Smile of a Yamauba" was written within two years of the publication of Anaïs Nin's *Diary* and won silent sympathy of the women of the middle class. A Yamauba is a legendary old woman who, after long, suffering years (like Tomo in *The Waiting Years*), turned resentful and secluded herself from human habitation. She became an object of fear as she was said to play tricks on innocent villagers, and as often as not to do mischief to young men. A typical Great Mother figure, Japanese literature is full of such Yamaubas. Minake Ohba's Yamauba is an all-seeing woman who takes good care of her husband and children, carefully disguising herself as a loving and forgiving mother, always with a smile on her face. Her smile is borne all through her life to her deathbed. She wears her smile even after death, and the family members nod to each other in acknowledgment of the very happy life she must have had. This is somewhat like Fumiko Enchi's *Feminine Masks* written in 1958, but Ohba Minako's Yamauba is far more resigned and speechless.

Generally speaking, the women's literature of the 1970s and early 1980s accents isolation, resignation, impasse, and feelings of failure after fruitless attempts to seek the core of being. Women who experimented on new modes of being two or three decades ago seem to have been thwarted. Minako Ohba's much-praised novel, *Formless*, may be an indication that when all leading ideologies have failed, destruction takes over and that formlessness is the mode of being closest to nature. Her philosophy of life seems closer to the Taoist submission to the ever-changing flow of cosmic energy. Taeko Tomioka's *White Light*, written in the mid-1980s, expresses a middle-aged woman's desolation at the failure of her experiment on a family. A small commune of men and women loosely tied through sexual liaisons is considered by her to be an ideal family, and she has an adopted son with whom she has sex, too. But the son-lover runs away and her idealism collapses. Her initial attempt was to deprive men and women of their socially fixed roles and identities, and to reduce them to sexual—therefore natural—human beings. But they become confused, lacking the strength to cope with her scheme. Mizuko Masuda's heroines stubbornly choose isolation and deny others in order to maintain individuality. Yuko Tsushima started out as a young author exploring the depths of the feminine psyche—obsessions, aspirations, nightmares, and demoniac drives, but as she matured she turned to the eternal theme of maternity. *Child of Fortune* deals with an imaginary pregnancy of a middle-aged woman, which alludes to the hollowness a woman feels in herself when she is deviated from motherhood. Later, in the mid-1980s, Yuko Tsushima lost her only son to an accident, and her theme of the mother-son bond was raised to a more spiritual level, as if to make manifest the very psyche of our culture. Kazuko Saegusa takes her stand against the over-glorification of maternity with her emphasis on women's infanticidal impulse. This is expressly tinged with the Yamauba motif. All in all, it seems as though women have been driven to extremes as the Japanese society, built on the morals of self-effacement, grows less tolerant of women's pursuit of personhood.

I took to writing fiction toward the end of the 1970s when my own attempt to integrate myself as a maturing person seemed to come into a deadlock. I too had been trapped into assuming the role of an almighty mother, but I was more obsessed with the potential, unlived half of myself than most of my contemporaries. This frustrated half might have its root in my long-forgotten teenage days in America, or in my narcissistic bondage to the father-figure. I was to anatomize my own psyche. For my first heroine, I opted for a woman intellectual who had failed in her career and was at a loss in her mid-thirties. She chanced to study for a year in an American university where her husband was invited as a visiting professor. She met people on campus who reminded her of her long-forgotten past. With them as psychopomps, she was awakened to the psychic dimension of being where suppressed fears and desires made prey of the soul. Through this psychic trip she came to realize that she had been unconsciously conforming herself to the norm of the society, seeking her value as a Japanese woman, at the sacrifice of her individual self. The split, I found as I wrote, was really soul-consuming and was shared by many of my contemporaries who were strong enough to assert themselves halfway, but not strong enough to stand alone. I titled my first novel *Glimpses of a Woman*, and it won a prize in 1979. I was attacked from all quarters, the main reason being that the novel was mere jargon, a sheer fabrication of an intellectual woman, irrelevant to reality. One male critic said, "What, a woman talking about the self? How impertinent!" Women confessed to me that they wanted me to write about an ordinary woman. Since then I have published three more novels, and I am currently writing a full-length novel about another intellectual woman who has been persecuted as an erratic mother. It will summarize the forty-six years of my life as a Japanese woman with Western influence. It will also typify the state of marriage many of my contemporaries have fallen into: a woman supporting her baby-husband as a good mother-wife until she realizes that she has failed in a true partnership.

Anaïs Nin's *Diary* was reprinted this year [1992] in paperback. The seventeen-year interim between the first and second edition may have been long enough for the betterment of women's social status perhaps because of the influence of feminism or with general change in the social structure. Opportunities for career and higher education have doubled and even tripled as the economy kept growing. The most recent statistics show that more than fifty percent of married women now have part-time or full-time jobs. With increasing shortages in the labor force, women's working conditions have been improved to a certain degree, although they are still far from satisfactory. A new consciousness has arisen, accordingly, concerning marital relationships among younger generations. More men now feel that they must share housework, and more young women choose to remain either unmarried or childless. Sex has become far more casual than before with the divorce rate rising both among young people and among the older generations. The concept of partnership between sexes is more accepted, and more women in their thirties and forties seek what they want to do. These phenomenal changes do not of course sustain that the whole society has been permeated with a new consciousness. Society's motivation having been a wholesale desire for a better living on a materialistic basis, the majority, say eighty percent, of the population persists in a cozy discomfort, which is peculiar to the middle class sentiment, dispersing their frustrations by chasing sensual pleasures of a luxurious sort. Popular literature reflects this trend frivolously. Yoko Mori, one of the best-selling authors of my age, has been providing the masses with images of urban sophistication and luxury fringed with horror. She is capable of serious writing, but she sells the least when she does so.

A curious mixture of self-affirmation and resignation features the present-day women of my age. Women who have learned limitations as

49

they matured through the ever-prospering decades are happy to remain within their limits, afraid to risk and lose what they have attained. They affirm themselves within their domain, but, having bypassed self-scrutiny in a desperate race to conform and out of fear to look within to confront what might prove to them that they are different from others, they remain strangely selfless. Fear of being alone seems to have seized their psyche, and prudence is now their favored code of conduct, which I call "general hushing." In order to ascertain their own righteousness, they tend to reproach those who are different, and their manner is copied by their children, who have created the "ijime" phenomenon at school, "ijime" meaning collective bullying. Their mixed emotions and unconscious drives are so subtle and complicated that they have so far been evaded by contemporary female authors except, perhaps, by Agata Hikari, a divorcée and mother of two children who dealt with "ijime" in *The Yellow Hair.*

Frustrated as they are, mothers have free outlet on child-raising. They can project their fears and desires on their children while the father-figure is totally absent from home. I have seen many youngsters caught under the thumb of domineering mothers. Boys have to fulfill their mothers' dreams. They are tamed, protected, kept on safe roads to success and, worst of all, doted on even erotically. Girls, too, are governed by their mothers' fears and so controlled as not to grow bigger than their mothers. The Great Mother syndrome is everywhere. Just as boys are expected to remain in their mothers' bosom forever, girls are expected both by their monstrous mother and by their intimidated fathers to remain *Peulla Æterna.* The childishness of young women is a very conspicuous phenomenon. Girls' fantasy comics have pervaded the society over the past two decades, and young women, well-fed with them, seem to cling to their fantasy world, safely sheltered from the threat of the outside reality and, particularly, of their mothers. They wish either to extend their fantasy onto reality or to stay within the dream world intact. Either way, they have opted to preserve their narcissistic immaturity, which may be their unconscious resistance against their selfless but domineering mothers. Besides, what is the good of maturing into a selfless monster? Girls' comics are, as it were, psychodramas full of sorrow and pains of living under parental pressures.

In 1988 Banana Yoshimoto, the young daughter of Ryumei Yoshimoto, astonished the world with her novel *The Kitchen* and instantly became the most popular female author not only among her peers but also among men and women of older generations. It is an unrealistic novel, very much like a girl's twisted fantasy, but it grotesquely reflects the reality of the psychic situation we are in. The image of "kitchen" itself is symbolic of the minimized woman's domain, but in Banana Yoshimoto's kitchen there reside a boy and his father who, after his wife's death, turned into a woman. They play "mother and son" as they cook, eat and live in the kitchen. Noriko Mizuta comments in *Beyond Feminism* that it presents the most fundamental act of living to which we reduce ourselves when all meanings of life have failed, but the text is also open to depth-psychological reading. A question may be asked as to why the father became a mother to the son, and why they confine themselves in the kitchen as if it were a womb for the two. The mother-figure is erased from the beginning and yet there it is. *The Kitchen* reminds me of a scene in the movie "Kramer versus Kramer" in which the father feeds the son in the kitchen, but the sentiment is entirely different. Kramer, after his wife is gone, remains a man and father to his son, very true to the American psyche which has stressed the father-son bond. *The Kitchen* also reminds me of the oldest extant diary, *Tosa Nikki*, that begins with the line: "Woman as I am, I venture to write a diary which has hitherto been men's occupation." It was in fact written by a man in disguise of a woman. This kind of trans-sexism has a deep root in our culture, and it has indeed determined the very femininity of our literature. Whether Banana Yoshimoto is aware of it or not, *The Kitchen* made the readers feel at home. But it is, after all, a young woman's denial and ridicule of reality, with an ambivalent feeling about the mother-figure. Deep in the psyche of a young woman lurks the faceless domination of the mother-monster. She must kill the mother-monster in order to mature, or she must transform her into a more acceptable figure, which, in Banana Yoshimoto's case, is an effeminized father. On the psychic level there is a serious battle between Great Mother and *Puella Æterna*, and the only mediator of this archetypal conflict is the awareness of one's inner self, which our culture forbids. Discontinuity between girlhood and motherhood is felt stronger where the Great Mother archetype has a full grip of the psyche, and it becomes extra hard for women to mature, just as Erich Neumann discussed in *Amor and Psyche* the hardships Psyche had to go through in order to win the love of Eros, the son of the Great Mother Aphrodite. I came to realize as I wrote my novels that women of my generation had been too busy negating their conventional mothers as old fools to prepare themselves for womanhood before they married into a "mother and son" relationship, which is conventional itself, with their husbands. The consequence is that we are still seized by the Great Mother archetype.

Volume One of Anaïs Nin's *Diary* is an exhaustive struggle of a young woman who endeavored to grow out of neurosis into full maturity. Beauvoir was very critical of Anaïs Nin's concept of femininity, which really is open to criticism, and I myself have grown out of Anaïs Nin's influence. Yet her tenacity in self-analysis, her strength in pursuing her independent self and her will to live and bloom are worthy of renewed attention, I thought. She offered us a brave new image of tomorrow's woman, as far away from a Yamauba as a woman could be. Months have passed since publication, but the paperback edition of Anaïs Nin's *Diary* remains unnoticed.

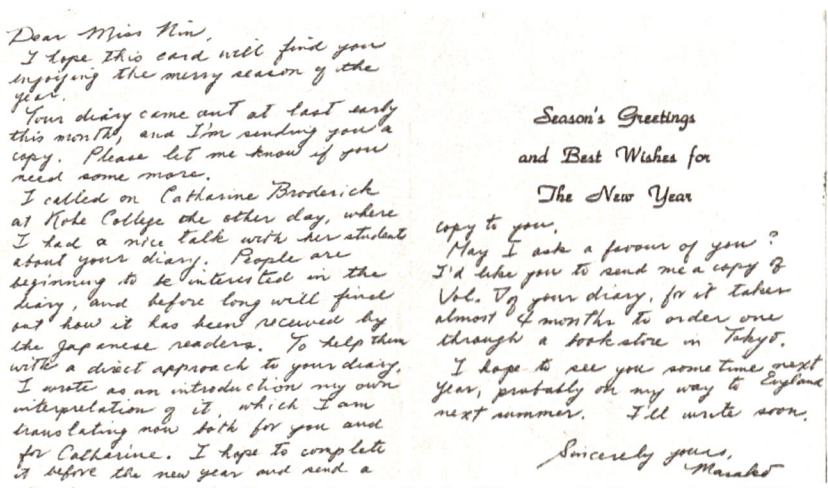

Card to Anaïs Nin from Masako Meio (Karatani), December 1974

Sumiko Yagawa

Anaïs Nin as Father's Daughter
True (?) Children's Literature

The Iwanami Collection of World Children's Literature will now have thirty volumes in total. I feel a bit awkward to bring up such a topic on this auspicious occasion, but I would like to frankly pose a simple question I have had for years about the term "children's literature."

There is a literary genre called Japanese literature, and there is foreign literature. There is modern literature, and also classical literature. Some classify literature by country, such as English literature and Chinese literature. Others by generation, such as youth literature and old age literature. Recently, there is even a dubious genre called "men's literature" as opposed to "women's literature." If literary works written by women are considered women's literature, then it is true that most of the masterpieces that have left their mark on the history of literature up to now have been men's literature.

According to this theory, children's literature should be the literature written by children, but for some reason, children have never been the authors of children's literature, and most of the works are written for children by adults. In other words, this is a phenomenon almost like women's literature written by men. As far as children's literature is concerned, this situation is taken for granted.

Adults have their own joys and sorrows. Children should have their own pleasures and griefs, but without a speaker of their own generation, children are probably just unfortunate readers who are forced to be content with what adults give them.

Why is it that children's literature written by children themselves does not exist? There may be many reasons, but the most fundamental one is that literary creation is an art, and it takes time to master it. The years change a child into an adult without any choice. It is rare to find a child genius who can write about a child as a child and express the joy, anger, sorrow and happiness of childhood.

I am also a little doubtful about whether children really want so-called children's literature. Children may always be ashamed of their immaturity and want to join the ranks of adults as soon as possible. Remember your frustration when people regarded you younger than your actual age. I think it was always my unfeigned desire to look a little older than my age, to read books that were as adult-like as possible, and to avoid the flashy packages for children, if possible.

Is there really no such thing as children's literature both written and read by children? I have recently realized that putting aside the case of fiction there could be such a thing in the case of documentary literature, memoirs and diaries.

A good example is *The Diary of Anne Frank*. Recently, a complete edition of *The Diary of Anne Frank* has been published and has become a hot topic of conversation, which is strange when you think it over. Because the deletions made to the original diary were undoubtedly just the meddling of adults.

Speaking of diaries, I have recently been absorbed in reading a diary written by an eleven-year-old girl, even younger than Anne Frank. This is a diary that has been praised as one of the greatest works of twentieth-century world literature, comparable to the confessions and diaries of St. Augustine, Abelard, Rousseau, and Proust.

The writer's name is Anaïs Nin. In the first part of her diary kept for more than sixty years, Anaïs's image as the eldest daughter of a single-mother family, forced to emigrate to a foreign country due to the sudden separation of her parents, comes out clearly and painfully in real time. When you think about her later works, the childhood diary feels even more interesting and I cannot bear to put it down. If I had encountered this kind of work when I was eleven years old, I would have felt a great deal of sympathy for her.

I secretly believe that children's literature in the broadest sense of the word, or in the true sense of the word, should include this kind of work.

There is one thing we must not forget about *The Early Diary of Anaïs Nin*, once praised by Henry Miller as being no less than those of Abelard, St. Augustine, or Proust, is that it was a part of the diary of a teenager. Anaïs Nin allowed her lover, Henry Miller, to read entries from her diary during the early days of their relationship in Paris in the beginning of the 1930s in order to help him understand her younger life before they met. It must be remembered that these entries were not from the then ongoing journal, but from a notebook written when she was a child.

I agree with Miller.

The memoirs of a divorce victim. The murmurs of the eldest daughter in an impoverished single-mother family. This record of a lonely girl's feelings in *The Early Diary* is a great piece of timeless and immortal literature that has been underappreciated in the pages of literary history.

Father's Daughter: On Anaïs Nin's "Incest"

One spring day, I went to see a premiere of the film *Father Fucker* directed by Genjiro Arato. With a remarkable cast, a masterpiece of hardboiled fantasy is born, as the director comments: "Every girl is a hero; every boy is a sissy."

I am not satisfied with one thing, however: the film's title, *Father Fucker*. It is undoubtedly the same as that of the bestselling novel, from which the film is adapted. However, I also feel uncomfortable with the novel's title itself.

It is a false and deceptive name in the first place. The man is not a father but a dirty pig who makes the heroine—the daughter of his girlfriend—call him "Father dear!" If it is based on the writer's autobiographical facts, as it is believed, some other title would do.

Had it been the confession of actual incest, the writer would not have dreamed of making it public. Incest is, without a doubt, a great taboo. It is rarely spoken of unless a speaker is brave, or a listener is a professional therapist. Yet, believing it was fiction, the general public did not hesitate to accept it and make it a bestseller. I even sense some kind of collusion between the writer and readers.

I now realize that the case of Anaïs Nin was the rarest of exceptions. My thoughts go back again and again to the exceptionally charming lady who some time ago captured my heart.

I wonder where else we could find an instance in which a history of incest and how the genuine father fucker is born is depicted minutely by the person concerned and is considered to be a monumental achievement in literature. We can only say that they were truly an exceptional daughter and an exceptional father. As it is from *The Unexpurgated Diary of Anaïs Nin*, we can trace what happened on specific days between the diarist and her father.

What exactly happened between them does not interest me very much. I would rather say that we can find rich, precious treasures in following the twenty years of complex and delicate psychological transformation of one girl prior to the physical act. Having recently read Anaïs Nin's works one after another, I wish to capture from them the archetypical image and symbolic meaning of Father for a girl.

— *Translated by Atsuko Miyake*

Sumiko Yagawa, 1950s

Atsuko Miyake

Modernist Women Writers on the Psychoanalysts
Anaïs Nin and H. D.

1. *Reasons for comparing H. D. with Nin*

If the interwar period of the twentieth century (1917-1939) is regarded as an age of modernism in the narrow sense, Anaïs Nin (1903-1977) and H. D. (1887-1961), who lived in that period, have many interesting similarities, even though there was little chance of them having met each other and no evidence of them reading each other's works. The only researcher who compares Nin with H. D. is Helen Tookey, who deals largely with similarities in the creation of self-image in their work. As she argues, the similarities between the two women writers can be described as an interest in the correlation between autobiography and fiction, a legend of the self created through psycho-analysis, and a passion for film as a synthesis of new art forms (Tookey 3). However, what is particularly noteworthy is the relationship with their psychoanalysts and the literary works they created based on this relationship. Modernism in literary works is still difficult to define, and Anaïs Nin has not been clearly categorized as a part of the modernist genre, partly because her work was widely published in the 1940s and 1960s. Recently, however, attempts have been made to secure a place in literary history, particularly in recent research by Jarczok (2017) and Oropeza (2019). Although it is not uncommon for two writers who share a common age to equally reflect the period and the culture of the time, the purpose of this paper is to clarify one of the literary historical reasons that Anaïs Nin should be confirmed as a modernist writer by comparison with H. D.

The fateful coincidence between the two women writers is that in the same year, 1933, H. D. and Nin received psychoanalytic treatment by Sigmund Freud and Otto Rank, Freud's disciple, respectively.

2. *Attitudes of H. D. and Anaïs Nin toward psychoanalysis*

In the experience of psychoanalysis, an interesting parallel between the two writers' attitudes is that they both sought to become apprentices of the psychoanalysts. First, H. D. wrote in a 1932 letter to Bryher (born Annie Winifred Ellerman), the daughter of a British millionaire (whom H. D. had met in 1918 and had been her partner and later a member of the family), after her four months' of sessions with Freud, "I will work, however, toward some professional status, as I think it more serious and also I need it, and can be useful if necessary" (*Analyzing Freud,* 12). Barbara Guest's authoritative biography of H. D., *Herself Defined: The Poet H. D. and Her World,* states H. D. herself and those around her referred to her as "a pupil" and she "wanted to learn Freudian techniques" (207). It appears that she continued to exchange letters with Freud even after his analytical treatment, while H. D. continued to study through self-analysis. She says that she spent time with friends such as the poet Robert Herring as a consultant in a kind of analysis (*Analyzing Freud* 354).

In the case of Anaïs Nin, she first visited Otto Rank, who had come to Paris after rebelling against Freud, to have herself psychoanalyzed in order to clarify her own problems, but later she became his assistant. In 1933, Nin met Rank in Paris through the introduction of Henry Miller to discuss her anxiety about being divided into various social roles (daughter, wife, lover, writer, woman). She then went to the psychology center at Cité Universitaire, where Rank was a lecturer, and gradually, according to *The Diary of Anaïs Nin, Vol. 1 1931-34*, she began to tell people around her that she was studying psychoanalysis under Dr. Otto Rank (372). Later, in the *Diary, Vol. 2,* Nin and Rank went to New York together, and she became his assistant. She wrote about studying, typing his papers, sometimes talking to his patients, and working as an apprentice. And suddenly Nin goes back to Paris, the reason for which is revealed in the third volume of the *Unexpurgated Diary, Fire: From "A Journal of Love": The Unexpurgated Diary of Anaïs Nin, 1934-1939,* published after the death of those concerned (mainly her husband and Henry Miller) in 1995. Miller, who at that time was her lover, came to New York to pick her up, begged her to leave, and took her back to Paris. The unexpurgated version of the *Diary* narrates her sexual relationship with Rank, and it seems to be true that she stayed at a hotel in New York and acted as a therapist and assistant to some of his musician patients.

3. *The reaction of the psychoanalysts*
The reactions and attitudes of the psychoanalysts to H. D. and Anaïs Nin show interesting similarities. Both Freud and Otto Rank were interested in the psychology of women, artists, homosexuals, and bi-sexuals, and they found their two writer patients very good subjects to study. H. D. became ill when her husband left her for his mistress and she was pregnant with Perdita, her child from another lover. Bryher loved H. D. and saved her life. Bryher and her husband adopted Perdita,

contacted Freud through her own analyst, and paid for everything, including H. D.'s stay in Vienna. Bryher, her husband, Perdita and H. D. were an unusual family living together in Switzerland. Susan Stanford Friedman writes, "In some sense, what she represented was the breakup of the patriarchal nuclear family, the blending of sexual and gender identities, and the growing recognition of the full spectrum of desires that has come to characterize the changing landscape of family life in the twenty-first century" (xxxii). As she says, Freud was greatly intrigued in his later years not only by homosexuality and bisexuality but also by the concept of family.

Otto Rank wrote *Art and Artist: Creative Urge and Personality Development*, for which Nin wrote a foreword in a later edition, and he studied the relationship between artists' psychology and the unconscious, and between female sexuality and incest. Anaïs Nin was a perfect research subject. This new treatment benefited both H. D. and Nin by giving them the opportunity to talk about whatever was on their minds and troubling them, and to meet a man who would listen and respond. At that time, it was considered impossible and forbidden for a woman to talk about the conflict between her self as an artist and her domestic role as a woman, or to talk about sexuality and gender, which were considered taboo. Since both of them were able to talk about these issues to their hearts' content, they were able to first sort out their own conflicts, and then they were able to regard their own creative imagination in a positive light.

4. *Expressing the psychoanalytic experience*

H. D. and Anaïs Nin, who were both pursuing avant-garde ways of thinking and living, expressed this precious experience of psychoanalysis and their relationships with the analysts in various ways. H. D. was told to take a break from writing the notes she had initially brought to the interview with Freud, and Anaïs Nin was told to stop her diary. Both were deprived of a firsthand record of their analytic treatment, but H. D. later recalled it in "Advent," published in 1974 in *Tribute to Freud*, and Nin recorded the content of an analytical conversation in the *Diary, Volume 1*, published in 1966. Both works are considered rare documents recorded by patients. In these two accounts, the analysts are revered as heroes, saviors, and gods. In *Tribute to Freud*, H. D. compares Freud to a soothsayer or priest. "I suddenly sensed a gap, a rupture or split in my consciousness, and I tried to hide it from him. It was a very tribal and telling attitude of Moses" (81). She also writes, "He is an infinitely old symbol of the soul, weighing the psyche on a scale (Daniel 5:27)" (120). Anaïs Nin also wrote about Rank as a charismatic prophet in November 1933 in the first volume of her *Diary*: "It is not easy to remember his words as he spoke them. His mere presence conveys all kinds of un-spoken teachings to others. He strikes down the past and its persistent demons by the concrete facts of his zeal, his interest, his adventurous spirit, his struggle against conventions, more than by mere words" (314). For both H. D. and Nin, the analysts who listened to their silenced self-narratives and gave them analysis were, in the first place, mentors and gods. However, the poet and the novelist, who are always looking at the internal conflicts of human beings, would not miss the complex com-munication methods and mental movements of their analysts, and soon the patients began to dissect and analyze the doctors. H. D.'s *Tribute to Freud* was written as a public tribute to the great psychoanalyst, and *The Diary of Anaïs Nin* was heavily edited from her original journal because the characters were still alive, so both works lacked much of what they wanted to say. However, the posthumously published collection of H. D.'s letters, *Analyzing Freud: Letters of H. D., Bryher, and their Circle*, describes Freud's use of transference, a phenomenon he discovered in his patients during counseling. The term "transference" is defined in the APA (American Psychological Association) Dictionary as "a patient's displacement or projection onto the analyst of those unconscious feelings and wishes originally directed toward important individuals, such as parents, in the patient's childhood." In the case of H. D., it was analyzed that she saw in Freud her father, her mother, and her older lover, Elise, with whom she had traveled to Greece. Freud's way of treating patients was full of tenderness, like a close man or woman, and he decoded H. D.'s most curious revelation, which she called "the writing on the wall," received in Greece, as well as other dreams, as the trauma of separation from her mother in the pre-Oedipal period.

According to *Analyzing Freud*, H. D. feels that Freud's attitude of singling her out is the method of pseudo-heterosexual transference he has found himself. After about three months of staying at a hotel in Vienna and completing one interview each week, H. D. begins to feel repulsed by Freud's fundamental theory of the Oedipus Complex and the scarcity consciousness of women. In a letter to Bryher dated March 10, 1933, she writes, "you must be careful as papa [Freud] is most slimy-ly dirt-ful," and "now you have been so frank, I will be frank with you— between ourselves— …My TRANSFERENCE seems to have taken place and what is it? This—Chiron [Ellis], big and remote and dumb is father-symbol and papa is a sort of old Beaver [Mother]. Isn't that odd?" (*Analyzing Freud* 69). It is possible that Freud also calculated this distrust and resistance to psychoanalysis and instructed H. D. to avoid writing letters and keeping notes as much as possible, which ironically became an important reason for H. D.'s visit to Freud: to help her overcome the slump that prevented her from writing poetry. H. D. wrote about Freud again and again in her letters, expressing her critical feelings about self-analysis, along with her great appreciation for Freud. "He has to stick to his scientific guns, but I have to stick to mine too" (*Analyzing Freud* 332). Although H. D. did not agree with Freud's theories, they maintained a long friendship until his death in England after he fled the Nazis.

In the case of Anaïs Nin and Otto Rank, it is clear from reading about their love affair in *Fire: The Unexpurgated Diary of Anaïs Nin 1934-1937* when they stayed in a New York hotel and opened a clinic to begin their work in the U.S. that they were in a state of reverse transference (the irrational feelings a therapist has for a patient in a transference situation). As Jean Bellemin-Noël says in *Psychoanalysis and Literature*, "In short, since literature embraces the unconscious, while psychoanalysis offers a theory of what escapes consciousness, it is natural that we should be tempted to join or even fuse the two" (16), literature and psychoanalysis seem to have needed each other. Like H. D., however, Nin rebelled against Rank's basic theories about artists and women. According to *Incest: From "A Journal of Love": The Unexpurgated Diary of Anaïs Nin 1932-1934*, on January 20, 1934, Rank says, "When the neurotic woman gets cured, she becomes a woman. When the neurotic man gets cured, he becomes an artist. Let us see whether the woman or the artist will win out. For the moment you need to become a woman" (301). In his *Will Therapy: The Therapeutic Applications of Will Psychology*, which later influenced the development of client-centered therapy in the U.S., Rank advocated a position of respect for the client's wishes, but he was also quite an egomaniacal lover of Nin, forcing her to translate his papers into English.

5. *Literary works brought to fruition*

The two writers who became patients were undoubtedly influenced by their legendary psychoanalysts, although they continued to receive treatment from other therapists. They then transformed their experiences into works of art. This is a literature in which one can find dissimulation and mythologization. H. D. portrays Freud in analytic therapy in her poem, "Master," which she adamantly refused to publish during her lifetime. The fourth stanza of the second section of the poem describes her unconvinced attitude towards Freud's analysis of her bisexuality:

I had two loves separate;
God who loves all mountains,
alone knew why
and understood
and told the old man
to explain
the impossible,
which he did. (*Collected Poems* 453)

In Ellen Friedman and Miriam Fuchs' feminist criticism classic, *Breaking the Sequence: Women's Experimental Fiction*, the expression "two separate loves" is said to refer to H. D.'s own bisexuality. And we can see that the poet's persona feels that no analysis or explanation is possible for this.

The fourth section has a strong tone:

I was angry with the old man
with his talk of the man-strength
I was angry with his mystery, his mysteries,
[. . .]
I could not accept from wisdom
what love taught,
woman is perfect. (455)

Freud was considered the chief reinforcer of negative gender images of women in late twentieth century feminist criticism. Half a century earlier, H. D. intuitively indicated the gender bias of psychoanalytic medicine. In the following stanzas, we see the poet admiring the master's unique mind-opening techniques even as she criticizes them. "And it was he himself, he who set me free / to prophesy" (458). "Freed to prophesy," H. D. went on to create many more long poems and prose for the rest of her life.

Anaïs Nin creates a human portrait of a psychoanalyst who appears to be Otto Rank in "The Voice," a novella in the collection *Winter of*

Artifice. Unlike the version of "The Voice" published in Paris, the one republished in the U.S. in 1942 is more compact, with the characters and episodes limited to the relationships between the Voice, Lilith, with whom he has a romantic relationship, and her female lover, Djuna. The text of the American version will be used in this essay. In the elevator of the Hotel Chaotica in New York City, Djuna is dizzy from the "the resonance to wind, to lament, to pain, to desires" (91) that leak from the hotel rooms. This poetic prose novel, like a series of dream scenes, begins with the analogy of dizziness caused by the elevator's ups and downs and continues with the stories of the patients, especially Lilith's family and her first husband with whom she did not get along. A man called "the Voice" speaks from behind a person lying on a couch and is described as "a modern monk," "a perfect man," "an alchemist," and "a sphinx who knows mysteries" (110). To Lilith, the Voice performs the role of "part of herself," "was in her to bring to light" (110), helping her to regenerate. Soon, however, Lilith proposes a role exchange as follows: "Suppose, just for once, that you lie here on the couch and I sit in your chair—like this—and now I'm you and you're me. What did you dream last night?" (111) This is the moment when the analyst and the patient switch places.

The Voice, whom Djuna reveres as a special human being, like God, gradually reveals his own desires. He says he has not experienced a human bond in his life devoted to research. His confession continues: "When they open secrets to me, they are in my power. But I want them to know me, and they don't. Even when they love me, it is a love that is not addressed to me. I remain anonymous. [...] You are the first one who has asked me a question about myself" (110). As Lilith listens, the Voice begins to cry. The psychoanalyst who appears here is not found in the first volume of *The Diary of Anaïs Nin*, published before the death of the author, and actually resembles Otto Rank in Nin's posthumously published *Fire*. The inversion of the love-affair roles is interesting in that the Voice loses his previous reason and speaks at length in an emotional and rambling manner, completely reversing his position. Gradually Lilith thinks, "[H]e is no savior. He is trying to save himself too. [...] Then when he became a man and ran after me I was very angry—it seemed to prove that he was only human" (118). She becomes frustrated, but dominant in the romantic relationship. And at the last climax the analyst gradually becomes trivialized and finally is presented as just an abstract voice. "The child that she awakened in him was like the child in those who had come to him for care, unsatisfied, lamenting, tearful, sickly. Neither her powers of illusion nor her dreams had worked the miracle. He remained nothing but A VOICE" (125-26). The last capitalized "VOICE" no longer seems to be human, but the originally unnamed analyst seems to have been invisible to the patient whose back is turned to the doctor.

Otto Rank died in 1939, and for the rest of her life Anaïs Nin mentioned him many times in her diary with gratitude and affection for the magnitude of his achievements; but in her literary work she lets the uninhibited Lilith transcend transference and countertransference, and abstract the human beings. The transitive relationship between therapist and patient seems to be discussed from many angles in the twenty-first century, but the figure of the male, predominantly gendered psycho-analyst as an authority, as Anaïs Nin sees it at that time, is interesting in its mythologization or deformation.

6. *The modernists' creations*

Both H. D. and Anaïs Nin, like other modernists, sought and created their own literary style as distinct from existing poetry, fiction, and especially Realism, and as a work that embraced the atmosphere of the particular era. In one of the most frequently cited modernist studies, Malcolm Bradbury and James McFarlane's *Modernism: A Guide to European Literature, 1890-1930*, modernism is characterized by "a quality of abstraction and highly conscious artifice, taking us behind familiar reality, breaking away from the familiar, from the functions of language and conventions of form...the violation of expected con-tinuities, the element of de-creation and crisis" (24), and both H. D and Anaïs Nin's works are characterized by these qualities, especially the discontinuities that capture the mood of the age. Also, the abstract nature, which is detached from reality, can be seen in their works.

The form, as well as the content itself, incorporated the most advanced science and thought of the time: the psychoanalyst and the patient. As Michael Bell notes in "The Metaphysics of Modernism," just as modernist literature was influenced by Einstein's theory of relativity and Roentgen's X-rays, these two women writers actually experienced Freudian psychiatry, which revolutionized the paradigm, and brought it to fruition in their works. Psychoanalysis, a new science, has influenced a great deal of subsequent scholarship and thought, including psychiatry, psychology, gender studies, and queer studies. H. D. and Anaïs Nin were involved as patients in the early days of the discipline, and both created interesting literary works that treated the analyst and the patient as equals in an experimental manner, while challenging the position of women in the discipline. And Anaïs Nin, who not only counseled Otto Rank but also kept a diary record of their relationship, sublimated and created a mythologized and fantastic poetic novel, like H. D. should be considered a writer in the modernist literary history.

Works Cited

By and on H. D.

H. D. *Analyzing Freud: Letters of H. D., Bryher, and Their Circle.* Ed. Susan Stanford Friedman. New Directions, 2002.

----. "The Master." *Collected Poems:1912-1944.* Ed. Louis L. Martz. New Directions, 1925; 1983, pp. 451-61.

----. *Tribute to Freud.* 2nd ed. New Directions, 2012.

Guest, Barbara. *Herself Defined: The Poet H. D. and Her World.* Quill, 1984.

By and on Anaïs Nin

Jarczok, Anita. *Writing an Icon: Celebrity Culture and the Invention of Anaïs Nin.* Ohio UP, 2017.

Nin, Anaïs. *The Diary of Anaïs Nin, Volume 1: 1931-1934.* Ed. Gunther Stuhlmann. Harcourt, Brace Jovanovich, 1966.

----. *The Diary of Anaïs Nin, Volume 2: 1934-1939.* Ed. Gunther Stuhlmann. Harcourt Brace Jovanovich, 1967.

----. *Incest: From "A Journal of Love": The Unexpurgated Diary of Anaïs Nin 1932-1934.* Harcourt, Brace and Co., 1992.

----. *Fire: From "A Journal of Love": The Unexpurgated Diary of Anaïs Nin, 1934-1937.* Harcourt, Brace and Co., 1995.

----. "The Voice." *Winter of Artifice: Three Novelettes.* Swallow Press, 1948, pp. 87-130.

Oropeza, Clara. *Anaïs Nin: A Myth of Her Own.* London: Routledge, 2019.

Rank, Otto. *Art and Artist: Creative Urge and Personality Development.* 1932. With a New Foreword by Anaïs Nin. W. W. Norton, 1989.

----. *Will Therapy: The Therapeutic Applications of Will Psychology.* W. W. Norton, 1936; 1978.

Tookey, Helen. *Anaïs Nin, Fictionality and Femininity: Playing a Thousand Roles.* Oxford UP, 2003.

On Modernism

Bell, Michael. "Metaphysics of Modernism." *The Cambridge Companion to Modernism.* Ed. Michael Levenson. Cambridge UP, 2011, pp. 9-32.

Bradbury, Malcolm and James McFarlane, eds. *Modernism: A Guide to European Literature 1890-1930.* Penguin, 1976.

Friedman, Ellen G. and Miriam Fuchs, eds. *Breaking the Sequence: Women's Experimental Fiction.* Princeton UP, 1989.

Kazuko Sugisaki

Translating Anaïs Nin's *Incest* into Japanese
Inciting the eye of a Yin woman

I shall begin with a story.

One fine day you are invited to a castle on the top of a mountain and given a tour of the place. It is a beautiful castle built of marble, colorful tiles and glass. It has several towers, countless rooms, windows and doors. Mirrors are everywhere. Fires are burning in fireplaces. One staircase leads you underground. There you find intricate labyrinths in which you are almost trapped. You are told that a woman has built this castle, all alone, devoting all her life to it. You are awed by its splendor.

"I wonder if you could build another castle just like this, an exact replica, in a foreign land," a voice says. "I'll give you one hundred dollars for the work." Of course, you could say, "No," and flatly decline the ridiculously unrealistic offer. But, there is something irresistible about the tone of the voice, and besides, you are so fascinated by the castle. You think and hesitate, but finally decide that maybe you have the ability to do it. So you say, "Yes, I'll try my best."

Now, it turns out that in the foreign land where the new castle is to be constructed none of the material used for the original can be obtained. So you have to use some ordinary stone instead of marble, paper instead of glass. You have a lot of other things to use—rocks, pebbles, wood, bamboo, sea-plants, flower petals. You work desperately hard, and since you are a good craftsperson one day the castle is complete. It looks just like the original and is just as intricate and beautiful. The only problem is that you know it is *not* the exact replica of the original.

This is precisely what I am experiencing translating Anaïs Nin's *Incest* into Japanese. It is an enormous project. The book is four hundred and three pages thick, and it demands that I pay very scrupulous attention to every detail of it in terms of meaning, ideas, expression, and the harmony of the whole. Very often while crafting this and that I find myself lost in Nin's unending labyrinths.

Translation of literature is hard work! It requires time, effort, persistence, perseverance, patience, literary sensitivity, and above all, you yourself must be an artist to create literature in the receptor language. In the end, your work brings you neither fame nor money.

Then why do you do it? Why do you spend months, years sometimes, laboring over someone else's artwork, trying to transform it into another language? It seems such an unrewarding labor. You do it, I suppose, just for the love of it. You read a particular work of literature, and you fall in love with it. You feel you understand it well enough to want to share the experience with someone else, with those around you, and with many others who don't know the original language. You also admire the writing style so much that you are tempted to recreate it in your own language. It is a challenge, a tormenting, yet enjoyable and exciting challenge.

There is something very different in translating English into Japanese from that into any of the European languages. First of all, letters we use are worlds apart. One word Nin is obsessed with, *love*, becomes *ai* in Japanese. It does not look anything like French *amour*, or German *libe*, does it? I feed the word *shoka* to the machine. It is another favorite word of Nin's. Very faithfully the computer gives forty-seven possible choices. Depending on the characters you use for the same pronunciation, meanings are totally different. It can mean digestion, fire extinguishing, children's song, department of business, merchant, and forty-two other things. With Nin, it is always this *shoka*—sublimation. (After repeating the conversion process thousands of times, one evening, my computer refused to do the job!)

And there is the problem of *I* and *you*. There are countless ways of saying *I* and *you* in the Japanese language depending on the speaker's gender, age, social status, occasions, situations, etc. It is obvious that Anaïs's *I* (*watakushi*) should be different from Henry's *I* (*boku*). But should Henry's *I* be different from Hugo's? What about Anaïs's father's *I* and Rank's? Should it be an imposing *I* for father or gentle and humble? By choosing a particular *I* for a particular person, we can almost define his or her character.

In the episode in which Allendy proposes flogging Anaïs, he says, "…Henry hasn't beaten you, has he? I'm going to possess you as you never have been possessed. You devil."[1]

Mocking and slighting *you* (*omae*) in this case certainly should be different from admiring and endearing *you* (*anata*) when Rank uses it:

> "I have been looking for a name for you," I (Anaïs) said.
> "I, too," said Rank, "and I can only think of YOU. When I say YOU, you stand before me."[2]

One of the main issues of literary translation is whether a translation should read as a contemporary of the original or as that of the translator. If, for instance, Shakespeare is read and spoken in 17th century Japanese, our contemporary audience would have a hard time understanding him. On the other hand, the text must give some texture, some favor that indicates its origin.

What I feel to be unique and remarkable characteristics of Nin's writing style is that, even though most of *Incest* was written in the early 1930s, it is amazingly modern. Translating it seventy years later, I have no concerns whether or not faithful reconstruction of any Nin passages may sound too archaic.

It is because, perhaps, she writes almost exclusively about her inner world where her own private climate prevails, the climate whose air is charged with the psychological, the emotional, and the sensual. Kissing, caressing, desire, joy, exaltation, understanding, jealousy, hurt and love. All of us understand love as love, sexual ecstasy as sexual ecstasy, spiritual and emotional hunger as exactly that. Time does not lay any patina on them.

And her language is direct and strong, using terms that describe what is happening right then and there.

About her affair with Father, Nin writes:

> Ecstatic, his face, and I now frenzied with the desire to unite with him…undulating, caressing him, clinging to him. His spasm was tremendous, of his whole being. He emptied all of himself in me…and my yielding was immense, with my whole being, with only that core of fear, which arrested the supreme spasm in me.[4]

Take one moment and consider *The Tale of Genji*, a long novel written by a woman in the 11th century. The very crucial scene of the first love union between the Prince Genji and his young protégé, Princess Murasaki, is described simply: The princess stayed in bed late this morning.

For someone like me born and raised in a culture whose literature traditionally relies heavily on images of natural beauty to describe the tangible and the intangible, on creating images to hint, to suggest, it is somewhat strange to realize that not even one flower is mentioned in the four hundred and three pages of *Incest*. There, no pine trees sway, no moon reflects on a quiet pond, no clouds announce approaching storms that might mow down pampas grasses and violate the pristine garden of the palace. *The Tale of Genji* is full of symbolism of this kind. The land where I intend to transplant Nin is indeed a very different place. And there is a danger that the translated text could meet a cool, impassive reception.

Times are changing, however, and we have women writers who write with braver, bolder and more direct strokes. One writer, Takako Takahashi, comes to mind as having Nin-like qualities. I quote below short passages I selected and translated from her work.

What interests me most of all is me, myself who have been hurt and unhappy. Ever since I can remember, I have been concerned with myself, watching and observing my unhappy self.[5]

This is perfect, at least something close to perfection, just being here now, like this... It is true that I love this man, but what I am waiting for is my own desire that reaches me through this man. Carried by this desire, from the deepest depth of myself, an unmanageable strange woman appears. It is a woman much thicker than my ordinary self, almost a mad woman, naked, violent, vora-cious, simple as a killer, gathering in herself the life that is too full. It is a woman strange to me, yet I feel I have known her all my life, no, not all my life, even before I was born. If I ask her, "Who are you?" the woman would reply, "I am you."

This is the person I really love, Michiko thought. But to meet this woman Michiko had to sleep with a man.[6]

I want to destroy Sister Sasaki, Yayoi thought. I want to expose that fresh wound hidden under her black nun's attire, make it bleed again. Imagining the nun screaming with pain, Yayoi felt excite-ment, exaltation. The hunger I have could be connected with this imagined sensation.[7]

"You have immense hunger for something, don't you?" asked the nun.

Yayoi didn't say anything, but she realized that she had had this unbearable hunger, thirst all her life. In the past, to pour water into her burning throat was the only reason for her to live, and it will be also for this reason that she will live in the future.[8]

These short quotations hardly do justice to Takahashi's voluminous writing, but I hope even they could incite some literature lovers in America to translate her delicate yet deeply complex work into English.

Anaïs Nin represents to me a Yang woman who had walked in light all her life. Being a Yang woman, she has that tiny black eye with which she can see into the heart of a Yin woman, her Japanese counterpart. The Japanese Yin woman may be still in a shadow, but she too has the small white eye with her. And that eye may sparkle with excitement when she reads Anaïs Nin.

When Ezra Pound published *Cathay* in 1915, his translation of Li Po poems, he hardly knew Chinese. But the poetry he recreated was so superb that it was received with tremendous enthusiasm. T. S. Eliot called Pound "the inventor of Chinese poetry" because "through his translation we really at last get the original."[9]

By no means do I claim to be the inventor of the Nin *Diary*, but at least I hope to be her Japanese shaman, the woman through whom Nin's spirit speaks.

Notes

[1] Nin, Anaïs, *Incest*. New York: Harcourt Brace Jovanovich, 1992. 147.

[2] Ibid. 339.

[3] Ibid. 275.

[4] Ibid. 209.

[5] Takahashi, Takako. "Going into My Self." Tokyo: *Waseda Bungaku*, Waseda University, July 1976. 83.

[6] Takahashi. *Waste Land*. Tokyo: Kawadeshobo Shinsha, 1980. 156-57.

[7] Ibid. 120.

[8] Ibid. 66.

[9] Eliot, T. S. Introduction to *Ezra Pound: Selected Poems*. Ed. T. S. Eliot. London: Faber & Gwyer, 1928. 14.

Yoshiho Satake

Body Image in *House of Incest*

In Anaïs Nin's prose poem *House of Incest*, various descriptions of *body* exist. What follows here is an examination of what lies behind these descriptions.

In regard to the first section of the book, in which the birth of the narrator is depicted, Lynette Felber says:

> Nin's self-proclaimed woman's "myth" associates Sabina and the narrator (June and Anaïs) with the preoedipal state of mother-child fusion that initiates the process of gender identity and prefigures Lacan's account of the narcissistic "mirror-stage." Replete with fluid, feminine images suggestive of Kristeva's semiotic *chora*, the *House of Incest* sequence places the narrator, an "uncompleted self," in the maternal "giant bosom" of the sea. (Felber 315)

It seems reasonable to suppose that the narrator has, to borrow Felber's phrase, the preoedipal "peace of mind before the awakening" because the narrator is "breathing in an ecstasy of dissolution" (*House of Incest* 5).

In the second section, the relationship between the narrator and Sabina is described. Gunther Stuhlmann points out that Anaïs Nin, in describing Sabina, "presented her own, multi-dimensional image of June [Henry Miller's second wife] as an extension, a missing aspect, a kind of 'Doppelgänger,' of her own fragmented multiple selves" (Stuhlmann x). The narrator finds they have many things in common and says, "one lies down at peace as on one's own breast" (*House of Incest* 11). Two good points seem to exist in their relationship: first, they have peace of mind; second, they understand each other. It may be assumed that both are the result of the similarity between them.

There is evidence indicating that Sabina loses the faculty of procreation when it is stated that "she [Sabina] was losing the human power to fit body to body in human completeness" (11). The similarity between the women may be depriving Sabina of this faculty. Furthermore, she is "at war with the sun and light" (11). "[T]he sun and light" are connected with procreation. In other words, darkness is connected with sterility. We read that "half the universe belonged to him [the sun]" and Sabina is "turning her serpent back to that [the sun] alone which might overshadow her own stature giving her the joy of fecundation" (11-12). It is likely that "fecundation" needs a balance between light and darkness.

After Sabina is lost, the narrator wonders if Sabina is only an imaginary character. The following is an example of how Sabina is considered one of the narrator's multiple selves: "I see two women in me freakishly bound together, like circus twins" (16). Yet, whether Sabina is really an imaginary person remains ambiguous. In any case, the relationship between these two similar people—narcissistic love—is fruitless.

In the third section, darkness is connected with pain: "I fall into darkness after the collision with pain" (21) and "I cannot tell the truth because I have felt the heads of men in my womb. The truth would be death-dealing and I prefer fairytales... But the moment I step into the cavern of my lies I drop into darkness" (25). The latter of these two examples makes it clear that the narrator thinks "men" hinder her "telling the truth" and they are her fetuses to protect. It seems logical that the narrator cannot "tell the truth" because "the truth would be death-dealing" for her fetuses, that is to say, for her "men." We see from the narrator's connecting her "lies" with "darkness" that they are considered fruitless.

Virginia Woolf acutely points out in *A Room of One's Own* that women are supposed to withhold criticism of men in order to better serve "as looking glasses possessing the magic and delicious power of reflecting the figure of man at twice its natural size" (Woolf 37). One may say that Nin's opinion on woman's role in protecting men is similar to Woolf's since it is likely that Nin was in the same situation that Woolf observed, considering *House of Incest* and *Room* were written during the same era. Although Nin has been sometimes criticized for telling "lies" in *The Diary of Anaïs Nin*, this view is quite unsatisfactory, because it is possible that such lies were the direct result of the imposition of woman's role by men.

In *Diary 1*, Nin says that she will live as a mother not of children, but of men. Yet, even if such a way of living that refuses childbirth was new, we cannot say the same of the role of a mother protecting men. In fact, we may say that she could not escape from traditional gender roles. One explanation for the impossibility of escape may be that these gender roles were too dominant in those days. Even Miller, who was against traditional sexual morals, expected women to fulfill the role of a mother who bore the reproductive labor: "I wanted the dark fecundity of nature, the deep well of the womb" (Miller 70). The role of mother is characteristic of Nin's sexual identity, as can be seen in the following quotation: "It was being such a mother that made me feel I was a woman" (*Diary 1* 290). It is likely that living as a mother to men caused her to "drop into darkness" and that she suffered from it. An example is a passage from the novella "Winter of Artifice," in which she depicts a conflict between a father who cannot tolerate any criticism and a daughter who wants the truth and suffers from his intolerance. Nin expresses the vanity of the relationship between them. There are several other examples. Viewed in this light, her "lies" can be regarded as an expression of suffering from a division between a desire for the truth and the gender role of a mother to men.

In the fourth section, we meet Jeanne, whose leg is deformed and who loves her brother. It is obvious that she is narcissistic because "she picked up a mirror and looked at herself with love" (*House of Incest* 28). There is a suggestion here that her love of her brother is an extension of this narcissism: "Our love of each other is like one long shadow kissing, without hope of reality" (31). What is immediately apparent in this extract is that the relationship between Jeanne and her brother is vacant. While their love lacks reality, her suffering from the narcissistic relationship is real. Her suffering is expressed by imagery of the physical pain, "until my nerves were twisting and curling inside me," and "until my flesh contracted and shriveled with pain, and the blood spilled out of my ears" (29). From all these things one may say that only pain is real for Jeanne. Why she wishes for "martyrdom" (28) can be regarded as a wish to feel the utmost pain. We can assume that Jeanne has no energy to procreate since she declares that she gets "tired of playing the guitar, of knitting and walking, and bearing children" (28). It seems likely that her narcissistic love of her brother deprives her of the faculty of procreation, like the relationship between the narrator and Sabina deprives Sabina of the same. Thus, we see that in *House of Incest* the lack of energy to procreate represents the fruitlessness of love between similar people, and that the word "incest" is extended to cover the notion of narcissistic love.

The narrator talks to Jeanne, who wants to both stay in her "isolation" (30) and get out of it as well, as can be seen here:

> But Jeanne, fear of madness, only the fear of madness will drive
> us out of the precincts of our solitude, out of sacredness of our

solitude. The fear of madness will burn down the walls of our secret house and send us out into the world seeking warm contact. Words self-made and self-nourished are so full of ghosts and monsters. (30)

The narrator holds a negative view of "solitude," and her hope of an escape from their "solitude" will nurture the possibility of their getting out of the world of "words self-made and self-nourished"—in other words, to escape the world of narcissism.

The suffering of Jeanne is expressed best when she says: "as soon as I utter a phrase my sincerity dies, becomes a lie whose coldness chills me" (30). We should not overlook here that the narrator reminds us that Nin sympathizes with Jeanne. This justifies the assumption that Jeanne is "an extension…of her [Nin's] own fragmented multiple selves" just as Sabina is. Although what makes Jeanne lie is not clearly described, it is possible to build up a hypothesis: the cause of her lies as well as that of the narrator's is their assumption of the imposed role of protecting men from seeing themselves.

Let us, for the moment, consider the narrator's relationships with men. It is no exaggeration to say that they are narcissistic because the men in her womb are part of herself. Her relationships with men are considered fruitless since the narcissistic relationships are represented critically. It seems reasonable to conclude that the narcissistic relationships with men which are maintained on the basis of women's "LIES" create "SOLITUDE" (46).

In the fifth section, Jeanne takes the narrator into "the house of incest" (33). Direct communication is absent in the house: "no room was on a level with another…one might talk in the dark from room to room, without seeing the other's face" (33). The narrator continues: "Everything had been made to stand still, and everything was rotting away" (34). Here, we notice that absence of change is considered contradictory to vitality. Nin uses the expression "the collision between their resemblances" (34) to put "incest" another way. This furthers the argument that the word "incest" is extended to cover the notion of narcissistic love. Nin goes on to say: "their love like the ink of squids, a banquet of poisons" (34), which makes it clear that "incest" is considered corrupt. Absence of truth in "the house of incest" is expressed in the following quotation: "I [the narrator] looked upon a clock to find the truth" (36). Reflection on some of these statements makes it clear the narrator thinks there is no hope of love there.

In the last two paragraphs of the section, the narrator comes upon a forest of sculptured trees, which she regards as "dead figures inside of live trees" (37) because what she sees are "decapitated trees," "fragments of bodies," "bodies armless and headless" (36). However, hope of life is suggested: "the cut-down tree lying there produced a green live branch that laughed at the sculptor" (37).

Turning now to the relationship between Jeanne and her brother, it is useful to quote from the sixth section: "I [Jeanne's brother] fell in love with your portrait, Jeanne, because it will never change… I was wishing you would die, so that no one could take you away from me, and I would love the painting of you as you would look eternally" (42). This example suggests that a wish for constancy leads to death. This is linked with changelessness contradictory to vitality, as mentioned earlier. Thus, we see that one can never gain a love full of life without accepting change.

In the last section, we meet the paralytic, who feels a sharp pain because he was born "without skin" (47). A close look at the descriptions of his body, such as "lips edged and withered by the black scum of drugs" (47) reveal that over-sensitiveness is considered morbid. The narrator calls him "the modern Christ, who is crucified by his own nerves, for all our neurotic sins!" (47) "Neurotic sins" can be regarded as the circumstances whereby people cannot form relationships with others beyond the narcissistic and incestuous ones because "the modern Christ" says, "if only we could all escape from this house of incest, where we only love ourselves in the other, if only I could save you all from yourselves" (48). Although the narrator refers to barren narcissism, one may notice that in her calling him "the modern Christ" there is the suggestion of the possibility of salvation.

Let us, for the moment, return to the portrayals of "the house of incest" and consider the following:

> But none of us could bear to pass through the tunnel which led from the house into the world on the other side of the walls,…where there was daylight and joy. We could not believe that the tunnel would open on daylight: we feared to return whence we had come, from darkness and night. The tunnel would narrow and taper down as we walked; it would close around us, and close tighter and tighter around us and stifle us. (48-49)

From this extract one may conclude that "the house of incest" is connected with the womb and that an escape from it is compared to the delivery of the child. It follows that this imagery of the womb is used to express a narcissistic and incestuous relationship. It is no exaggeration to say that "the house of incest"—the womb—is the place where women are obliged to protect their men, who assume the role of fetus. We can assume from this view that the suffering in the house originates from patriarchy, and that the crucifixion of "the modern Christ" is needed to save the people in the house from this patriarchy. Furthermore, Nin describes several times how she has conquered the Electra complex through her experience of stillbirth. Because of her experience, she creates the paralytic to fulfill the role of her dead baby, namely, the role of holy sacrifice. One may say that the necessity for sacrifice shows just how unbearable suffering from patriarchy really is.

In the latter part of the last section we meet the dancer who is "dancing the dance of the woman without arms" and "danced as if she were deaf" (49). It must be noted that "her dancing was isolated and separated from music and from us and from the room and from life" (49). Like Sabina and Jeanne, she lacks vital power. We are also told that "my [the dancer's] arms were taken away from me" and "I was punished for clinging" (49). A few lines later, however, she gets back her arms. It is useful to quote from the last part of the story: "she relinquished and forgave…permitting all things to flow away and beyond her…she turned with the earth turning, like a disk, turning all faces to light and to darkness evenly, dancing towards daylight" (51). We notice that a body without disability is connected with a release from "clinging" and with the balance between "light" and "darkness."

In *House of Incest*, we are shown various characters who have some form of disability including the sterile Sabina, the sterile and crippled Jeanne, the paralytic, the dancer—Nin connects the descriptions of these disabilities with "darkness" in mind. Another illustration of the same point is in "Winter of Artifice," in which the narrator is disillusioned by her father, who is connected with his own disability. In Nin's works, a sound mind resides in a sound body in the world where "light" and "darkness" balance out. We should notice that Nin's serious consideration of the correlation between body and mind has something in common with D. H. Lawrence's pursuit of life through sex.

The word "incest" can be regarded as a symbol for overall unsoundness. We can see that both the relationship between similar people and fear of change are considered unsound. To put it another way, a sound mind can be considered the state in which people are released from narcissism, fear of change, and imposed gender roles. Nin describes the process of moving from "the preoedipal state of mother-child fusion" to a full release from the "gender identity" which had been imposed by patriarchy. There is one point, however, that we should notice: in spite of the "feminine images suggestive of Kristeva's semiotic *chora*," Nin has one important difference from Kristeva. Kristeva sees the possibility of shocking the patriarchy in this semiotic *chora*, which is abstract and impossible to realize. Nin tries to relieve the patriarchal suppression through a release from narcissism, or rather the patriarchal self-consciousness, which, according to Luce Irigaray and Hélène Cixous, shows that the integrated self is a phallic self. Nin's views have much in common with the theories of the new French feminists, which are associated with the idea of "*écriture féminine*," in that Nin aims "to write as a woman" (*Diary 1* 128) against the logic of men, which stems from patriarchy. Yet, we should not overlook that her approach is different from theirs in that she does not try to solve the problems of patriarchy only in the abstract world. It is important to bear in mind that as early as the 1930s, Nin, while recognizing the patriarchal side of the self, noticed that it was important "to write as a woman." Moreover, she escaped the impossibility of this realization. These things should be highly regarded.

We may say that the balance between "light" and "darkness," which the dancer achieves at last, represents the balance between body and self-consciousness. It is entirely fair to say that the dancer is harmonious with nature because "she turned with the earth turning." We can recognize from the descriptions of the dance in the closing paragraph that Nin describes this harmony as a goal self-conscious people should seek to attain. The *body* image in *House of Incest* is a mirror of the mind with Nin suggesting that it is today's self-conscious people who will find it possible to recover a sound mind within a sound body.

Works Cited

Felber, Lynette. "The Three Faces of June: Anaïs Nin's Appropriation of Feminine Writing." *Tulsa Studies in Women's Literature* 14.2, 1995. 309-24.

Miller, Henry. *Tropic of Capricorn*. London: Calder, 1964.

Nin, Anaïs. *The Diary of Anaïs Nin, 1931-1934*. Ed. Gunther Stuhlmann. New York: Swallow, 1966.

----. *House of Incest*. Athens: Swallow, 1994.

----. "Winter of Artifice," *Winter of Artifice*. Ohio: Ohio UP, 1961.

Stuhlmann, Gunther. Foreword. *House of Incest*. vii-xv.

Woolf, Virginia. *A Room of One's Own*. London: Hogarth, 1929.

Anaïs Nin: A Guidebook by the Anaïs Nin Study Group in Japan

Toru Nakamura

Resonance of Anaïs Nin's Voice in Henry Miller's Texts
The Resisting Double of June Miller

1. *Dialogue between Miller and Nin about June and criticism of their relation*

It is a well-known fact that Henry Miller paid great attention to Anaïs Nin's opinions while developing a character modeled on his second wife, June, and that Nin's views of June contributed to the author's creation. However, controversy arises in how we are to consider the collaboration between Nin and Miller. Most feminists and other critics who are interested in power relations concerning gender have regarded their relationship negatively. Moreover, Nin herself complained that Miller had appropriated her idea, noting in her diary, "He has taken all my sketches for her portrait" (*Diary I* 128). Critics who sympathize with Nin tend to see Miller's involvement with Nin negatively based on her accusation of Miller (Bair; Petrequin). Meanwhile, there are different kinds of critics who regard her relationship with Miller negatively although they do not sympathize with Nin's accusation. In his biography of Miller, Robert Ferguson argues that Nin imitated Miller's representation of June, and both of them together portrayed her with bias. Ferguson's contention is embodied in his explanation that "Nin quickly aped" Miller's "deindividualization of June" (Ferguson 198). In her study of Nin, Lynette Felber criticizes the author's assistance to Miller, considering it as her conspiracy with a male writer.

Contrarily, in her essay intended to defend Miller from the attack of feminists, Erica Jong evaluates Nin's involvement with Miller's writing from the aspect of gender. A chapter in her book on Miller, *The Devil at Large*, titled "Must We Burn Henry Miller? Miller and Feminist Critique," argues that the novelist "absorbed Nin's writing and let its influence enliven his own art" (204). She emphasizes "the androgyny" of Miller's writing, which he supposedly gained through his interactions with Nin (205).

Some critics who defend Miller against feminist critics follow Jong's argument. For example, Anna Lillios refers to Jong's understanding of Miller when she emphasizes that the novelist celebrates the "common humanity" of women and men (Lillios 92). Another critic, Allison Palumbo, whom Lillios relies on to support her own argument, stresses the similarity between Miller's writing and what Hélène Cixous calls *écriture féminine*. Palumbo's view may have a connection with Jong's argument about "the androgyny" of Miller's writing, though she does not refer to Jong directly. Regarding the relationship between Miller and Nin, though, both Lillios and Palumbo consider Nin as someone who understood Miller properly; neither of them paid attention to their interactions in the context of his treatment of June.

The position of this paper is similar to Jong's stance to some extent: The relation between Miller and Nin is viewed positively in response to the scathing feminist criticism against it. The typical accusations against Miller are epitomized in Kate Millett's essay, which insists that Miller presents a distorted image of women created by male fantasy in which women do not have any subjectivity or individuality. This study opposes such an accusation by reassessing the relationship between Miller and Nin. Although Millett argues that Miller does not confront a "challenging" woman (Millett 147), he was indeed faced with the challenging voice of a woman when he created works based on his wife, June. This challenging voice belonged to Nin, who read and continually criticized the manuscripts of his works.

The emphasis on Nin's intervention in Miller's writing does not imply that Nin's voice was absorbed in Miller's words, as Jong insists. In addition, this study does not view Miller's writing as androgynous or feminine. Contrarily, the hypothesis is that the voices of Nin and Miller never merge into one united voice, and Miller's works are written from the viewpoint of a male who cannot take a female position. The purpose of this paper is to show that by identifying with the depicted female object, June, Nin challenged Miller's point of view as the embodiment of male power. In turn, Miller created his works by responding to Nin's challenge. The resultant female character, called Mona or Mara, is a combination of June and her representative, Nin. Consequently, the character obtains her own voice, resisting the description forced by the male author.

To this end, this study investigates the process of dialogue between Miller and Nin by examining Miller's earliest works, *Crazy Cock* and "Scenario," and thereafter, *Tropic of Capricorn*, as well as Nin's criticism of the work.

2. *Seeking unity with a female lover: From "Crazy Cock" to "Scenario"*
Ever since Miller and Nin became acquainted, they continually discussed how to understand Miller's wife, June, and how to depict her

in a literary work. When Nin encountered Miller for the first time, he was struggling to write a novel about a kind of femme fatale based on June. This was propelled by the irritation he felt with June's endless lies and his desperate attempts to find the truth hidden behind them. In February 1932, Nin wrote in her diary that she criticized Miller's "relentless analysis of June," telling him, "You go about it like a surgeon with a scalpel. And as you cut, you kill what you cut into" (*Diary I* 58). In fact, in his first novel, *Crazy Cock*, the heroine, based on June, is described as the object of a surgical analysis, as Nin had pointed out. The following passage is a typical example of the kind of description in which the protagonist, seeking to find the secret of his wife, looks at her while she sleeps:

> He looked at her brow, so smooth, so peaceful, so absolutely impenetrable. A bundle of mystery, even to herself. What lay behind that wall of flesh and bone? ... So obsessed did he become by the thought of his helplessness that at last he closed his eyes and surrendered himself to a flight of fantastic, wanton cruelty. Like a cold, searching vivisectionist, he saw himself bending over her with scalpel, stripping away the flesh from the brain, sawing through the bone with steady hand to expose the soft, dull-gray convolutions, the delicate, palatable tangle of mystery which no one could unravel. (*Crazy Cock* 172-73)

The heroine is regarded as an object to be observed and described unilaterally by the male protagonist in his fantasy of dissecting her head. In this description, the observed heroine is completely passive, in contrast to the observing protagonist's imagined aggressiveness. The protagonist's attempt to view the heroine as a perfectly inactive object embodies his will to dominate a woman into a submissive presence and to make himself the absolute ruler. In addition, the above passage shows that regarding a woman from the privileged observer's position creates a psychological distance between the observed woman and the observer.

Nin's criticism that Miller conducts a "relentless analysis of June" just like "a surgeon with a scalpel" can be regarded as a protest against Miller's will to become a detached observer in order to rule the observed object, which is exemplified by his fantasy of dissection. Furthermore, according to Nin, such a protest was originally made by June herself— the object of observation for Miller's creativity. On December 30, 1931, Nin wrote that June had complained to her about Miller's depiction of

June in his work: "I don't want objectivity. I don't want distance. I don't want to be detached" (*Diary I* 24). If this testimony of Nin is to be believed, her criticism of Miller suggests that she spoke on behalf of June as a representative of her protest.

Nin certainly felt strong sympathy for June's protest against Miller's detachment expressed in June's words, "I don't want to be detached." She echoes June's protest in order to urge Miller to change his attitude, that is, to stop his detached observation of June. In her diary Nin wrote that she had explained to Miller the necessity of "compassion" to understand someone's mind, and that June's "need to be loved" aroused Nin's "compassion for June" (52). What Nin calls "compassion" seems to signify empathy, which enables an individual to understand other people's suffering and desire. Furthermore, Nin emphasizes that it is important to "think of June as a human being in trouble" (53). In her letter to Miller dated April 24, 1933, Nin writes, "I feel more than ever how much of her there is in me—I feel her lies, motives, raison d'être, reason for subterfuges, evasions etc." (*A Literate Passion* 148). She also stresses her "complete imaginative assimilation, similitudes" with June (149).

Following this explanation in her letter, Nin wrote a prose poem titled *House of Incest* in which she identifies herself with a female character based on June, who wants to be understood by other people while fearing the exposure of her mind. In *House of Incest*, Sabina, the character based on June, cries, "DOES ANYONE KNOW WHO I AM?" (13) Replying to Sabina, "I," the first-person narrator says, "Cease trembling and shaking and gasping and cursing and find again your core which I am" (14). The narrator "I" also says to Sabina, "I become you. And you become me" (13). Thus, the narrator of the book and the character based on June are unified completely in Nin's writing.

In *House of Incest*, Nin dramatizes what she calls the "complete imaginative assimilation" with June. Meanwhile, reading the prose poem, Miller was profoundly impressed and moved. Inspired, Miller tried to imitate Nin's writing on June. Thus, Miller composed his own work imitating the poem by Nin in which he rewrote Nin's surrealistic verse in the style of a scenario for a film. In fact, the work was named *Scenario* and carried an explanation under that title that reads, "This Scenario is directly inspired by a phantasy called House of Incest written by Anaïs Nin" (*The Cosmological Eye*, 75). This marks a great turning point in Miller's writings based on June. A fundamental change in Miller's attitude came about that involved a shift from the attitude of a detached observer who resembles "a surgeon with a scalpel" to the attitude of seeking what Nin calls the "complete imaginative assimilation."

Though Miller sought an "imaginative assimilation" with June, it was not a direct, but an indirect unification with her through an indirect assimilation. What Miller actually tried to achieve in *Scenario* is an assimilation with Nin, who had achieved imaginative assimilation with June in her own poem, and thereby attempt to realize an indirect assimilation with June. The fact that Miller imitated Nin's prose poem to create *Scenario* implies a kind of indirect assimilation. Moreover, the content of the poem suggests an indirect assimilation and unification.

Two female characters appear in *Scenario*. One is a character modeled on June, who also appears in *House of Incest* and whom Miller borrows from Nin. She is named "Alraune," a character borrowed from the "Alraune" in the manuscript of *House of Incest*, who was finally given a new name, "Sabina," in the published version of book. The other character, who is obviously modeled on Nin, is named "Mandra." She lives in a gorgeous mansion and is a "frail," "slender [,] Spanish woman" (*The Cosmological Eye*). Nin herself was wealthy, physically weak, and a woman of Spanish descent. These two female characters have been regarded in *Scenario* as a united presence, represented by their faces reflected on a mirror merging into one.

Furthermore, in the same work, a male character appears who is a double of Miller, and he is assimilated into Mandra who has been merged with Alraune. In Nin's *House of Incest*, the first-person narrator is "in the soft current of water and desire" as if she is in a womb (5). Correspondingly, in *Scenario*, the male character is merged with Mandra in water. In one surrealistic scene of *Scenario*, the male character, who is in his room, notices a woman in a map and finds her singing. This woman is Mandra, and both of them are swallowed into the sea that surrounds her. The state of being sunk into the sea is depicted as "the joy of endless spiral movement, of endless ecstasy, of endless song" (*The Cosmological Eye* 93). Thus, the man who listens to a woman's voice is united and passively assimilated with her, in contrast to the aggressiveness of the male in *Crazy Cock*.

This description of ecstatic unity can be considered to be based on Miller's own experience when he read *House of Incest* with fascination and happily felt the sense of unity with Nin through this fascination. In a letter dated December 29, 1934, Miller uses the metaphor of soaking water to describe the sense of unity with Nin that he felt while reading

House of Incest—a metaphor that is associated with the above-mentioned scene of *Scenario* in which a man is drawn into water. He wrote to Nin, "I was saturated with you" while writing *Scenario* (*A Literate Passion* 288). Thus, in his own writing, Miller tries what Nin calls the "imaginative assimilation" into a speaker by listening to the female voice expressed in *House of Incest* in which Nin dramatizes her own "imaginative assimilation" with June.

Though Miller accepted Nin's criticism of his writing and changed his attitude by seeking fusion and unity with June, it did not necessarily lead him to the correct understanding of the inner mind of the described woman. The author's lack of confidence and sense of uncertainty in his understanding of June can be inferred from the way in which the fusion of Mandra and Alraune is described in *Scenario*. In the scene of the two character's unification, which seems to be based on Nin's statement in *House of Incest* that "I become you. And you become me," Miller made some significant revisions that are different from Nin's original poem. One important revision is the use of mirror image. In *Scenario*, the female characters' act of looking at a mirror is presented in the scene where Mandra and Alraune appear; this kind of act is not shown in *House of Incest*. Consequently, the description of the two female characters is not that of their real, substantial presence, but the description of their image reflected in a mirror. In other words, it is just a projected image, lacking substance. In this scene in *Scenario*, Mandra shows Alraune's image to her in a mirror at first. Alraune gazes into the mirror, which is followed by an additional explanation, "We see in the mirror not the face of Alraune, but the face of Mandra" (*The Cosmological Eye* 85). If the real-life relation between Nin and Mandra is considered, it can be said that Miller's explanation of the mirror image in this scene implies Nin's representation of June, which shows Nin's own self-image projected on June, rather than the truth about June.

In the following scene, the reflected images of Mandra and Alraune overlap and merge into one in the mirror into which they gaze. Here as well, additional revisions were made by Miller. The situation itself in which the faces of the two women merge into one is not present in Nin's original prose poem. However, a more remarkable change is that in Miller's *Scenario*, the first-person plural narrators, "we," who are different from the two female characters, see the unification of the female characters, whereas in *House of Incest*, the first-person narrator "I" is united with another woman called "you." In *Scenario*, the merging of the

85

two women's faces is described as follows: "there is a blur and then the faces fuse and we have a composite face of Mandra and Alraune" (*The Cosmological Eye* 85). In other words, *The House of Incest* emphasizes the ability of understanding shown by the narrator "I," who can grasp the inner mind of "you" as her double, whereas *Scenario* stresses the difficulty of distinguishing the images of the two women or the indistinctness of their figures, which is evident in the expression, "there is a blur," from the viewpoint of "we" who are different and separated from the two women.

Such a difficulty in distinguishing the images of the two women and their lack of distinction in Miller's poem can be interpreted as an expression of his confusion and uncertainty. Miller was probably uncertain about the extent to which Nin's representation of June reveals the latter and to what extent it talks about Nin herself, apart from June.

In fact, it is certain that Miller felt the image of June represented by Nin and the image of Nin herself to be overlapped and fused. He explains this feeling clearly in his letter to Nin dated December 27, 1934, referring to Alraune, whom Nin presented in *House of Incest* as modeled on June. As to his impression of Nin's face that he remembers, Miller says:

> I thought of the look on your face when I left you at the door of your house early in the morning. It reminded me of your description of Alraune's face swimming in the taxi. It haunted me for a long time. I felt profoundly uneasy. (*A Literate Passion* 277)

This explanation clarifies that for Miller the image of the fictional character that Nin created modeled on June seems indistinguishable from the image of its creator, Nin herself. Thus, it can be deduced that the overlapping of Nin's representation of June and the image of Nin herself, which Miller felt in his real life, is shown in the description of the two fused faces of the women in a mirror in *Scenario*.

Though Miller tried to emulate Nin's writing to create his own literary work based on June by applying her method of "imaginative assimilation" in the composition of *Scenario*, he inevitably found the process problematic and difficult, which he expresses in the work. This problem with the treatment of June continues without resolution in Miller's later writing based on her, especially *Tropic of Capricorn*.

3. *Miller's struggle for an imaginative assimilation in "Tropic of Capricorn"*

In Miller's autobiographical work *Tropic of Capricorn*, which was completed in 1938, his life in New York before the beginning of his literary career is recalled in a fictionalized form. The most significant topic of that recollection is the memory of Mara, a character modeled on June. In the storytelling of the memories of her, the detachment and analytical attitude of an observer is not assumed unlike in *Crazy Cock*, and what Nin called an "imaginative assimilation" is exactly what is attempted. In the process of reminiscence, the first-person narrator "I" tries to understand Mara as "a human being in trouble," just as Nin suggested in her conversation with Miller. His explanation of Mara is sympathetic as he attempts to understand her hidden trouble that she cannot reveal directly. This kind of storytelling about Mara can be seen as a consequence of Miller's change of attitude after *Crazy Cock* in response to Nin's criticism of the cruelty and detachment of the male narrator seen in his earlier writings.

In the later part of *Tropic Capricorn*, a female character, who is just called "her" and seems to be Mara, is said to be "struggling to free herself, to make herself clean of love's pain," and "with each struggle" she is "sinking back into the wound, mired, suffocated, writhing in blood" (*Capricorn* 231). Furthermore, in the concluding part of the text, there is a reminiscence in which "I" attentively listens to Mara talking, who avoids telling the truth directly, but, nevertheless, tries to make herself understood. The narrator explains, "I listened with such tense alertness that I fell into a trance," which shows how thoroughly he was drawn to Mara's speech (341). In addition, recalling the ecstatic condition of being fascinated by Mara's speech, the narrator says, "her words inundate me; wave after wave rolling over me." This confession reveals that the psychological distance between the speaker, Mara, and the listener, "I," disappeared in the moment of her speech (343).

Yet, the first-person narrator's absorption in Mara's speech and the disappearance of distance between Mara and him does not guarantee his understanding of her. In *Tropic of Capricorn*, it has been emphasized that the narrator's empathy for and attachment to Mara does not lead to his grasp of the woman. Though the narrator is drawn toward what Mara tells him, he admits his inability to understand her saying, "I am unable to form the slightest image of her being" despite the fact that "she speaks of nothing but herself" (*Capricorn* 343). Such an impasse, in which the understanding of Mara is impossible in spite of an ecstatic sensation of union with her, seems to be linked with Miller's dilemma in *Scenario*, where he emphasizes the difficulty of understanding the twin-like women Alraune and Mandra while expressing the ecstatic union achieved by listening to the voice of Mandra.

Miller's explanation of this difficulty in understanding Mara suggests its linkage with *Scenario* and his past discussions with Nin about understanding June. To grasp the hidden meaning of Mara's confusing speech, the narrator, "I," tries "looking into her eye and trying to find there some reflection of the significance of her words"; however, he could "find nothing, nothing except my own image wavering in a bottomless well" (343). Similar to the image of Alraune reflected in a mirror in *Scenario*, the difficulty in understanding Mara is expressed by the use of the image of unclear reflection. In addition, the unclear image of Mara is regarded as an image projected on her by her interpreter.

Furthermore, in *Tropic of Capricorn*, the narrator tries to understand Mara's mind by listening to her talk about a specific fictional character with whom she identifies herself. Such an attempt reflects Miller's effort to listen to Nin's explanation of June, whom Nin identified with, and to understand June through the fictional character in *House of Incest*, Alraune, whom Nin created to represent June. In *Tropic of Capricorn*, Mara identifies with a female character named Henriette, and she tries to express her deepest thoughts by projecting her own emotions onto the fictional character. In his recollection, the narrator refers to his long conversation with Mara about Henriette, saying, "Almost the whole evening we have been talking about Strindberg, about a character of his named Henriette." Thereafter, he narrates Mara's reaction to that character: "Henriette! Almost immediately the name was mentioned she began to talk about herself, without ever quite losing hold of Henriette... Henriette is me, my real self, she seemed to be saying" (*Capricorn* 341).

The fictional work referred to in this part of *Tropic of Capricorn* must be August Strindberg's drama *There Are Crimes and Crimes* in which a female character named Henriette appears. Strindberg's play encourages the readers to believe that Mara's image in the text is created as a composite of Nin and June, just as the "composite face of Mandra and Alraune" in a mirror whose models are Nin and June. Mara struggles to "make herself clean of love's pain," and her identification with Henriette suggests that Mara's "love's pain" comes from her love and hatred toward her father. This is because in Strindberg's play, Henriette expresses her family members' strong hatred for her father. In *There are Crimes and Crimes*, Henriette says to her lover, "Have you ever heard that a person could be hated to death? Well, my father incurred the hatred of my mother and my sisters, and he melted away like wax before a fire" (Strindberg 45). Henriette does not clarify whether she herself hated her father. Yet, because this statement of hers is a reply to another character's request, "Tell me about your crime," it can be inferred that she feels guilty for what she calls her father's "death," and is extremely ambivalent toward her father. Intriguingly enough, the love and hatred for a vanishing father suggested by Henriette, whom Mara identified with, is precisely the main theme of Nin's work. Furthermore, the above statement of Henriette, which expresses her family members' extreme hatred for her father, sounds surprisingly similar to what Nin wrote in her diary. For example, on May 16, 1933, Nin notes in her diary her brother Joaquin's resentment against their father who left home and deserted them, saying "Joaquin furious," and conveys how he blames him: "Father lives in a nonhuman world" (*Incest* 166).

Indeed, the image of Mara—a woman who emphasizes how much her father was hated and imagined his death caused by such hatred—is similar to the image of June that Nin has in her mind—a woman who both loves and hates her father, which is strong enough to destroy him, as is shown in Nin's diary. In her diary on November 16, 1932, Nin writes, "My little June [...] You punish yourself, you punish yourself for also having loved your father. You punish yourself by destroying the love you most wanted" (43).

Considering this correspondence between the image of Mara as a double of Henriette and the portrait of June imagined by Nin as her double, and considering Miller's dialogue with Nin and his emulation of *House of Incest* in order to understand June, it can be said that the portrait of Mara in *Tropic of Capricorn* is a collaborative work that Miller created with Nin through his listening and reading of her interpretation of June.

Yet, as already specified, this collaboration does not mean that Miller's writing of Mara in *Tropic of Capricorn* results in his possessing androgynous or feminine features. In contrast to Nin's confidence of her understanding of June as the same kind of woman and the confidence expressed in her writings, such as her diary and *House of Incest*, Miller expresses a lack of confidence and bewilderment caused by a female character modeled on June in *Tropic of Capricorn*. Although the narrator of this novel, "I," keeps listening to Mara and is fascinated by her speech, the content is impenetrable for him, which leaves him puzzled and confused.

4. *Miller's response to Nin's criticism in "Tropic of Capricorn"*

Mara continues talking while the narrator passively listens to her; through her speech she entices, tantalizes, overwhelms, and eventually stuns the narrator. In this aspect, she is completely different from the other female characters, who are just the object of coitus for the male narrator. Little attention is paid in the text to what they say.

Reading the unfinished manuscript of *Tropic of Capricorn*, Anaïs Nin criticizes Miller's general presentation of women in the novel. She stresses the specialness of June, who could cause Miller pain. The author's exceptional presentation of Mara in the published version of *Tropic of Capricorn*—a woman who puzzles and torments the narrator— looks like Miller's sincere response to Nin's criticism during the composition of *Tropic of Capricorn*. The following argument of this paper is centered around the possibility of regarding the representation of Mara as Miller's response to Nin's criticism of his work in progress.

Nin had criticized him, saying that most women in *Tropic of Capricorn* did not seem to have any personality. In the published version of this work, before Mara appears in the very last part of the story, several female characters who are almost indistinguishable from one another are described. Nin had probably read the manuscript before Miller started to write about Mara. Certainly, in *Tropic of Capricorn*, before the con-cluding part on Mara, the narrator's encounters with numerous other women and his careless sexual escapades with them are endlessly recounted. Nin wrote in her letter to Miller in March 1937:

> I glanced over what you were writing in Capricorn, and there it was, the great anonymous, depersonalized fucking world. Instead of investing each woman with a different face, you take pleasure in reducing all women to an aperture, to a biological sameness. That is not very interesting. (*A Literate Passion* 307)

Following this criticism of the depersonalization of women, Nin argues that for Miller the only woman with individuality was June:

> My God, Henry, the only personal, individual thing that ever happened to you was June, because she tortured you and so she finally was able to distinguish herself from the sea you make. (307)

Through this insistence, Nin estimates June's act of torturing Miller as a woman's independent and active deed, and claims that June is thereby free from the objectification forced by a man. In addition, Nin believes that Miller's sufferings caused by June signify intense human interaction between the two, and she regards his painful experience as meaningful. Nin's criticism of his description of women certainly shocked Miller. He replied to Nin in a letter, saying "I'd loathe myself" if what Nin points out is true (309).

If Miller's explanation of Mara, whose model is June, is read as his immediate response to Nin's criticism and her analysis of his relation with his wife, it makes sense and aids in understanding his presentation of Mara in *Tropic of Capricorn*. First, Mara is regarded as a special woman who tortures the narrator "I," and this painful relation between Mara and the narrator is presented as a significant and meaningful experience that deserves to be narrated in detail. In the published version of *Tropic of Capricorn*, the narrator recalls Mara as an unforgettable woman who had given him pain. Initially, the memory of a certain woman, who is just called "her," is referred to, and the memory is described as the narrator's "open wound" (*Capricorn* 231); this woman seemingly signifies Mara. Thereafter, Mara's shocking confession is revealed. More concretely speaking, the narrator's painful memory is recounted, in which Mara tells him an unexpected anecdote while he is listening to her ambiguous and elusive talk and trying to understand her, a very short and fragmented story about a man's sudden sexual treatment of her:

> ...now it's about Henriette again, or is it Dostoevsky?—I'm not sure, but anyway, suddenly I realized that she's not talking about any of these any more but about a man who took her home one night and as she stood on the stoop saying good-night he suddenly reached down and pulled up her dress. She pauses a moment as though to reassure me that this is what she means to talk about. I look at her bewilderedly. (344)

The narrator "I" is puzzled and confused at being told suddenly about this sexual experience of Mara. He wonders about the identity of the man she mentioned, asking himself "What man?" (344). He could not understand why she told him about this man's behavior toward her. After all, nothing is clarified in her explanation. Although Mara implies that the man she mentioned is already dead, the narrator is doubtful about the information. Meanwhile, it is certain that the narrator is deeply hurt to hear about the incident. He says, "I can't picture the man as dead; I can only think of him as he stood on her stoop lifting her dress." Moreover, he confesses that the man's image of "lifting her dress" is fixed in his mind and calls him "a man without a name but alive and perpetually fixed in the act of bending down to lift up her dress" (344). This fixed image can be seen as the center of what the narrator calls his "open wound." The image of an unknown man's sexual treatment of his beloved obsesses the narrator and continues to cause him anguish. Whether his agony comes from his empathy with Mara or from his jealousy over that unknown man is uncertain.

The response of the narrator reveals that Mara's disclosure of her sexual experience has damaged him mentally and the memory of her words traumatizes him. Mara's statement about the man's sudden lifting up of her dress is repeated in the text once more, and this repetition shows that the narrator's experience of being told about another man's sexual treatment of his lover has become a repeated nightmare and unforgettable wound for him. After the reminiscence of Mara's confession about her sexual experience, the narration shifts to the narrator's inference about the unknown man she talked about. The narration almost reaches the ending page of the text without arriving at an answer to the question. In the concluding section of the text, Mara's words, which bewilder the narrator, are referred to once again:

> Again her words…"suddenly for no reason at all, he bent down and lifted my dress." (346)

This repetition not only reveals what an enormous impact her confession has made on the narrator but also clarifies that Mara is not an object described and defined unilaterally by the male narrator of the text, but a subject who has her own independent voice apart from and not submissive to the narrator's discourse. The independence of Mara's voice is shown by the fact that although her sexual experience is paraphrased by the narrator at first, her confession is rewritten in the form of direct speech in the concluding section, as is apparent in the above citation. Through the rewriting, Mara's confession is eventually retold in her own words.

Furthermore, Mara's confession of her sexual experience retold in her own words does not simply repeat the content that the narrator had paraphrased previously. In Mara's statement expressed in direct speech, just after the adverb "suddenly," which is used to describe the act of the man who lifted up her dress, an additional explanation—"for no reason at all"—is inserted, so that the unfairness of the act is definitely declared. Consequently, the feature of Mara's statement as her protest against that man's act is clarified. Although in her past sexual experience Mara was treated as a passive and sexual object, by willfully recounting the painful experience in her own words, she strongly protests the man's thoughtless sexual treatment, which is characterized by complete indifference to her emotion and reaction. Mara's voice of objection is powerful enough to be equal to the voice of the first-person narrator of the whole text, and it might be even possible to think that the protesting voice of Mara overwhelms the voice of the narrator "I." This is because the narrator of the text cannot do anything in his confrontation with Mara's challenging voice. He cannot interpret her words nor give them a meaning or include them as an organized part of his own narrative. Consequently, Mara's words expose the limit and powerlessness of the narrator's words.

Therefore, Mara's words, which are presented repeatedly, puzzle and torture the narrator, and this kind of formidable capacity makes her an independent subject, different from the other almost anonymous female characters. This feature of Mara's words completely matches Nin's compliments for June in her letter to Miller. As already mentioned, in her letter Nin highly estimates June's ability to torment Miller, saying "she tortured you and so she finally was able to distinguish herself from the sea you make." Considering this remarkable connection between Nin's words and the presentation of Mara, it would not be a strained interpretation to regard the insertion of Mara's confession in *Tropic of Capricorn* as Miller's sincere response to Nin's statement that June, the model of Mara, is special for Miller because of the pain she gave him.

Mara's confession, however, does not merely indicate Miller's response to Nin's assertion that the pain June gave to him was meaningful. The confession seems to resonate with Nin's own voice, which is engaged in a long-term dialogue with Miller. This is because Mara's inner trouble, suggested by her confession, precisely accords with the central theme of Nin's literature—her incestuous love for her father.

After mentioning the man who suddenly lifted up her dress, Mara's wayward storytelling of her personal life shifts to other topics. While the narrator follows her erratic outpouring, he has an intuition that Mara was trying to suggest that she drove that man to suicide. Moreover, while listening to Mara's ambiguous talk about her personal life, the narrator vaguely realizes that her father and a man whom she loved fervently are mentioned besides the man whom she drove to suicide. He has the startling impression that these three men are not different persons. The narrator says, "between this man who was her father and the man with whom she was madly in love I can make no separation." In addition, regarding the man whom Mara madly loved, the narrator explains, "I'm not sure that was not the man who lifted up her dress nor neither am I sure that it wasn't a man who committed suicide" (344). Her elusive storytelling ironically implies the drama of an incestuous love in which the man whom she loved madly, her own father, and the man whom she fiercely hates, hoping for his death, are the same person. This kind of incestuous love and hatred is precisely what Anaïs Nin repeatedly expresses in her diary and fictions.

Indeed, it is hard to imagine that Miller would have presented Mara's incestuous love and hatred toward her father if Nin had not shared with him her interpretation of June when he was writing *Tropic of Capricorn*. This is because the motif of incest does not appear at all in *Crazy Cock*, which Miller wrote before his encounter with Nin. In addition, this motif disappears again in *Sexus*, *Plexus*, and *Nexus*, which Miller wrote based on his relation with June after he separated from Nin.

As has already been argued in this paper, by focusing on Mara's identification with Henriette, who expresses her ambivalence toward her father, Mara assumes the composite features of June and Nin. Nin projects her inner struggle onto June, and June's image held by Nin is mingled in Mara's representation. It can be said that as a result of this kind of mixture, the resonance of Nin's voice is felt in the words of Mara.

However, instead of using the expression "resonance of Nin's voice," it can be said that the words of Nin, who regards herself as the double of June, are thrown into the text of *Tropic of Capricorn*. In fact, Miller himself uses the expression "throw into" in the text. In his letter to Nin dated August 16, 1932, after he tells her that he intends to send her the first few pages of *Tropic of Capricorn*, he says, "I think it's marvelous of you to throw yourself into my work as you do. You will be in it too—watch and see" (*A Literate Passion* 98).

To point out the assimilation of Nin's words in Miller's text does not, however, mean that they were appropriated by Miller. Nor does it mean that the words coming from individuals of two opposite sexes are merged into one, as Erica Jong assumes when she emphasizes the androgynous aspect of Miller's writing.

What needs to be stressed instead is that the words of Nin, which are echoed in Mara's words in *Tropic of Capricorn*, are essentially a form of female protest criticizing the writing of Miller, which comes from a male point of view. The words of Nin can be described as an alien presence in the text, which consists of the first-person narrator's words created by the male author. The female words, as an alien presence in the male text, resist the assimilation and absorption into the discourse of the male narrator of the text. Furthermore, it can be said that Mara, who delivers such formidable words, has succeeded in gaining her own voice, one that is completely independent of and equivalent to the voice of the male narrator.

In summary, this paper argues that Miller's works based on his relationship with June, including *Tropic of Capricorn*, which he wrote after *Crazy Cock*, are a product of his efforts to face and respond to the challenge of Nin, who identified with June and spoke for her. Though in his own texts Miller continually attempted to apply what Nin called "an imaginative assimilation," the author was confronted with the difficulty of putting that method into practice. This dilemma of Miller is evident in *Scenario* and *Tropic of Capricorn*. In the aforementioned novel, the voice of Anaïs Nin, who speaks for June as her double and her representative, resonates in Mara's words, achieving the power to encounter the words of the male narrator of the text.

Works Cited

Bair, Deirdre. "Writing as a Woman: Henry Miller, Lawrence Durrell, and Anaïs Nin in the Villa Seurat." *ANAIS: An International Journal.* 12 (1994): 31-38.

Felber, Lynette. "The Three Faces of June: Anaïs Nin's Appropriation of Feminine Writing." *Tulsa Studies in Women's Literature.* 14.2 (1995): 309-24.

Furguson, Robert. *Henry Miller: A Life.* New York: W. W. Norton and Company, 1991.

Lillios, Anna. "'A Dirty Book Worth Reading': Henry Miller's *Tropic of Cancer* and the Feminist Backlash." *Henry Miller: New Perspectives.* Ed. Decker, James and Männiste, Indrek. New York: Bloomsbury Publishing, 2015. 85-94.

Miller, Henry. *Crazy Cock.* New York: Grove Press, 1993.

----. *The Cosmological Eye*. New York: New Directions, 1961.

----. *Nexus*. New York: Grove Press, 1965.

----. *Plexus*. New York: Grove Press, 1965.

----. *Sexus*. New York: Grove Press, 1965.

----. *Tropic of Capricorn*. New York: Grove Press, 1961.

Millet, Kate. "Henry Miller." *Critical Essays on Henry Miller*. Ed. Ronald Gottesman. New York: G. K. Hall and Co., 1992. 145-64.

Nin, Anaïs. *The Diary of Anaïs Nin*: Volume I, 1931-1934. Ed. Gunther Stuhlmann. New York: Harcourt Brace and Company, 1966.

----. *House of Incest*. Athens: Swallow Press, 1958.

----. *Incest: From "A Journal of Love": The Unexpurgated Diary of Anaïs Nin 1932-1934*. New York: Harcourt Brace Jovanovich, 1992.

Palumbo, Alison. "Finding the Feminine: Rethinking Henry Miller's Tropics Trilogy," *Nexus: The International Henry Miller Journal*. 7 (2010): 145-76.

Petrequin, Marie-Line. "The Magic Spell of June Miller: On the Literary Creation of Female Identity in Anaïs Nin's *Diary*." *ANAIS: An International Journal*. 6 (1988): 43-57.

Strindberg, August. *There Are Crimes and Crimes*. Trans. Edward Björkman. New York: Charles Scribner's Sons, 1912.

Hidekatsu Nojima

A Woman of the Diary: Anaïs Nin

and before the throne there is as it were a sea of glass, like crystal.
—*Revelations* 4:6

O, wert thou for myself! but, Suffolk, stay,
Thou mayest not wander in that labyrinth,
There Minotaurs and ugly treasons lurk.
—Shakespeare, The first part of *Henry the Sixth,* Act V, Scene III

L *abyrinth of incest*
"I was eleven years old when I walked into the labyrinth of my diary." This is the first line of a short story, "The Labyrinth," in *Under a Glass Bell* (Anaïs Nin printed the book by her own hand in 1944). In 1913, when Anaïs was ten years old, her father, a famous pianist in Europe, Joaquin Nin, and her mother, a singer, Rosa Culmell, separated. Joaquin was a dandy who looked upon himself as a modern-day Don Juan. Everywhere he traveled for his concerts, he won women's hearts. After a reunion with his daughter twenty years later, he was bold enough to boast that he could recreate a world map using all the women's names as the cities' names. In 1914, Rosa left Barcelona and emigrated to New York with Anaïs and her younger brothers Thorvald and Joaquin Jr. Immigrating from the joyful, lavish, and sophisticated southern part of Spain, where luminaries such as Pablo Casals often visited the family, to the somewhat cold and austere New York, was a great shock for an eleven-year-old girl. The shock was beyond the abrupt change in the environment, as well as the fact that Anaïs's feeling that it was she who was deserted by her father.

Anaïs first began her diary as a long, plaintive, and continuous love letter in which she longed for her father to come back. "The diary began as a diary of a journey, to record everything for my father. It was written for him, and I had intended to send it to him. It was really a letter so he could follow us into a strange land, know about us" (*Diary I* 202). Anaïs hated New York, but for her father she described it as a brilliant, shining city. She desperately hoped that her father would be lured into rejoining the family if she mentioned the place as attractive. "Though she detested New York, she painted a picture of it in glowing terms, hoping that it would entice him to come" (*Winter of Artifice* 63-64).

The "labyrinth of the diary" she stepped into when she was eleven years old was, first of all, a labyrinth of incestuous emotions akin to Electra's love for her father. On April 18, 1915, Anaïs wrote, "My heart is full of a slow sadness and I feel like crying… I pour a heavy heart into my diary. This morning I took Communion, and during Communion I just murmured, *God, France, Papa!* God knows what that means and, like my diary, He will understand" (*Linotte* 58). In a subsequent diary when Anaïs was twenty-nine, she recalled the entry of her eleven-year-old self and wrote, "When I took communion at Mass, I imagined it was not Christ who visited me in this heart shaped like a room, but my father" (*Diary I* 90). Anaïs had an obsession with her father. She imagined her situation similar to the story of a father and daughter reunited after a long absence in the myth of Pericles later portrayed by Shakespeare. Her obsession is the theme of the novella "Winter of Artifice": "During her teen years she felt her true God was her father. At communion it was her father she received, not God. She closed her eyes and swallowed the white bread with blissful tremors, embracing her father in holy communion. Her exaltation was fused into a semblance of holiness. She aspired to saintliness in order to conceal the secret love which she guarded so jealously in God, the joy without name when she stood in his presence, the inexplicable bliss at communion, because then she talked with her father and she kissed him" (*Winter of Artifice* 65).

For Anaïs, God was her father's double, the body of Christ and "holy communion" as substitutes for the caress of her father, the "semblance of holiness" as compensation for sensual intoxication, blasphemies against sanctity by a young girl! Anaïs's writing appeared desperate and pitiful. In addition, by keeping her secret feelings of love towards her father to herself in the diary, she astutely created a public façade of religious piety that allowed her to suppress her inner emotions. This early act of self-deception was the initial phase of Anaïs's life as a woman in the labyrinth. Certainly, Anaïs must have been playing her role as a devout girl well enough. She found Communion difficult because the bread used in the ritual of the Eucharist represented both the body of Christ and that of her own father. If this were true, her inability to swallow the holy bread was an unconscious urge against incest. Wasn't the Christ figure that entered the chamber of her mind a "holy guest," a double of her father? Her welcoming of Christ into the pure and orderly chambers of her heart was her unconscious desire to welcome her father again to her life. After all, Anaïs had carefully cleaned and decorated the room and her surroundings to receive him. Anaïs was obsessed with the reason her father deserted her, and she was plagued by thoughts that it was because she was an ugly girl.

Neither Christ nor the Church brought Anaïs's father back to her. Thus she began to feel that not only was her Catholic faith meaningless, but that it also created difficulties in her real life. Even after dedicating herself to Christ and thinking of Him as a double for her father, Anaïs still kept searching for her father's face among other earthly men. "A man so strong...with very white teeth, a pale mysterious face...a grave walk, a distant smile...I would like him to tell me all about his life, a very sad life, full of harrowing adventures...I would like him to be proud and haughty...to play some instrument..." (*Winter of Artifice* 66). The "labyrinth of the diary" was, at first, "the house of incest."

In May 1933, Anaïs's father finally returned to her. By a curious coincidence, he had been absent for the same length of time, twenty years, as was Pericles, the father of Marina, in Shakespeare's *Pericles, Prince of Tyre*. By this time Anaïs was in her thirties and married. In March 1923, she had married a banker named Hugh P. Guiler, whom Anaïs called Hugo, and who was later known as a filmmaker and a copper engraver using the name Ian Hugo. Hugo and Anaïs were living in Louveciennes in 1931 when she met Henry Miller there. Even though Henry's style was that of a self-abandoned urban Satyr and the utter opposite of her father's penchant for perfect fashion and manner, he was a double for her father. "I became a child listening to Henry, and he became paternal. The haunting image of an erudite, literary father reasserted itself, and the woman became a child again" (*Diary I* 80). And in Anaïs, perhaps, Henry himself realized a beautiful, ideal mother, a double for his real mother who was a cold-hearted woman of German descent who never treated him gently and for whom he felt both awe and hatred. Henry was cursedly restrained and obsessed with his mother his whole life. In 1935, he wrote in his unpublished "Dream Book" (which he dedicated to Anaïs): "And thinking of...the questions Anaïs and others put to me about my mother, my possible worship of her (unconsciously) and of how this affected my whole love life, I must confess there is an enigma here worth penetrating. Because I see that in the woman I loved there was always a dual nature—I...worshiped them, trusted them blindly, *and* I regard them as *cruel*. And perhaps the root of it lies in my attitude towards my mother... I transferred this dual nature of love (the worship and hatred) to all the women I encountered, and created each time anew the same conflicts, even when there may have been no reason, no necessity for them..." (*Always Merry and Bright* 284).

For Henry, his wife June was both femme fatale and, deep within herself, mother. The duality of Henry's love for June, "the worship and hatred," corresponded to his feelings of love and hatred towards his mother. Henry believed that his inability to complete his book on D. H. Lawrence was because, like Anaïs with her father, he too was held prisoner between conflicting emotions.

After all, while discussing Lawrence, Henry could not help thinking about the cursed fate of mothers by both Proust and Joyce. "Molly Bloom is water, tree, and earth. She is mystery, she is the devourer, the ocean of night in which the lost hero finally plunges, and with him the world. She is the quintessence of the great whore...like the sea itself... With Molly Bloom, *con anonyme*, woman is restored to prime significance—as womb and matrix of life" (*The Cosmological Eye* 133). Miller also wanted to write about Rimbaud who was condemned by his mother as an *enfant terrible*. "Rimbaud stressed the fact that he wanted *liberty* in salvation... All this has one meaning for me—that one is still bound to the mother. All one's rebellion was but dust in the eye, the frantic attempt to conceal this bondage... 'Outside! Forever outside! Sitting on the doorstep of the mother's womb.' I believe those are my own words, in *Black Spring*, a golden period when I was almost in possession of the secret. No wonder one is alienated from the mother. One does not notice her, except as an obstacle" (*The Time of Assassins* 49-50). It was only when the eighty-five-year-old Henry Miller published *Mother, China, and the World Beyond* in 1977 could he finally reconcile with his mother. There, Henry dreamed of the scene of a reunion with his mother in the region of the dead. "When I looked up I perceived my mother some distance away. She appeared to be on her way out. Looking more carefully, I observed that she was waving to me, waving good-bye. With that I stood up, my eyes wet with tears, and giving a mighty shout, I cried: 'Mother, I love you. I love you! Do you hear me?'" (*Mother, China, and the World Beyond* 25)

To sum up, in 1931 Paris a daughter with an absent father met a son with an absent mother. And each could recognize in the other a double of a father and a double of a mother. At that time, Anaïs was undergoing therapy with the famous French psychoanalyst, Dr. René Allendy. Her motivation to consult with him was her anxiety and dissociated personality issues as noted in the *Diary*: "I feel that an initial shock has shattered my wholeness, that I am like a shattered mirror" (*Diary I* 103). Obviously, "an initial shock" means the shock caused by her father's deserting her. Eventually, Anaïs came to desire the father figure in Allendy. Anaïs was disappointed that his analysis, which was focused on her emotional difficulties (trauma), did not release her creativity. Finally, she decided to part with Allendy, and reading what she wrote in the *Diary* we can rather easily surmise her feelings: "I have no guide. My father? ...It saddens me to have become again an independent woman. It was a deep joy to depend on Allendy's insight, his guidance" (*Diary I* 194).

At the initial consultation with Allendy, Anaïs confessed in detail about when she was deserted by her father and how the holy host at communion took the place of her father's flesh. She talked about her misfortune as a woman who was unable to mature because of her father's curse:

> Anaïs: "June is my ideal of what a woman should be. I am underweight. A few more pounds would add greatly to my self-confidence. I feel like an adolescent girl. Will you add medicine to your psychic treatment? My breasts are too small."
>
> Dr. Allendy: "Are they absolutely underdeveloped?"
>
> Anaïs: "No."
>
> As I flounder in my descriptions, I say: "To you, a doctor, the simplest thing is to show them to you." And I do. And then Dr. Allendy began to laugh at my fears.
>
> Dr. Allendy: "...perfectly feminine, small but well shaped, well outlined in proportion to the rest of your figure, such a lively figure..." (*Diary I* 90-91)

If Allendy is a substitute for her father, does this conversation betray the daughter's bold seduction, her desire to seek Allendy's love? She wrote that she would abandon her father's substitute, that she would not cure her neurosis: "...when the 'cure' was finished, our relationship would end and I must lose him" (*Diary I* 114). She added, "I also wanted to know whether he would miss me" (*Diary I* 114). Allendy, who was already captured by his "daughter" Anaïs's allure, honestly told her: "If you dropped me now, I would suffer as a doctor from not succeeding in my cure of you, and I would suffer personally because you are interesting. So you see, in a way, I need you as much as you need me. You could hurt me by dropping me" (*Diary I* 115). There is nothing to do but to attest to the doctor's disqualification. Anaïs accurately offers this diagnosis: "Allendy has lost his objectivity" (*Diary I* 131). Allendy, who declares Henry Miller a "dual personality" and "schizophrenic" (*Diary I* 131) and thinks it is wrong and dangerous to have relations with him, calls her "*ma petite Anaïs.*" "I bow my head so he will not see me smile" (*Diary I* 131). He loses his credibility as a father figure completely for playing the clown. Moreover, Anaïs cruelly and coolly writes, "An analyst in love is as blind as anyone else in love!" (*Diary I* 162) Her diary continues, "I think it's humorous that I should have gone to Allendy to get cured of a lack of confidence in my womanly charms, and that it should be those very charms he has succumbed to" (*Diary I* 163). Here Anaïs is well aware of the ironic humor in the reversal of roles in which the patient had become the analyst and the analyst the patient.

Anaïs's quest for her father's love continued. It was Otto Rank who then appeared in the place of Allendy. Although Rank was the top disciple of Freud, he opposed Freud's objective and passive psycho-analysis: treating the patient's neurosis by finding out the causes of past trauma in the deep unconscious and trying to return him to social life by this awareness. Rank's resistance brought Freud's wrath down on him, and he was purged from the Viennese academic circles. Rank not only searched for a personal cause of disease in his patient's trauma, he comprehended a mythical, symbolic meaning there like Jung's collective unconsciousness. Then Rank led the patient to recover the connection between an individual who was beyond the social norm and the universe. Rank's analytical practice following his break with Freud was at variance with that of orthodox Freudians in that it attempted to utilize the individual's creativity in order to understand his personality, a method that he called the Pericles myth in *The Trauma of Birth* (1924). That Anaïs's coming together with Rank was fortuitous can be seen in their shared interest in the work of D. H. Lawrence. Rank had read Lawrence; Anaïs had written *D. H. Lawrence: An Unprofessional Study* (1932). The pair were well suited. As Anaïs explained to Rank, "Perhaps I came not to *solve* anything, but for another adventure, to dramatize, to enlarge upon my conflicts, to discover all that they contain, to seize upon them in full. My experience with Allendy was a new conflict added to my life, added to the old. Perhaps I want to go on juggling. I am again at an impasse. So I shift my ground, displace my objective. Conflict insoluble, so I will interest myself in my talks with you" (*Diary I* 272). For Rank, with his unorthodox approach resolving his patient's difficulties, Anaïs must have seemed like a marvelous gift, a daughter in search of a father. Am I the only person who sees this? In this search she rejects Allendy in favor of Rank but writes that she does not expect to "solve" anything because her inner conflict is "insoluble." Obviously, this conflict is one between her search for her father and her obsession with him as the object of her incestuous desires. This conflict cannot be solved, and it should not be solved. To search for her lost father, her identity and the reason for her existence, if there was any, could be only placed in such a dangerous "juggling."

Anaïs carried her diary everywhere she went in order to record her impressions of the moment and place as they were. One day after the analysis, when she was about to leave, Rank's eyes caught sight of her diary, and he said, "Leave that with me" (*Diary I* 275). "I was startled. It was true I had brought it…[b]ut I had also written in it the fabrications I had intended to tell Dr. Rank. And to suddenly expose it all to someone frightened me. What would he think? Would he lose interest in me? Would he be shocked, startled? It was a bold stroke. He interpreted my carrying it as a wish to share it. He challenged my 'offer.' I hesitated, and then I placed it on the low table between the two armchairs. And I left" (*Diary I* 275). Was Anaïs really frightened? No, by this time she had already let Henry read her diary. It was not the first time to "suddenly expose it all." Rank, whose therapeutic method involved harnessing the patient's own creativity, rejected the use of Anaïs's diary entries as part of this process because he regarded them as a form of passive self-defense. Rank recommended she give up the diary. "Is this what Rank wanted, to throw me into my novels, books, out of the intimacy of the diary?" (*Diary I* 285) Rank read the part about June in the diary, and he understood that it was not lesbianism but an imitation of her father who courted women. Following this analysis, that the androgynous and incestuous fusion with June, which was born out of longing for life, was actually carried out with her father.

Rank asked her, "What did you feel when I asked you to leave your diary?" Anaïs answered, "First of all, I was afraid of what you would think of the lies I was going to tell. Then I felt a feminine elation, like that of a woman who is asked to give all her possessions, all of herself. You demanded everything in one blow. I felt an elation due to a recognition of power, of mastery. Was it not power and mastery I was looking for?" (*Diary I* 284) So surely Anaïs recognized her father in Rank. She continued, "You realized that the diary was the key. I always kept an island, inviolate, *to analyze the analyst* (my emphasis). I had never submitted. If I did look for a leader in Henry, a man of experience, he very soon became like a child, or at least an artist I must take care of, and who could not guide me" (*Diary I* 284). In continuance of her search for her father, Anaïs shifted her attention from Miller and Allendy to Rank. Anaïs now dedicated her diary of secrets, her "inviolable island" to Rank as a representation of her father. It was as if the diary was a woman's body, and she offered it as her secret, sensuously, feeling "a feminine elation."

Anaïs wrote in the diary about Rank's way of analysis and therapy: "He does not put any ideas in my mind as the priests in the confessional put sin in my mind by their devious questions: 'You have not been impure, my daughter? You have not enjoyed the sight of your own body? You have not touched your body with intent to enjoy, my daughter?'" (*Diary I* 289) The problem was that Rank was made to read such a diary and to share his impressions of it. Then, was his male heart *elated*? Once again Anaïs called the diary an inviolate island on which to analyze the analyst. Before long, Rank would respond to her written portrait of him: "'I like what you wrote about me immensely, immensely'" (*Diary I* 301). Anaïs wrote, "And his expression was full of gratitude, the eyes seemed almost as if about to dissolve in tears" (*Diary I* 301). Then Anaïs made a sarcastic remark: "As Henry was. Kill the diary, they say; write novels; but when they look at their portrait, they say: 'That is wonderful'" (*Diary I* 301).

Now it is definite that the father Rank was caught in the labyrinth of the diary by the daughter Anaïs, in which he himself had forbidden her to write. As with Allendy, Anaïs turned the tables on Rank, and once again the patient became the analyst's analyst. Thus, Rank became the victim of a humorous fate. Before long Rank would confess to Anaïs: "I denied myself life before, or it was denied me, first by my parents, then Freud, then my wife" (*Diary I* 336).

In Paris, Rank had fewer and fewer patients and then went bankrupt. He went to New York and sent Anaïs a letter: "I am dying now. Come to my rescue" (*Diary I* 359). It was November 1934. "Rank's last SOS" (*Diary I* 360) is the last phrase in *The Diary of Anaïs Nin, Volume 1*. Now, would Anaïs rescue the father Rank in the role of faithful daughter, or in the role of femme fatale? Responding to Rank's SOS, Anaïs went to New York and lived with him at the "Hotel Chaotica," as she called it. The conflict of her inner mind at that time can be reimagined through her novelette "The Voice." Here the psychoanalyst is referred to only as the Voice. In the end he loses objectivity in the relationship with his patient.

The Voice wrote a letter to Lilith, the neurotic woman he fell in love with and "slipped it under her door. Tied to it was a diminutive frog. 'This,' he wrote, 'is my transformation, to permit my entrance through the closed door'" (*Winter of Artifice* 166). Lilith, a she-demon found in both Mesopotamian and Judaic mythology and supposedly the first wife of Adam, was apparently cast out of the Garden of Eden for disobedience.

Parting from her father

In May 1933, Anaïs's father finally returned. Anaïs had still mourned his loss, but she had also evolved into a mature woman. When she received a letter from him, she wrote: "My father comes when I have gone beyond him; he is given to me when I no longer need him, when I am free of him. In every fulfillment there is a mockery which runs ahead of me like a gust of wind, always ahead... Yet the child in me could not die as it should have died, because according to legends it must find its father again. The old legends knew, perhaps, that in absence the father becomes glorified, deified, eroticized, and this outrage against God the Father has to be atoned for. The human father has to be confronted and recognized as human, as a man who created a child and then, by his absence, left the child fatherless and then Godless" (*Diary I* 203). In Anaïs's eyes, her "glorified, deified, eroticized" father should not have aged during his absence; he was still handsome with clear-cut features and a dandy, but he had more wrinkles, and his face was like a mask that had lost its vigor. "The skin did not match the skin of his wrists. It seemed made of earth and papier-mâché, not pure skin" (*Winter of Artifice* 67). His persona as a dandy no longer seemed natural. Instead, there was "[t]he great uneven flow of life with its necessary disorder and ugliness" (*Winter of Artifice* 82). This is reminiscent of the dandy Shokichi Kuga, a character in *Hanran* (*Flooding*), a novel by Sei Itoh.[1] In the novel, Shokichi lives the life of a philanderer, and his way of life with the "*mensonge vital*" is to play his role in order to live. However, in a reverse, he is gradually living in order to play his role. At the end of his life, Shokichi realizes that in his efforts to be free, he has been playing the role of a free man instead of developing his own identity. By the time the character realizes what he has been doing, it is too late.[2]

The father Joaquin looked at his daughter Anaïs and said, "You have become beautiful. Lovely, that black hair, green eyes, red mouth" (*Diary I* 211). He looked at her long, tapered hands, and Anaïs's reaction was: "I pulled away my hands brusquely, hit the glass bowl with the crystal fish and stones, and it broke, and the water ran down the mantelpiece to the floor" (*Diary I* 211). In this glass bowl there were glass fish and glass ships just like in the opening sentence of *Winter of Artifice*: "She is waiting for him. She was waiting for him for twenty years. He is coming today" (*Winter of Artifice* 55). The glass bowl was "the sea for her and the ship which carried her away from him after he had abandoned her" (*Winter of Artifice* 55). The scene is reminiscent of the sailboat that Anaïs, as a young girl, drew in her diary on December 9, 1914, a sailboat floating on the sea when she landed in New York with her mother and younger brothers. "I wanted to draw the way it looked when we arrived from Spain, with the moon reflected on the water" (*Linotte* 33). Indeed, the glass bowl's breaking, the glass fish popping out and the glass ship falling to the floor could be symbolic like the rite of passage of parting from a father and of becoming a woman. Additionally, Anaïs was born under the sign of Pisces, so she may have had affinity with or sensitivity to water. When the glass bowl broke, her sensitive fixation on her father that bound her and the prison of Electra may have been crushed as well.

Another time, father and daughter were driving to the south of France. He took off his shoes and socks to rest. As he did that, his daughter glimpsed his feet and saw *her own bare foot*: "It was her foot—the very same size and the very same color, the same blue veins showing" (*Winter of Artifice* 91). "A confusion of feet. She is not alone in the world. She has a double. He sits on the running board of the car and when he sits there, she does not know where she is. She is standing there pitying his foot, and hating it, too, because of the confusion. If it were someone else's foot her love could flow out freely, but here her love stands still inside of her, still with a kind of fright. There is no distance for her to traverse; it chokes inside of her, like the coils of self-love, and she cannot feel any love for this sore foot because that love leaps back into her like a perpetually coiled snake, and she wants always to leap outside of herself. She wants to flow out" (*Winter of Artifice* 91-92).

It was necessary to flee from the ouroboros of father-daughter, the labyrinth of incest. The time to escape was approaching. *Winter of*

Artifice ends with the scene of the daughter having a stillbirth of "a little girl with long eyelashes and slender hands." (*Winter of Artifice* 119). "The little girl in her was dead too. The woman was saved. And with the little girl died the need of a father" (*Winter of Artifice* 119).

The Diary of Anaïs Nin, Volume I also ends with a climactic scene as recorded by the stream of consciousness of an obsessed and sensual woman: a miscarriage six months into a pregnancy.[3] Again, Anaïs's work would mimic or copy her life. "Legs tied and raised, the pose of love in a cold white operating room…" (*Diary I* 340). "These legs I opened to joy, this honey that flowed out in the joy—now these legs are twisted in pain and the honey flows with the blood. The same pose and the same wetness of passion but this is dying and not loving" (*Diary I* 344). "Perhaps I was designed for other forms of creation. Nature connived to keep me a man's woman, and not a mother; not a mother to children but to men. Nature shaping my body for the love of man, not of child. This child which was a primitive connection to the earth, a prolongation of myself, now denied me as if to point up my destiny in other realms" (*Diary I* 346).

When Anaïs suffered her miscarriage, the maid in Louveciennes, Henry Miller, and Otto Rank, who had rushed back from London, were the ones who visited her in the hospital. The father of the stillborn child was unknown. It was Marta Traba, the Latin American novelist, who made an ironic comment: "In August 1934, Anaïs Nin gives birth to a fatherless child (almost like a literary product!)" (*Under the Sign of Pisces: Anaïs Nin and her Circle*, Winter 1976 9). Traba also added her thoughts on Anaïs's *Diary I*: "I think this book is dangerous for us women, but especially suitable for masculine reading" (*Under the Sign of Pisces: Anaïs Nin and her Circle*, Winter, 1976 14).

Anaïs had always written about her physical meeting with God through the sacrament of communion or her surrogate fathers: "I still miss something: it must be God. But I want a god in the flesh, not an abstraction, an incarnated god, with strength, two arms, and a sex" (*Diary I* 261). During the process of her convalescence, Anaïs was stricken by immense joy. At this moment, she became aware of "communion with God" as she wrote: "This joy which I found in the love of man, in creation, was completed with God" (*Diary I* 348). She added: "The moonlight shone in the room. Heaven was a bower, a hammock. I swung in infinite spaces, beyond the world. Slept inside of God" (*Diary I* 348). It was Soseki who felt the bliss of *sokutenkyoshi* [4] during his own convalescence after violently vomiting blood due to a stomach ulcer. Soseki describes an out-of-body experience during which he felt himself to have been fused with the clear, perfect blue sky he could see through the window of his hospital room. Anaïs was fused with the moon in the night sky and sleeping in bliss. Again, a combination of both sexes is represented by the daytime sun as a symbol of the mythological principle of the male, and the night moon, a symbol of the mythological principle of the female. Anaïs wrote, "Nature connived to keep me a man's woman, and not a mother; not a mother to children but to men" (*Diary I* 346), and in her diary she added, "Man can never know the kind of loneliness a woman knows... Man lies in her womb and is reborn each time anew with a desire to act, to BE. But for woman, the climax is not in the birth, but in the moment when man rests inside of her" (*Diary I* 106). The suggestion here is that even at the moment of climax during the sexual act the woman is alone, her true union being with the moon.

Inside the whale of the black diary

"In the spring of 1932 Hugo Guiler, assisted by Allendy, did Henry's 'interesting but unfortunate' chart. Hugo remarked that Henry's ruling planet, Mars, was 'out of harmony' with the rest of existence, but to everyone's surprise, Anaïs spoke out: 'Mars is the planet that has only one friend—Venus. My ruling planet is Venus'" (*Always Merry and Bright* 265). It is a matter of common knowledge that Venus's husband is an ugly smith, the Vulcan, and Venus's lover is the god of war, Mars. After this, whenever Hugo remained absent on his business trips, Venus/Anaïs wrote a letter from Louveciennes to Mars/Henry: "Come and be my husband for a few days" (*Always Merry and Bright* 267). "They left little notes around the house for each other to find, even love notes on the pillow of the sleeping one... He called her *Schneewittchen*, Snow-White" (*Always Merry and Bright* 267). Certainly, he was happy as a fairy-tale prince who awakens a sleeping beauty in order to love her. Yet in this case, the sleeping beauty had already been awakened and was shining like the morning star, Venus, and who allures the god of war or love. This god of war or love, Henry, called Hugo "a man without ecstasy" and assured Henry's friends "that in his opinion Anaïs could not remain married to Hugo." And in 1932, he said decisively to his childhood friend in Brooklyn, Emil Schnellock, that "My next wife is Anaïs" (*Always Merry and Bright* 268). Unfortunately, Henry Miller's rose-colored dream never came true. Anaïs wrote, "I want to live only for ecstasy" (*Diary I* 174), but she will not cease to be the wife of "a man without ecstasy" (*Always Merry and Bright* 268). Henry thought of Anaïs as a Snow-White figure as opposed to the femme fatale, who was June. He also saw Anaïs as Ariadne, who would spin the thread that would enable him to escape from June's black labyrinth. At the same time, Anaïs herself was a woman in a labyrinth, albeit a white one.

Moreover, this woman in the white labyrinth was chasing after the woman in the black labyrinth, following her around, crowned by an illusion of ecstasy in Lesbos. Henry did not know the secret of the dangerous relationship between the woman of white and the woman of black then. The first time he began to suspect this secret was due to Anaïs's letter to him. That was when Henry, working as an English teacher at a middle school in Dijon, was absorbed and obsessed with a mysterious woman, Albertine, and possessed by Marcel Proust while Henry was immersed in *Remembrance of Things Past.*

Henry wrote to Anaïs Nin: "In your letter there are two or three paragraphs which torture me...'this world, etc. you are not meant to enter.' True, but I will never cease to bang my head against the doors. If I don't get a glimpse of that world I shall go mad. No, I do not want it symbolically. You are making it too difficult. It is already obscure enough and now you want to tack on a long vestibule through which I must grope painfully. Already in these lines you mystify me. You are talking a language that is beyond me. And the elusiveness of it enrages me" (*Letters to Anaïs Nin* 55). After Henry returned to Paris, he demanded that Anaïs explain whether Albertine was a pseudonym for June. The clue Anaïs gave him was that Albertine could actually be Albert, and that Proust described a homosexual relationship. Then, are Albertine = June and Anaïs homosexual? Is Anaïs another Jean Kronski, the woman who came to live with Henry and June in 1926? Is Anaïs the same kind of madwoman who, posing as Rimbaud, once threw Henry into utter despair in Brooklyn? No, according to Henry, Anaïs is "the full box" (*Diary I* 49). That is, someone who is both beautiful and richly cultured. That's why she may be fascinated by "an empty box" (*Diary I* 49) like June. Was it a foolish act for Henry, being contrary to his expectations, to bring these two women together? Do these women, one black and one white, conspire secretly to bring Henry to ruin?

One day, in April 1932, a different Henry came to Louveciennes, "A new Henry, or rather, the Henry I sensed behind the one generally known, the Henry behind the one he has written down" (*Diary I* 62). "He looked so serious. His violence has burnt itself out. The coarseness, in the alchemy, became strength. He had received a letter from June, in pencil, irregular, mad, like a child's moving, simple cries of her love for him. 'Such a letter blots out everything.' I felt the moment had come to expose the June I knew, to give him June, 'because it will make you love her more. It's a beautiful June. Other days I felt you might laugh at my portrait, jeer at its naïveté. Today I know you won't. I let him read all I had written about June. What is happening? He is deeply moved, torn apart. He believes. 'It is in this way that I should have written about June,' he says. 'The other is incomplete, superficial. You have got her" (*Diary I* 63).

Henry was mesmerized by the labyrinth of the diary because of its sensitive and enchanting passages about a woman's hunger for the fulfillment of her life, her courage in pursuing her own ideal of how she should live, her beautiful descriptions of a woman's passion, her devotion to being a free spirit despite the inherent dangers this entailed. In order to live deeply and really, a woman turns life into a symbolic ceremony. Henry surely read these bitter words in the diary: "June eats and drinks symbols. Henry has no use for symbols. He eats bread, not wafers" (*Diary I* 35). Henry, a coarse and violent realist, as Anaïs realized, could never enter the world of two women.

Anaïs asked him, "If I had the means to help you get June back to Paris, would you want me to do it?" Henry winced from her words and suffered only to respond, "Don't ask me, Anaïs, don't ask me" (*Diary I* 64). But later, when June reappeared in Paris after a prolonged absence, the three of them began to face their dangerous relationships, and their season of Hell began. Only when this was over could Anaïs finally escape from June's madness and danger and from being a captive in a nightmare. "Flight. I always look for the exit" (*Diary I* 238). Furious, jealous, brandishing some of the letters from Anaïs Henry had kept with him, June challenged him to put down the woman she thought he loved, telling him she was merely a little lesbian. But such words meant nothing to Henry who had already read Anaïs's diary, and he was charmed by the labyrinth it contained. Henry, who had been allowed to read her diary, was fascinated by both it and its author. Because of this, Anaïs was able to maintain her relationship with Henry while, at the same time, remaining untouched by the collapse of Henry's relationship with June.

This white woman of the labyrinth was a beautiful and mysterious Minotaur, but she always prepared a thread of Ariadne for herself. "I want to be June" (*Diary I* 89). This desire to "become June" suggests a desire for some sort of androgynous and incestuous relationship with her. However, at the same time, Anaïs wrote finely and callously, "I let June go to the very end of her perversities. We love best those who are, or act for us, a self we do not wish to be or act out" (*Diary I* 330).

That Anaïs expressed desire to "be June" shows itself to be a calculated act through which she could live out the life she desired. June, a woman of the black labyrinth, was Anaïs's double, and Anaïs doubled herself as well. Inevitably, June burnt herself out. On the other hand, as a matter of course, Anaïs saved herself from perversities. During the earliest stages of the relationship with Henry and June, she had written, "The artist goes beyond the neurotic. He glorifies his personality. Henry has done that. I do it **through June** (my emphasis), portrayed in *House of Incest*" (*Diary I* 200-201). Anaïs did not want to part with her neurosis, which she believed enabled her as an artist to escape the bounds of what others might consider a normal life. As Anaïs writes, "The artist goes beyond the neurotic" (*Diary I* 200). Thus she accepts her own neurosis and seeks to release her inner madness that until now has been confined by the requirements of social norms in the world of everyday life. June's real life of perversities was a victim of Anaïs's double. Clearly, Anaïs described *House of Incest* as "my Double book" (*Diary I* 333).

Anaïs's cruelty here is certainly a fact, but artists are always cruel. Anaïs was correct in stating, "The same thing which makes Henry indestructible is what makes me indestructible. The core of us is an artist, a writer. And it is in our work, by our work, that we reassemble the fragments, recreate wholeness" (*Diary I* 69). Even before she met June whom she only knew from Henry's conversations, Anaïs wrote in her diary, "Poor June is not like me, able to make her own portrait" (*Diary I* 16). June could never imitate the actions of such an artist as Anaïs because of the mess of June's real life. Even if Henry tried to draw her faithfully or to make her an eternal figure, it could not be the true June. June could only say that such a depiction was not how she really was.

Anaïs never tired of creating her own portrait, the one she kept locked in the chamber of her inner mind. The diary had been Narcissus's mirror for Anaïs and her persona ever since she began writing it. The diary of her twelve-year-old self included a one-page drawing by pencil. There is a big anchor in the center diagonally, and, in the middle of it, "*Mon Journal*" is written. Two little birds, which seem to be linnets, are drawn: one is up on the right arm of the anchor, and the other is down at the left fluke of the anchor. On respective breasts of the birds, "Anaïs" and "mon âme" (my spirit) are written. "Linotte" was a nickname the young Anaïs gave herself (*Linotte* 69). In addition to these sketches, at the corner in the upper right, "force" is written pretentiously, surrounded by short, radiant lines like arrows of light. The meaning of this picture is simple: the *Diary* served Anaïs as both anchor and fulcrum. The one held her fast to her visions of her life; the other provided her with the force required to live that life. Later, Anaïs called her diary "a protective cave" or "my snail shell" (*Diary I* 300). Her diary was truly the labyrinth where she could protect herself by hiding there. Or, as Anaïs wrote, "My diary-writing is a vice…this is the way an opium smoker prepares for his opium pipe" (*Diary I* 89). Moreover, she repeatedly called her diary "my drug, and my vice" (*Diary II* 310). Like an addict, Anaïs could not stop creating a record of everything she thought and did.

As for the woman in the black labyrinth, there was no protective cave or snail shell. June's self was entirely exposed. If there was something to cover her naked body, it was only the black cape she wore. It fluttered about her when she went out at night. June's Icarus-like fall was inevitable for she did not know the cunning of Daedalus, the creator of the labyrinth. To me, Anaïs was another Daedalus, creator of the Cretan labyrinth, while June was Icarus, destined to fall from the sky. Actually, Anaïs wrote, "I have often wondered whether June was not the sincerest one of all because so easily discovered" (*Diary I* 205). Anaïs was right. Among the dangerous relationships of Henry-June-Anaïs, it was only June who revealed her jealousy which was her **honest**, sincere mind. It was June who withdrew from dangerous relationships, not Anaïs, as she wrote in the diary. Is the diary an accurate representation of her life as she claimed, or is it a recording of the life she wished she had led? "I have always believed in Bergson's '*mensonge vital.*' The trouble is not with my lies; the trouble is that we were all brought up on fairy tales. We were poisoned with fairy tales. Women expected love to always take lyrical form, a romantic expression. We have all expected wonder, the marvelous. You yourself wrote me a few days ago: 'I expected so much, so much of the world and it all fell short.' I was more poisoned by fairy tales than anyone. *Only I decided to work miracles. I decided that when somebody said: 'I want' that I would fulfill this want.* I decided to be the fairy godmother who made things come true" (*Diary I* 246-47). If the diary is filled with untruths, then they are untruths that were required in order to live. The diary reveals that Anaïs believes in the *mensonge vital*

(*Diary I* 246), the lie that gives life. I have no doubt that this diary was like a secret rose that blooms in a woman's innermost being. After all, Anaïs herself calls it the labyrinth of the diary.

Or, by confessing that Anaïs was untruthful in her diary, the poison of the lie is immediately neutralized, and Anaïs is freed from any sense of guilt. For example, when she wrote, "I have often wondered whether June was not the sincerest one of all" (*Diary I* 205), she added, "When I'm admired I think I am duping the world. I begin to add my lies and to tremble. I have to say to myself: 'Either I am just a cleverer liar and actress than June, or I'm real'" (*Diary I* 205). One year before, she wrote, "It is quite possible that I may be even more secretive than June. More fearful than June to reveal myself" (*Diary I* 47). Do not misunderstand because Anaïs's diary is not just her own secret confessions. She shows her diary to other people, and, needless to say, she does not do this pretentiously. She reveals herself elaborately, with perfect timing, with a graceful manner as she did to Miller and to Rank. Besides, though she wrote she was fearful to reveal herself, she wrote fearlessly, "In my dreams I sleep with everybody. The twelve rooms in the dream? Past, present, and future?" (*Diary I* 227) The twelve rooms? Do they represent the twelve signs of the zodiac? Anaïs was, after all, very interested in astrology. Or does the number represent the twelve apostles? The twelve apostles to serve Anaïs. Here are her words from the *Diary*, Winter, 1942: "It is a difficult, a deep problem for woman to commune with the cosmic. She can only achieve it by a universal motherhood or else the priestess prostitute way" (*Diary III* 240). Are her dream-lovers her apostles and she the universal mother?

To be certain, Anaïs shared her diary with the men she loved. Henry Miller and Otto Rank were not the only ones who were captured by the labyrinth of the diary, but also Antonin Artaud, the genius behind the Theater of Cruelty, and Gonzalo, a son of revolution in Peru. All the men Anaïs loved became captives in the labyrinth of the diary. It was Miller who wrote to the world about her diary, "Everyone who comes under her glance is lured, as it were, into a spider web, stripped bare, dissected, dismembered, devoured and digested" (*The Henry Miller Reader* 303). In addition, her father, Don Juan = Joaquin, called her diary "[m]y only rival" (*Diary I* 215), and he was jealous of it. In the fall of 1937, the writer of *The Black Book*, Lawrence Durrell, also read her diary and was certainly fascinated by it and called the diaries Anaïs's "black children" (*Diary II* 265). Undoubtedly the reason why Durrell named it so was not only because her diary notebook was bound in black. Anaïs herself clearly wrote, "I was the Whale of the *black diaries*" (*Diary II* 272, my emphasis). Really, the labyrinth of her diary swallowed every lover, one after another, like Leviathan, the whale, who swallowed Jonah.

A woman who loved too much

The Minotaur, the monster with the body of a man and the head and tail of a bull living in Daedalus's labyrinth, according to Apollodoros,[5] also has the name Asterion. According to Karl Kerenyi[6] in his book *Labyrinth Studien*, this name is derived from Asterios, a star that can be found in a labyrinth-like constellation, the pattern of which changes with the phases of the moon. Kerenyi explains that this fearsome figure transforms into the star Asterios in the middle of a labyrinth. Thus, the labyrinth, which is a place of darkness and death, can also represent infinite possibilities of rebirth (*Labyrinth Studien* 86). To me, there is no doubt that Anaïs wanted to be like a godmother to the men in her life and share the world of light and rebirth.

Actually, Anaïs did help both materially and spiritually many poor artists like Henry. Certainly, she seemed like the star that gave them light and life as an eternal woman. For example, Miller told her, "What I feel is that I want you to save me from June" (*Diary I* 129). According to him, Anaïs sometimes playfully called herself "une étoilique" (*The Henry Miller Reader* 294). The word lunatic, which is a state of madness brought on by the moon, might just as well be replaced by the word "étoilique," a state of madness brought on by a star. Let us recall the scene where Anaïs became a woman by sacrificing her dead baby and was fascinated with the bliss created by fusion with the moon in the night sky; then there is Sabina, a character in *A Spy in the House of Love*, who was fascinated by the idea of moonbathing rather than sunbathing. As Anaïs wrote, "Someday I'll be locked up for love insanity. 'She loved too much.' This could be on my tombstone" (*Diary II* 205). So we should not be surprised by the starry connection between the Minotaur and Anaïs.

At the same time, it can be argued that the reverse is also true. For the woman in the labyrinth, the inside is also the outside, and light is also darkness. The fairy godmother, creature of goodness and light, can turn into a negative figure as Anaïs does with June.

"We fight this part of ourselves which is unknown, which we instinctively fear because it was feared, and so we stifled it. Since it was stifled, we must breathe it *through others*. (The June in myself? In other women? The Henry in myself, friendly to the whole world? The Gonzalo in myself, rebel and untamed?)" (*Diary V* 124, my emphasis) This quotation is from the end of the summer diary in 1953. In order for Anaïs to live both as a person and an artist, she had to transform those she loved into, first, a double of herself, and then a scapegoat, a substitute that could be sacrificed in place of herself. So June became the double who was destroyed instead of Anaïs herself. To pamper a favorite and then destroy it is a common pattern in human history. Anaïs, who took for her motto the words of Jung, "Proceed from the dream outward" (*The Novel of the Future* 5), was the dreamer who was not destroyed by her pursuit of fulfillment. Anaïs, the woman who loved too much, said her dominating star was Venus, and welcomed Henry Miller = Mars to her house. Anaïs's love that she described as "love[ing] too much" (*Diary II* 205) was Venus's love. Certainly, her love was like that of the goddess who was both tender and cruel. It is similar, perhaps, to that of Augusta Goraldin Almeda in the *Gondal* poems of Emily Brontë. Passionate and cruel, she is another femme fatale born under the sign of the planet Venus. Anaïs wrote, "Through love it is I who fall into traps, yet when I was a girl I did not like to play the fairy princess, but the dark, evil, crafty queen. Through love I am enslaved, as I am enslaved by the helplessness of Helba and Gonzalo, but another side of me seeks ruses by which I could escape" (*Diary II* 330-31).

In addition, Anaïs wrote, "Flight. I always look for the exit" (*Diary I* 238). Flight here refers to the double who must be discarded, sacrificed when that person fails to act out the dream scenario, which Anaïs has prepared. Describing the parting with June, she wrote, "I could not explain the breaking away, the withdrawal that took place in me" (*Diary I* 150). This word, withdrawal, is inwardly a hidden keyword throughout the *Diaries*. Henry seemed able to see through the artifice in her flight. He thought that Anaïs's way of parting was not by breakdown, but a quiet and clever escape in order to elude. Since Gonzalo was the double for her violent dream, the double for her dangerous and free life, the double for June, the passionate guitarist who lived with her in the houseboat on the Seine, a son of revolution in Peru, had the same fate as June.

"Henry wrote about June: 'I thought I had found a female Vesuvius.' He was as deceived about June as I was about Gonzalo. I thought Gonzalo's volcanic nature would bring a new kind of freedom. I thought with the fire and faith in him he would burn all the chains, start a new world. But he is bound like an animal. Strange that, like Henry, I was always awaiting the one who would represent evil and lead me into dark experiences...June could have done it. Gonzalo and June were really alike... There was no great evil in either Gonzalo or June, just great adventurousness, but both change in relation to me" (*Diary II* 321).

The words "change in relation to me" accurately describe what happens when the double betrays the dreams and expectations of the dreamer. The relationship between the two, maker and surrogate, shifts, and the double is soon put aside. "My own way is always to do so very gradually, drop by drop, so that the abandonment is hardly felt..." (*Diary I* 307). And then another relationship with a new double begins. Anaïs also recalled in her diary, "I had my diary in which I traced the character of people for a long time and recorded changes, recorded a different aspect for each relationship" (*The Novel of the Future* 123).

Anaïs had a habit of buying two of the things she liked. For example, if you wear out a favorite dress, you can wear a spare one. If you lose one sandal, you have another. This was not all; she wanted to wear that sandal with a woman she loved. Anaïs gave the same sandals she wore to June. On the day of their last parting, June came to the station to say goodbye wearing the same pair of sandals as Anaïs, except in a bigger size. What about the bracelets they wore? Following the style of Rank, who cannot be satisfied until he finds a symbolic meaning for everything, she interpreted the two bracelets as "Duality? Two loves? One representing the woman who wanted to be enslaved (slave's bracelet), the other to bind the other, the one I loved? Was I going to wear them together, like twins..." (*Diary II* 40). The yearning to be enslaved and the desire to enslave the other: this demonstrates the duality inherent in a sadomasochistic relationship. Within this duality, the way out is the flight from the danger of loss of self that is inevitably deprived in fusion, the dream of the androgynous union, and the secret trap door was superbly prepared. Actually, Anaïs wrote, "I liked *play*. I did not want tragedy, destruction. I had cultivated elusiveness, means of escape, magician's tricks" (*Diary II* 40).

Yet, Anaïs said to Henry that she did not like clowns, that it was madmen she preferred. The double must in some sense be mad in order to liberate her own inner madness while at the same time not allowing it to bring about her own ruin. Surely June, Gonzalo, and Artaud were all mad. Perhaps what Anaïs loved about Henry Miller were those moments when he seemed to release the madman inside himself, acting violently, losing his self-control. But in reality, Henry was a clown who only pretended to give way to madness as a kind of game. Even though he kept proposing marriage to Anaïs, she avoided answering him, elusively and mysteriously. In 1935, when she was staying at the "Hotel Chaotica" in New York as an assistant to Otto Rank, Miller followed her to the States, but she told him that she must go back to her husband, Hugo. (This was when Henry was choked up by reminiscences of days passed, like passing in front of the Wilson dance hall where Henry and June's love began.) Then on July 14, 1939, with World War II approaching, Anaïs saw Henry off to Greece from Marseille and rejected him by telling him she would never part from her husband. Was that refusal because of his commitment to being a clown? There was no place in her fantasy life for a clown. To Anaïs, it was nothing like her role-playing in the *mensonge vital* in order to live. Naturally, Henry, too, changed due to his relationship with Anaïs.

Hugo was the better husband for Anaïs even though he refused to finance the publication of Henry Miller's novel *Tropic of Cancer* and later asked to be expunged from the published version of the diaries. Perhaps Anaïs did not have the will to marry Henry from the beginning. He received some fame through *Tropic of Cancer,* but it was all notorious, and he was still penniless. She definitely needed a home with an eternal husband, a domain, a place of refuge, a safety zone for her self-protection, and a financial base in order to keep supporting the doubles, one after another.

According to Jay Martin, Anaïs and Henry "never really made a conclusive break or had a devastating argument" (*Always Merry and Bright* 386). Gradually, "drop by drop," they became estranged. Her ability for flight remained a keen skill. But "he heard from friends that she regarded him as a traitor" (*Always Merry and Bright* 386). Henry was a traitor because he was not the "demon" she hoped he would be, but a clown. As she wrote in the diary, "I have my own demons... All of us have our demons. Mine is caged in the diary" (*Diary III* 163-65). Henry could exorcise the demon in June, the woman in the black labyrinth, but I wonder whether Henry was able to exorcise the demon in Anaïs, the woman in the white labyrinth. Either way, no one knows if that was Henry's happiness or misfortune.

Anaïs continued to contemplate hidden selves that many dare not think about, preferring instead to repress and hide them. She wrote, "But the revelation of this aspect in those we love becomes the threatening enemy. We cannot come to terms with it. The proof of this truth is the reversals which take place. Henry and I are estranged, and I have to do my own living and writing. Gonzalo returns to France, and I have to achieve my own violence" (*Diary V* 124).

However, Anaïs was not the type to make her own violence; she was too wise to venture into such danger. To work through the labyrinth of her own being, it was necessary for Anaïs to have a double to carry out acts she dared not execute or experience herself. After June, Henry and Gonzalo, she continued to expect and search for her double, a loving victim. An example that comes to mind is Margaret Fuller, a dark figure of nineteenth-century America, who valued a friend in order to obtain "a golden key to unlock all caskets of confidence" (*Memoirs of Margaret Fuller Ossoli, Vol. II* 40). For Anaïs, the "caskets of confidence" are the labyrinthian diaries that act as her confidante. In order to navigate Anaïs's labyrinth in the diaries, a friend or double is necessary for her to live through vicariously.

"DOES ANYONE KNOW WHO I AM?" (*House of Incest* 26) Precocious thirteen-year-old Anaïs wrote in her diary, "Is there anyone who will understand me? I do not understand myself" (*Diary I* 246). Throughout her life, Anaïs often asked "Who am I?" because the solution to this self-doubt was constantly changing. The reason for this was that Anaïs felt her identity to be directly related to the people around her at any given moment and her relationship with them as individuals. In 1968, 65-year-old Anaïs wrote: "The self is a conductor of emotion by which we make contact with others" (*The Novel of the Future* 36). After all, her identity of being, if any, existed only in relation with others, her identification with others with whom she related, whom she pursued, and whom she followed and held. Her identity was encapsulated in the double, the others she loved. Anaïs wrote, "My madness is that of perpetual identification with others" (*Diary II* 188). This madness is like that of the vampire feeding on the blood of its victim until it has killed the one who has given it sustenance. So Anaïs's love was destructive because she loved too much. The need of identification with others must have come from Anaïs's desperate longing for her own identity. Her identification with others is reminiscent of John Keats's idea of "negative capability." (As Keats explained in a letter in 1817, "I mean Negative Capability, that is, when man is capable of being in uncertainties, mysteries, doubts, without any irritable reaching after fact and reason" (*A Glossary of Literary Terms Eleventh Edition* 235). It is to bring one's self to naught, and it is an ability to change, transform to other selves.

It is nothing in itself but everything at the same time. At such a moment, Keats said, the inherent color of being is like that of a chameleon. Henry also thought Anaïs chameleon-like. Anaïs wrote, "My mellowness is strange. He finds that, like a chameleon, I change color in the café" (*Diary I* 56). If that was the case, is it not odd? Because identification with others in order to prove one's identity causes one to lose one's self instead. Keats searched for his own self throughout his short 26 years, as he burned through life like a meteor. And Keats called himself a chameleon poet who kept creating unrivaled masterpieces by embodying the negative capability to lose himself and morph into the other's self for the sake of his poetry. It is rather strange that Anaïs did not mention Keats's negative capability anywhere in her massive diary. However, Anaïs Nin's pursuit of identity and her anxiety about losing herself to schizophrenia are similar to Keats's negative capability. "My neurosis is utterly different from Henry's or Artaud's, or Helba's, or Gonzalo's. It is as if by a fluid quality, a facility for identification with others, I became like water and instead of separating from others, as Henry does, I lose myself in others... Then I got confused. This for me is the labyrinth. Identification, projection. My identification with my father which had to be broken. Myself in June. I see the double, the twins of others" (*Diary II* 285).

As Anaïs wrote above, if she wanted to live, she needed to live with her neurosis. Rank told her: "When the neurotic woman gets cured, she becomes a woman. When the neurotic man gets cured, he becomes an artist" (*Diary I* 291). The neurotic woman who is cured and becomes a new woman suggests to me a true daughter of Adam. However, in the case of Anaïs, after becoming a woman, she tries to become a completely new woman, not one formed of Adam's rib. Anaïs wrote: "Man must fear the effort woman is making to create herself, not to be born of Adam's rib" (*Diary I* 276). She should not be a man's copy; "*It is the woman who has to speak.*" (*Diary I* 289). Thus, Anaïs writes, "I chose to retrogress into my neurosis and obsessions" (*Diary I* 282). Anaïs does not want to cure her neurosis completely because she feels that some of her artistic talents are derived from it. She adds, "the woman's role to live for a man, for *one* man, was denied to me by my neurosis" (*Diary I* 294).

Anaïs describes her neurosis as "a fluid quality, a feeling for identification with others" (*Diary II* 285). She asks, "Is it this deep psychological truth I will explore to the limit and make the base of my Proustian edifice? It is at the basis of my life, analogy, interchange of souls, of identities. Doesn't love mean just that, this growing into the other like plants intertwining their roots, this interchange of soul and feelings? Not an abyss then, but a new world. Not madness, but a deep truth. A principle moving us, our inner fatality" (*Diary II* 285-86).

Instead of a cure for her neurosis, she sought a means of living with it, one she described through the metaphor of "plants intertwining their roots, this interchange of soul and feelings" (*Diary II* 285-86). She was moved by the principle of love in which one grows into the other while intently searching for inner fatality in her own mind. Yet, as mentioned before, identification with others leads to the loss of self, and rejecting a woman's role to live for *one* man causes schizophrenia, self-division. Anaïs's diary, the record of her feelings of inner fatality, begins to reflect the Proustian labyrinth which refers to the endless description of a human mind, so she keeps writing about her identification with others, the loss of her own self, her relations with her beloved doubles, and so on. Her endless diary was nothing but a vicious circle, the uroboric coil of longing and loss of such an identity. Much like the dual figure of Asterios/Minotour, Anaïs continued to attract lovers/victims at the same time as she went ever deeper into the labyrinth of her self.

In all her love affairs, Anaïs made sure she had an exit strategy, the metaphor for which might be that of the thread spun by Ariadne that enabled Theseus to find his way out of the labyrinth after he had killed the Minotaur. What she could not escape from, however, was the world she created in her diary. This was her labyrinth, and it was of her own making. "*L'enfer, c'est les autres*" ("Hell is other people") is the last line of the end of the play *No Exit* by Sartre. Anaïs would have said: "Hell is me."

From Snow White in the land of mirrors to a woman of water, Arethusa

We should not forget, to begin with, that the diary was begun as a snail's shell or a protective cave. When Anaïs used the diary to analyze an analyst, Rank also analyzed it: "The diary is your last defense against analysis. It is like a traffic island you want to stand on" (*Diary I* 284). The model of the Voice is certainly based on Rank, and the Voice told Lilith: "You would not move. Everything else around you could move, change, but you, because of your mistrust of pain and loss, refused to move. You would be the island, the fixed center. For fear of a second loss, a second abandon, a second wound. That is why you never again gave yourself, that is why you are cold" (*Winter of Artifice* 105). The outer reality being deserted by her father, being harmed by trauma, prevented discourse with human beings. As a double of Anaïs, Djuna in "The Voice" is aware of being hurt by relationships; another double who had been a model and Spanish dancer when she was young, Stella, the movie actress in "Stella," mentions a situation in which "nearness brings wounds" (*Winter of Artifice* 7). Note that the name's etymology is "star."

Being hurt by a relationship is similar to the fear of one's existence, which R. D. Laing refers to in *The Divided Self.* This fear caused Anaïs to hide herself in the labyrinthian diary. For her, this diary becomes a sealed room, a "protective cave" (*Diary I* 282) in which she can maintain her dream of a fulfilled life. Even if she left the safety of the island, the cave of self-protection, and related to people, she dared not discard the cave altogether. The cave of self-protection was the lie, the performance that Anaïs used to relate to other people. Anaïs Nin was a mysterious woman capable of changing herself like a chameleon changes its coloring. Anaïs wrote: "I like to think me puzzling, mystifying and unpredictable. I feel that I keep my real self a mystery" (*Winter of Artifice* 103).

Antonin Artaud, playwright, actor, poet and essayist, devised a form of theatrical performance that broke with established theatrical tradition in that it sought to free the human subconscious by approaching performance as a type of exorcism. Artaud wrote to Anaïs, "You must surely know similar mental obsessions, but you cannot have lived—I hope you have never experienced—such horrible states of mental constriction, of exacerbation, of emptiness which, in me, manifest themselves outwardly by a constant role-playing, a lie" (*Diary I* 220). Though he hated acting and lying, his intense honesty of agonizing for this self-contradiction of being an actor inevitably pushed Artaud into the abysm of schizophrenia. Anaïs, who received this letter, wrote in the diary, "[T]o assume a false role was a natural way of protecting one's true self from some inimical places" (*Diary I* 222).

Anaïs kissed Artaud at the café Couple, and "invented for him the story that I was a divided being" (*Diary I* 228). And she "looked at his mouth, with the edges darkened by laudanum, a mouth [she] did not want to kiss" (*Diary I* 229). "I have a love for the poet who walks inside of my dreams, for his pain and the flame in him, but not for the man. I cannot be physically bound to him" (*Diary I* 234). So Anaïs "invented the myth of [her] divided love, spirit and flesh never uniting" (*Diary I* 229), murmuring "not to hurt him" (*Diary I* 229). Artaud said, "I never thought to find in you my madness" (*Diary I* 229). Artaud was totally deceived by Anaïs's inventions. "Because I imagine people need those lies as much as I need them. Truth is coarse and unfruitful" (*Diary I* 241). Here Anaïs could have said how humorous it was.

But Artaud's honest and sincere eyes saw through Anaïs's lies and acting. "What a divine joy it would be to crucify a being like you, who are so evanescent, so elusive" (*Diary I* 234). Let us remember that young Artaud acted splendidly as a monk accompanying Jeanne d'Arc who was burned to death at the stake in the silent film masterpiece, *The Passion of Jeanne of Arc*, directed by Dreyer. Artaud called Anaïs the "plumed serpent" (*Diary I* 231), and then ended with "I hated you at first as one hates the all-powerful temptress, I hated you as one hates evil" (*Diary I* 235). And he added, "You give everyone the illusions of maximum love. Furthermore, I do not believe I am the only one you have deceived. I sense that you love many men. I feel you hurt Allendy, and perhaps others" (*Diary I* 245). Anaïs was silent and denied nothing, but she felt he was wrong to interpret her deception as "premeditated" (*Diary I* 245). For Anaïs, the word "premeditated" was incorrect because she did not feel that any of her actions towards others were planned beforehand. She treated each person she met as an individual. With Artaud, she responded to him as one whose work identified him as a poetic figure already existing in her dreams. The fact that the phrase of Jung's "from the dream outward" was so important in her life is the key to understanding why she felt Artaud was destined to be another of her doubles, a means for her to progress. But Artaud declined to act the part, telling her, "I believe in your absolute impurity" (*Diary I* 245).

Anaïs wrote, "I felt I would rather have him think me a Beatrice Cenci than one who had pretended to love him" (*Diary I* 245). In Artaud's version of *The Cenci* in the Theater of Cruelty, Beatrice is the heroine. The play was already written when Anaïs put the above quote into the *Diary*. Yet, Anaïs's writing of her wish rather having him think her a Beatrice was not only out of such association with the drama. In the labyrinth of the diary, she had already symbolically committed incest with her father. Additionally, patricide is symbolically countenanced by her rifling through the minds of men like Miller, Allendy and Rank. Anaïs must have been aware of all these implications, and then she wrote about her wish of having Artaud call her a Beatrice.

After all, her diary, her lies, her acting were contrivances for her own self-protection. The *mensonge vital* was also a disguise. In this conundrum lie the secrets of Anaïs's duality.

"This diary is my drug and my vice. This is the moment when I take up the mysterious pipe and indulge in *reflections*. Instead of writing a book I lie back and I dream and talk to myself. A drug. I turn away from a brutal reality into *the refracted*... I must relive my life each day in the dream. The dream is my only life. I see in *the echoes and reverberations* the transfigurations which alone keep wonder pure. Otherwise all image is lost, and I awake to touch my prison bars. Otherwise the homeliness, the deformities, the limitations, gnaw into every gesture like rust. This is my diary and my drug" (*Diary II* 310-11, my emphasis). Actually, Anaïs intentionally left this page of the diary on the desk in the houseboat that was her love nest with Gonzalo, rented from the French movie actor Michel Simon, on the Seine, shrouded in mist. Reading this page, Gonzalo wrote the following note and left it on Anaïs's typewriter. "I prophetize that one day, there will come a day when Anaïs will see that these prison bars are precisely made of dreams, that she is imprisoned in a prison of dream. And her jailers will keep her there, feeding her on fantasy which will prevent her from turning into a rebel" (*Diary II* 311). Anaïs might never turn into a rebel as this passionate socialist revolutionary expected. However, Gonzalo's remark was right: the prison that held Anaïs was constructed from her own dreams and not her suppressed real life itself. He would have been even more accurate if he said that her diary itself was a prison, not just her dreams.

Let us pay attention to my own italicized words in the diary above. Both "*reflections*" and "*the refracted*" imply mirror images. Either word originally means reflected things. The labyrinth of the diary was one of mirrors. Here, as I mentioned before, I called Anaïs's diary her portrait in front of mirrors in the sealed room of her mind. All those doubles swallowed up the black diary. The living doubles that yearned for androgynous or incestuous unions and fusions, after all, were the reflections in the mirror of her labyrinth. Anaïs Nin's diary, her labyrinth, was, in a way, a narrative of a conflict with shadows. Her so-called doubles were, all of them, shadows. Certainly, the doubles must be the mirror images of herself in others she loved.

Anaïs's diary was one of doubles but at the same time a mirror world, one of self-reflections, of narcissism. In *Winter of Artifice*, Anaïs writes that "nearness brings wounds" (7). Real life, real-life relationships, may cause hurt. In a looking-glass world, hurt is less likely. However, in the world of intoxication of narcissism, this labyrinth of mirrors was nothing but a prison of enchantment with no way out, surrounded by reflections or images. In the looking-glass labyrinth, Anaïs's own image and those of her doubles were infinitely reflected one to the other and back again. Anaïs's words, "Ecstasy and anxiety are twins" (*Diary II* 133), were correct. Sabina, a woman of narcissistic unions or fusions with June, recollects Marcel Duchamp's well-known picture *Nude Descending a Staircase*. "Eight or ten outlines of the same woman, like many multiple exposures of woman's personality, neatly divided into many layers, walking down the stairs in unison" (*A Spy in the House of Love, Cities of the Interior* 452), "the figure design as the eye could see it, but empty of substance having evaporated through the spaces between each personality. A divided woman indeed, a woman divided into countless silhouettes" (*A Spy in the House of Love, Cities of the Interior* 453).

The character Stella from *Winter of Artifice*, who is given the line "nearness brings wounds," is an actress who as a young girl stands before a mirror acting out characters such as Joan of Arc, Marguerite, the doomed heroine of *La Dame Aux Camélias*, Mélisande, Thais, and Electra. "She is decomposed before the mirror into a hundred personages" (*Winter of Artifice* 32). In the mirror there is "[no] Stella, but a disguised actress multiplied into many personages" (*Winter of Artifice* 31). "Was it in these games that she had lost her vision of her true self? Could she only win it again by acting?" (*Winter of Artifice* 31)

Stella wants to go back to her true self. If she acts, "[s]he wants to act only herself. She is no longer an actress willing to disguise herself. She is a woman who has lost herself and feels she can recover it by acting this self" (*Winter of Artifice* 32). But who is she when she tries to act as herself? If there is any self, where in the world is it? The confusion in Stella's nature between her real self and the persona adored by her public mirrors a similar confusion in her creator, Anaïs Nin. "But who knows her? What playwright knows her? Not the men who loved her. She cannot tell them. She is lost herself. All that she says about herself is false. She is misleading and misled" (*Winter of Artifice* 32).

As an actress, Stella creates a series of characters, people she is only pretending to be, false selves, while at the same time she searches for the person she really is. In her diary, Anaïs creates characters who are versions of herself all the while seeking to discover the person she really is. It is a situation that in some ways echoes the labyrinthine plot of Pirandello's *Six Characters in Search of an Another*.[7] "The book is taking shape. The women have been divided into elements: Djuna, perception; Stella, blind suffering; Sabina, the free woman; Lillian, the one who seeks liberation in aggression" (*Diary IV* 41). Four characters in search of an author, Anaïs Nin, that is, the cities of the interior, the pilgrimage through women's inner psychological labyrinth, must be written by all means. To recover one's true self when living in a world peopled by many imagined selves, doubles, shadows, and mirrored images, it is necessary to leave the space inhabited by these creations and go out into the real world no matter how unsafe it seems. Anaïs confessed long ago: "Am I facing reality? Am I Stavrogin, who would not act but who watched Stepanovitch with fascination, as if letting him act for him?" (*Diary I* 70)

The description of Stella who swims in the ocean was: "All through the swimming she had the impression of swimming into an ocean of feeling…this great moving body of feeling undulating with her which made of her emotions an illimitable symphonic joy. She had the marvelous sensation of being a part of a vast world and moving with it because of moving in rhythm with another being" (*Winter of Artifice* 13). This sensation can be thought of as Freud's *Ozeanisches Gefuhl* (Oceanic Sensation), the feeling of coexistence with all things in the universe that Freud late in his life despairingly told himself that he could not feel. Anaïs wrote that "we have to find our own element. Mine is undeniably water. Now the ocean is admittedly a universal symbol for the unconscious. In reality, I am drawn to the sea and to ships, and I would have become a scuba diver in reality. Physical limitations thwarting that, I have to be contented with diving deep into the psyche. In fantasy I felt people could communicate through vibrations of intuition, through antennae rather than verbally. According to Dr. Otto Rank, some of these fantasies are 'return to the womb' fantasies, where there was neither cold nor heat nor pain nor consciousness. I describe such a fantasy in *House of Incest*: 'Far below the level of storms I slept. There were no currents of thought, only the caress of flow and desire mingling, touching, traveling, withdrawing—the endless bottom of peace'" (*The Novel of the Future* 120).

Certainly, a woman of mirrors like Anaïs was also a woman of water. It was Lawrence Durrell who called her "the submarine superwoman" (*Diary II* 196). We can understand that she was fascinated with the ocean and ships from her drawing of sailing vessels in her childhood or her love nest with Gonzalo in a houseboat on the Seine. But the houseboat was tied to the bank and never went out. Anaïs wrote, "a story of a boat in a garden. Suddenly I was sailing down a river and I went round and round for twenty years without landing anywhere" (*Winter of Artifice* 78). Anaïs described Djuna's dream: "This boat I was pushing with all my strength because it could not float, it was passing through land" (*Winter of Artifice* 173). Being fascinated by the ocean or water might be Anaïs's yearning for the flow of life. Yet, the boat is tied up or sailing in vain to nowhere, or it must be standing still on land. The diary is also filled with dreams, sometimes nightmares, about water: a frustrated dream that yearns for water, for the ocean; a bad dream in which the water seeks to flow out from where it is being held but is never released.

Conrad Moricand, a gifted astrologer, and a friend of Anaïs and Henry Miller, identified her with the Greek nymph Arethusa. "Arethusa, unable to reach for an impossible fulfillment in love, turned into a fountain, nourished others with her tears… Moricand says the fountain is the diary" (*Diary II* 315). The river god Alpheus falls in love with Arethusa but flees from him. Changed into a spring by the goddess Artemis, she traveled underground to Ortygia in Sicily where she emerged into the light. But Alpheus, who had followed her, flows into the spring himself and so is able once more to possess the nymph. Let me indicate here that this river god, Alpheus, is an archetype of the origin of the river in Coleridge's gothic masterpiece poem, "Kublai Khan." In the "forests ancient as the hills / Enfolding sunny spots of greenery," when "a waning moon was haunted," and "woman wailing for her demon-lover," through "caverns measureless to man," from "that deep romantic chasm," "Alph, the sacred river" ran, "meandering with mazy motion" (*The Norton Anthology English Literature* 440). Anaïs found the comparison of herself to Arethusa amusing. In her diary she writes, "A rather ridiculous personage, Anaïs, as ridiculous as Don Quixote" (*Diary II* 315). Did she wish to change as Arethusa was changed and become possessed by the river of life? Was that like Don Quixote's dream, the dream of impossible love?

By night on my bed
I sought him whom my soul loveth:
I sought him, but I found him not. (Song of Solomon 3:1)

In December 1946, Leo Lerman, the editor of *Harper's Bazaar*, asked Anaïs for a short autobiography, and she answered him: "That was one question I was hoping you would not ask me but answer for me…

My real self is unknown... I wrote, lived, loved like Don Quixote, and on the day of my death I will say: 'Excuse me, it was all a dream,' and by that time I may have found one who will say: 'Not at all, it was true, absolutely true'" (*Diary IV* 177).

Don Quixote may be analogous to Anaïs Nin, who continued to dream things about love that could possibly be realized. Her hunger for life was not enough to secure her release from her self-constructed prison of which these dreams were an integral part. And part of this problem was that she could not live in the real world *without* her dreams; no woman can. Anaïs wrote in the same letter to Lerman: "I am guilty of fabricating a world in which I can live and invite others to live in, but outside of that I cannot breathe" (*Diary IV* 177). In this letter, are not true feelings made clear? Is not the sorrow of Quixote's crazed quest for love laid bare?

The same letter continues, "I suffer from chronic loneliness. I am born under the sign of Venus, the one that appears in the sea shell every morning with a sad expression: 'Another long day of love to come.' I was intended to live the life of Ninon de Lenclos, my favorite woman. I will never settle down, never have a home. My symbol is a roving ship. I am a writer. I would rather have been a courtesan. The rest is in the diary" (*Diary IV* 177-78). De Lenclos seduced the Great Condé, La Rochefoucauld, Molière, Voltaire. Even one of her illegitimate children, not knowing she was his mother, fell in love with her and ended up killing himself. She, too, was the ageless, beautiful and alluring minotaur.

"It is my thousand years of womanhood I am recording, a thousand women" (*Diary VI* 400). This is one sentence in the ending of Anaïs Nin's last diary volume that will have been published by now. Anaïs Nin passed away due to cancer in Los Angeles, near midnight on January 14, 1977, when she was almost seventy-four years old. It was Rupert Pole, her 16-years-younger husband and more like a son, who attended her deathbed. According to Masako Meio, who made a complete translation of *The Diary of Anaïs Nin Volume 1* into Japanese, the newspaper in Los Angeles reported Rupert Pole as the bereaved husband and the newspaper in New York listed Hugh Guiler (*High Fashion No. 1 mid summer*, Anaïs Nin: A Secret Story 177). Three years before Anaïs's death, shortly after Ms. Meio met Anaïs and Rupert for the first time, Ms. Meio received a letter from Anaïs asking her not to tell anybody about Rupert for she did not want Hugo Guiler to know about him. Before Anaïs's death, Daisy Aldan, who had called on Anaïs, wrote, "I spoke with her on January 11. It was an experience. She was very beautiful. She seems very present" (*Under the Sign of Pisces: Anaïs Nin and her Circle* Winter 1977 1).

Anaïs Nin's body was cremated following instructions in her will on January 17, and her ashes were scattered over the Pacific Ocean. A woman of water, born under the sign of Pisces, a woman of Venus born out of the foam of ocean = the planet Venus, returned to the eternal recurrence of water as per her lifelong wishes.

Lastly, let me add, four months before Anaïs's death, Magda Bleier, the editor of the magazine *Châtelaine*, interviewed her. Bleier remarked that the diary did not speak of her marriage or love affairs and that some had reproached the author for being prudish. Then Anaïs stated that her silence did not stem from prudishness, but rather from respect for others' privacy. With her voice growing frail, she said, "But be assured, a day will come when all will be published. With all the details that I have so far kept secret. After my death the complete, the entire Journal will be published... You are still young. You will read it" (*Under the Sign of Pisces: Anaïs Nin and her Circle* Fall 1978 7). The labyrinth of the diary is, further and further, like uroboros, perpetually twisting and winding...

— *Translated and annotated by Toyoko Yamamoto*

Notes

[1] Japanese writer, poet, and critic, 1905-1969.

[2] See "Bergson's mensonge vital" in *Diary I* 246.

[3] In fact, the pregnancy was aborted.

[4] Natsume Soseki (1867-1916), scholar of British Literature, Japanese novelist. The four-character *kanji*, or Chinese characters, means *satori*, spiritual awakening or transcendence of the self to live following the natural way of things. The word was coined by Soseki.

[5] Greek writer in ancient Rome.

[6] A Hungarian scholar in classical philology and Greek mythology, 1897-1973.

[7] Luigi Pirandello (1867-1936), Italian dramatist, novelist, poet who was awarded the 1934 Novel Prize in Literature.

Works Cited (compiled by the translator)

Abrams, M. H., and Geoffrey Galt Harpham. *A Glossary of Literary Terms, Eleventh Edition*, Stamford: Cengage Learning, 2015.

----, and Stephen Greenblatt, eds. *The Norton Anthology of English Literature, Seventh Edition Volume 2*, New York: W. W. Norton & Company, 2000.

Fuller, Margaret. *Memories of Margaret Fuller Ossoli.* Independently published, 2018.

Hara, Masako. *Hai Fasshon (High Fashion) No.1 mid summer*, Anaïs Nin: A Secret Story. Tokyo: Publication Bureau of Bunka Fukuso Gakuin, 1979.

Martin, Jay. *Always Merry and Bright: The Life of Henry Miller.* Santa Barbara: Capra Press, 1978.

Miller, Henry. *The Cosmological Eye.* New York: New Directions, 1939.

----. *The Henry Miller Reader.* Ed. Lawrence Durrell. New York: New Directions, 1969.

----. *Letters to Anaïs Nin.* Ed. Gunther Stuhlmann. London: Sheldon Press, 1979.

----. *Mother, China, and the World.* Santa Barbara: Capra Press, 1977.

----. *The Time of Assassins.* New York: New Directions, 1956.

Nin, Anaïs. *The Diary of Anaïs Nin Vol. I 1931-1934.* Ed. Gunther Stuhlmann. New York: A Harvest Book, The Swallow Press and Harcourt Brace & Company, 1966.

----. *The Diary of Anaïs Nin Vol. II 1934-1939.* Ed. Gunther Stuhlmann. New York: A Harvest Book, The Swallow Press and Harcourt Brace & Company, 1967.

----. *The Diary of Anaïs Nin Vol. III 1939-1944.* Ed. Gunther Stuhlmann. New York: A Harvest/HBJ Book and Harcourt Brace Jovanovich, 1969.

----. *The Diary of Anaïs Nin Vol. IV 1944-1947.* Ed. Gunther Stuhlmann. New York: A Harvest/HBJ Book and Harcourt Brace Jovanovich, 1971.

----. *The Diary of Anaïs Nin Vol. VI 1955-1966.* Ed. Gunther Stuhlmann. New York: Harcourt Brace Jovanovich, 1976.

----. *House of Incest.* Chicago: The Swallow Press, 1958.

----. *Linotte: The Early Diary of Anaïs Nin* 1914-1920, Sherman, Jean L.

trans. New York: Harcourt Brace Jovanovich, 1978.

----. *The Novel of the Future*. Athens: Swallow Press/Ohio University Press, 1986.

----. *A Spy in the House of Love, Cities of the Interior*. Athens: Swallow Press, Ohio University Press, 1974.

----. *Winter of Artifice*. Chicago: The Swallow Press Incorporated, 1945.

----. *Under the Sign of Pisces: Anaïs Nin and Her Circle Winter 1976, Volume 7, Number 1*. Ed. Richard Centing. Columbus: Publications Committee, The Ohio State University Libraries, 1976.

----. *Under the Sign of Pisces: Anaïs Nin and Her Circle Winter 1977, Volume 8, Number 1*. Ed. Richard Centing. Columbus: Publications Committee, The Ohio State University Libraries, 1977.

----. *Under the Sign of Pisces: Anaïs Nin and Her Circle Fall 1978, Volume 9, Number 4*. Ed. Richard Centing. Columbus: Publications Committee, The Ohio State University Libraries, 1978.

Shakespeare, William. *The Riverside Shakespeare, Second Edition, The Complete Works*. Boston, New York: Houghton Mifflin Company, 1997.

Tanemura, Suehiro and Yoshiro Fujikawa, trans. *Labyrinth Studien* by Karl Kerenyi. *Meikyu to Shinwa*. Tokyo: Kobundo, 1996.

The Holy Bible. [authorized King James version] New York: Oxford University Press, 1976.

Japanese edition of *The Winter of Artifice*, translated by Yuko Yaguchi

Yuko Yaguchi

A Spy in the House of Sexuality
Rereading Anaïs Nin through "Henry and June"

Am I a unity? A monster? Am I one woman?
—Anaïs Nin, "Incest" (9)

The making of Anaïs Nin

The Diary of Anaïs Nin was launched into publication in 1966 and ended its seven-volume series in 1980 with the author's death intervening in 1977. One of the peculiarities of the work is that, unlike most published diaries of writers, the diary of an almost unknown author was published, thereby realizing the birth of a writer. In other words, *The Diary of Anaïs Nin* served also as "the making of Anaïs Nin."

It was in the late '60s. The *Diary* rode on the crest of the second wave feminism. Anaïs Nin, whom Kate Millet once called "a mother to us all" (Millet 3), was made into a type of cultural icon. Nevertheless, critical assessment of Anaïs Nin as a writer remains ambivalent and ambiguous thirty years after her death and after two decades of critical rereading and reevaluating American literature.

Henry and June was published in 1986 as the first volume of "The Unexpurgated Diary of Anaïs Nin," followed so far by *Incest* (1992), *Fire* (1995), and *Nearer the Moon* (1996). It will be considered another peculiarity that new titles keep coming out by a dead author like a series of postscript or letters from the other world (it is regrettable that we have not heard from her for a decade).[1] On top of that, major differences can be found between the original and the unexpurgated series of the *Diary*. Every time a new volume appears, readers are enticed and compelled to revise their portrait of Anaïs Nin. What Henry Miller described in his marvelous essay on Nin's diary, "Un Être Étoilique," never seems to cease: "that world which is constantly in the making" (16).

The aim of this essay is to reread Anaïs Nin, placing a focus on the unique or "notorious ménage de trio"[2] between Anaïs Nin, Henry Miller and his wife June, which came into light with the publication of *Henry and June*.

Female (sexual) bildungsroman?

"The impetus to grow and live intensely is so powerful in me I cannot resist it." So writes Anaïs Nin in the opening passage of *Henry and June*

(1). The determination coincides with the description on the last page: "Last night I wept. I wept because the process by which I have become woman was painful" (274). Is *Henry and June* given a frame as "female (sexual) bildungsroman," in which Anaïs is initiated into "the world of sex" with Henry and June as her guides and achieves a goal by "becoming woman"? At least it seems this is how the book is edited,[3] paralleling Otto Rank's patriarchal "plot" to force Nin to choose to be either a woman or an artist, implying the former is a preferable choice (*DI* 291).

Nin herself turns down the alternative choice and chooses "[t]o write as a woman" instead (*HJ* 233). She defines herself in another place as "a man's woman" (*DI* 346). The phrase is used in the context that Nin feels she was not born to be a mother, but determined to undertake metaphysical motherhood, so to speak, not for children but for art and men. However, it was interpreted almost solely as "a woman for men" or "a man-loving woman" and has been the target of criticism by feminists. Nin's words on women, femininity and feminism cover a broad range and include contradictions, some of which can be considered rather archaic or even reactionary in the light of the twenty-first century premise. What did Anaïs Nin mean by the term "woman"? Can we shed "yesterday's woman to pursue a new vision" there? (*DI* 204)

Between / Both Henry and June

The title of the book, *Henry and June*, is both suggestive and misleading, for the two persons named are neither protagonists of the story, nor is their relationship the main subject. The protagonist is Anaïs Nin, who is missing from the title; the subject is the triangular relationship between the three parties.

I wrote earlier that theirs is a unique ménage à trois. The uniqueness will come into focus when compared with other theories of triangle we have at hand.

What René Girard called "the triangle of desire" (Girard 3) is an isosceles triangle with a beloved as an apex, while Henry, June, and Anaïs form an equilateral triangle in which the three concerned are attracted to each other. If we place Anaïs's husband Hugo Guiler and sculptress Jean Kronski (who is believed to be June's ex-lover) outside the equilateral triangle, a number of triangles begin to be divided and multiplied in a chimerical manner. Between lovers exists "the mimetic desire," in Girard's terminology. "Between men" Eve Sedgwick found "the homosocial desire." Between Henry and June is Anaïs as a singular point of function.

In order to clarify the structure of this idiosyncratic triangle, we shall start with analyzing the relationship between Henry and June. Nin tells us in volume one of the *Diary*:

> From the very first day I could see that Henry, who had always lived joyously and obviously outside, in daylight, had been drawn into this labyrinth unwittingly by his own curiosity and love of facts... June must be like those veiled figures glimpsed turning the corner of a Moroccan street, wrapped from head to foot in white cotton, throwing to a stranger a single spark from fathomless eyes. Was she the very woman he had been seeking? (*DI* 13)

Day/night, outside/inside, reality/illusion, explorer/mystery, speaker /spoken, subject/object, and of course, man/woman. Following the example of what Hélène Cixous calls "[a]lways the same metaphor" (Cixous 37), the couple perform the role-playing game of artist/muse or man/femme fatale (stereo)typically and professionally, as if making a caricature of gendered dualism.

Anaïs, who confesses, "I am trapped between the beauty of June and genius of Henry" (*HJ* 48), places herself between them and wants both as objects of desire ("I want [Henry], and I want June" [120]). Furthermore, Anaïs is both Henry and June by being "a speaking woman," or at least wants to be them both. ("They are both in me: the woman who acts as Henry does and the woman who dreams of acting like June" [134].)

Standing in a privileged position of having Henry and June both as objects of desire and identification, what role does Anaïs play? First of all, she defines herself as "a translator":

> They need a translator!
> I was sitting on Henry's bed in Clichy, and doing just that, translating them to each other. (*DI* 151)

She must have been translating not only between Henry and June as two individuals, but between "two facts" (*HJ* 271), two genders, and two cultures.

Fritz Klein, juxtaposing a sexual category of bisexuals to that of racial interbreeding, presents a border-transcending existence of bisexuals as the "spy" or "traitor":

The bisexuals resemble the spy in that he or she moves psychosexually free among men, among women. As well, the bisexual resembles the traitor in that he or she is in a position to know the secrets of both camps, and to play one against the other. The bisexual, in short, is seen as a dangerous person not to be trusted, because his or her vision of party loyalty, so to speak, is nonexistent. (Klein 41)

The description brings to the mind of Nin's readers the title of her novel *A Spy in the House of Love.* If we apply Klein's theory, Anaïs Nin deserves the name of "a spy in the house of love and sexuality." When confronted as artist with the mystery named June, Henry and Anaïs make an alliance ("There is in both of us an obsession to grasp June... We both felt the need of allying our minds, our two different logics, in understanding the problem of June" [*HJ* 33]). But Anaïs rejects Henry's knowledge when she loves June, talking in "a secret language" with her:

What a secret language we talk, undertones, overtones, nuances, abstractions, symbols... What is this powerful magical thing we give ourselves to, June and I, when we are together? (26)
June was afraid that Henry would turn me against her. What does she fear? I said to her, "There is a fantastic secret between us. I only know about you through my own knowledge. Faith. What is Henry's knowledge to me?" (27)

Declaring "I feel like the greatest traitor on earth" (*Incest* 23), Anaïs Nin fluctuates between the two worlds of Henry and June and picks fresh and rich fruit from both. The way she acts certainly reminds us of a double spy. Now that we have read *Henry and June* and *Incest*, doesn't this spy in the house of sexuality look more "seductive," to use one of Nin's favorite words, than one of her old images as a fortunate woman who is gifted and loved (by men, especially her husband) and endowed with both art and marriage, the image rather heterosexist, white middle class, and reactionary?[4]
She not only takes away precious fruit from Henry and June but gives each one back to the other:

I felt the moment had come for me to release my June, to give him my June, "because," I said, "it will make you love her more." (*HJ* 86)

I want to write her and beg her to come back, because I love her, because I want to give up Henry to her as the greatest gift I can make her. (120)

Anaïs as a spy/translator/gift-giver soberly observes her own "love" and "evil" as well as her standpoint as an artist, and weaves language of her own. The following passage, taken from "Djuna" in *The Winter of Artifice* (1939), a novelization of *Henry and June* in advance, so to speak, shows this point clearly. Hans is modeled upon Henry, Johanna upon June:

While he caressed me I would poison him with the inextricable mixture of Johanna and myself. The deepest treachery to man ever played. I was a creator of images. Of characters and masks. I would recreate Johanna in Hans' mind. It was I who would tell Hans what dreams, what desires, what impulses Johanna had. And I would give Johanna these gifts which Hans made me of his passionate rages, his secrets, his mind's fertility. ("Djuna" 20)

A laboratory of body and soul

"A laboratory of the soul" is the expression often used as a metaphor for Nin's legendary house in Louveciennes as well as her (also legendary) diary. Passing through the unexpurgated diaries, however, we may feel enticed to call it "a laboratory of body and soul." Here we would investigate within the framework of this essay a series of experiments conducted in the laboratory.

Following "the equilateral triangle" theory we introduced earlier, we still have two sides to examine, those of Henry-Anaïs and June-Anaïs. First, let's look at the heterosexual relationship between Henry and Anaïs. One of the distinct attributes of this relationship is that in it sheer physicality/eroticism and literary comradeship/fraternity co-exist. Also worthy of notice is that while the combination of "feminine" Anaïs and "macho" Henry cannot but stimulate the heterosexual/heterosexist illusion of "marriage of the opposites," there happens at the same time the subversion of genders. Nin, at one point, writes in a "womanly" tone, "God, I have known such a day, such hours of female submission, such a gift of myself there can be nothing left to give" (*HJ* 83). Notwithstanding, she complains that the passive role of female gender restricts her in a sexual act and asks herself, "Rather than wait for his pleasure, I would like to take it, to run wild. Is it that which pushes me into lesbianism?" (101) On the other hand, Miller becomes "romantic" as their relationship deepens, whining "It isn't only fucking, is it? You do love me?" (109) "Yesterday I was worrying like a woman. How long will she love me? Will she get tired of me?" (181)

In fact, we should remind ourselves that Nin wrote when their relationship culminated sexually, "The tenderness of his hands, the unexpected penetration, to the core of me but without violence. What strange, gentle power" and reported Miller's question, "You expected more brutality?" (56) In a sense, it may be called a cliché that a man in love tends to be "sissy" and a woman virile. In "a laboratory of body and soul" named love and/or sexuality, both sexes are compelled at a critical moment to get rid of their gender stereotypes. When Miller experienced a period of temporary impotence, Nin covers up her disappointment by saying, "It is natural. It happens to women, too, only in women it doesn't show! They can conceal it." It then occurred to her that they both internalized the heterosexual/heterosexist myth, where Miller wanted to prove his potency and she desired to be the one to provoke the potency (180-82). Even more noteworthy are such descriptions as to convert heterosexuality into homosexuality and to show a possibility that the two can intervene with each other: "At the Hotel Anjou we lie like lesbians, sucking" (191) or "our last week of interpenetration" (230). We may remember this singular phrase "interpenetration" later, when we examine the relationship between Anaïs and June with a little help from Judith Butler.

Therefore, next and last, let us take a look at female homosexuality between the two women. "What is lesbianism?" is a question both Nin and Miller ask, undoubtedly one of the main motifs of the work. Miller, who is reported to "beat [his] head against the wall of [Anaïs and June's] world" (44), strikingly resembles Freud, who laments, "Throughout history people have knocked their heads against the riddle of the nature of femininity" (Freud 113), or Lacan who says jocularly, "[I]n all the time people have been begging [women] on their hands and knees...to try to tell us [of this jouissance], not a word!" (Lacan 75) Nin has once given a tentative answer to Miller: "The love between women is a refuge and an escape into harmony... Such love is death, I'll admit" (*HJ* 33). It is true that Nin repeatedly compares June's power to death. Yet she also writes about another "homme fatal" of hers, her own father Joaquín: "My Father only gave me death" (*Fire* 189). About Artaud, whom she calls "Brother, brother" ("Je suis" 65), she recalls his kiss was as if "to be drawn toward death, towards insanity" (*DI* 229). In other words, homosexual or heterosexual, love of the double is inevitably intertwined with death for Nin. Nevertheless, fatal love or love of death attracts her over and over. And the world she opens up there is a far cry from "an escape to harmony."

Between June and Anaïs there are not as many direct or distinct sexual descriptions as between Henry and Anaïs, but they are pervaded with almost ontologically dense eroticism. We may hear some responses there to Virginia Woolf's words, which expect a women's literature that "will light a torch in that vast chamber where nobody has yet been," it is "a laboratory" women share, which is "all half lights and profound shadows like those serpentine caves" (Woolf 80).

Nin writes of June: "A startlingly white face retreating into the darkness of the garden. She poses for me as she leaves. I want to run out and kiss her fantastic beauty, kiss it and say, 'You carry away with you a reflection of me, a part of me'" (*HJ* 15). Anaïs and June have often been categorized as two opposite types of women, such as intelligent and sensual, "the full box" and "the empty box" (45). But if we give it a cool second thought, we will notice that various attributes of June—lies, theatricality/multiplicity of character, the femme fatale complex (to coin a phrase)—can be applied without an exception to Anaïs as well. June has a voluptuous body and rich experience; Anaïs doesn't. Anaïs has her own words; June doesn't. Nevertheless and at the same time, June may be extremely close to Anaïs, almost a double.[5] A description in "Djuna" leaves no room for doubt:

If I were to unmask you, Johanna, I should only be revealing myself! You are the face of my unmasked self... We see the face beneath the mask, you mine, I yours, because it is the same face. ("Djuna" 78)

And in *Incest*:

We kissed each other passionately. I fitted my body against every curve of June's body, as if melted into her. She moaned. Her embrace was around me. I lost myself, I lost my consciousness in this bed of flesh. Our legs were bare and twined. We rolled and heaved together. I under June and June under me. Her light moth kisses showered on me, and mine bit her. (*Incest* 39)

Here we could witness what Luce Irigaray tried to indicate by saying "two lips…that caress each other" (Irigaray 24), the world of female genitals, auto-eroticism, and (homo)sexuality expressed in language so vividly and opulently.

Even more intriguing is the way Nin depicts, alongside with *écriture fémininesque* passages as above, what Judith Butler calls "the phallicization of the lesbian" (*Bodies That Matter* 51). In the mainstream feminism it is considered to be a taboo to discuss lesbian sexuality with the intervention of the phallus, which in return could lead to preserve the polarity and complementariness of genders. If lesbian sexuality is as constructed as any sexuality, Butler suggests, we could consider the transferability of the phallus and reconsider the possibility of the lesbian phallus as a useful fiction. We take it for granted that men cannot be penetrated. But the attitude may be a panic over feminization, lesbianism, and in particular the phallicization of the lesbian. Once this common sense is doubted, what are we going to witness or experience?[6]

What might happen if a masculine penetration of the masculine is authorized, or a feminine penetration of the feminine, or a feminine penetration of the masculine or a reversibility of those positions—not to mention a full-scale confusion over what qualifies as penetration anyway. (51)

Anaïs met June, "the most beautiful woman on earth," fell in love with her almost (melo)dramatically, and felt "like a man" within that day (*HJ* 14). When a woman loves a woman, does she have to transgress the bounds of womanhood/femininity? Anaïs Nin writes:

What excludes me forever is the reality of being a man. When the imagination and emotions of a woman overstep normal boundaries, occasionally she is possessed by feelings she cannot express. I want to possess June. I identify myself with the men who can penetrate her. (68)

However, in her dream their positions reverse:

I dreamed of June last night… I begged her to undress. Piece by piece I discovered her body, with cries of admiration, but in the nightmare I saw the defects of it, strange deformations. Still, she seemed altogether desirable. I begged her to let me see between her

139

legs. She opened them and raised them, and there I saw flesh thickly covered with hard black hair, like a man's, but then the very tip of her flesh was snow white. What horrified me was that she was moving frenziedly, and that the lips were opening and closing quickly like the mouth of the goldfish in the pool when he eats. I just watched her, fascinated and repulsed, and then I threw myself on her and said, "Let me put my tongue there," and she let me but she did not seem satisfied while I flicked at her. She seemed cold and restless. Suddenly she sat up, threw me down, and leaned over me, and as she lay over me I felt a penis touching me, I questioned her and she answered triumphantly, "Yes, I have a little one; aren't you glad?" "But how do you hide it from Henry?" I asked. She smiled, treacherously. (91)

It clearly tells us how Anaïs was fascinated as well as horrified by June, in the manner of Kristeva's abject. But the peculiarity here is that the abject, which is usually connected with the feminine, is linked to bisexuality and/or androgyny. In accordance with Butler's claim that the phallus is a taboo subject in lesbian sexuality, the little penis June possesses in Anaïs's dream appears to be a secret she (June or Anaïs or both?) has to hide from Henry.

Male or masculine sexuality and female or feminine sexuality definitely have different significations for Anaïs Nin. That said, she imagines the way of loving or being loved in the manner of "the feminization of the penetration," if we are to apply Butler's terminology. Nin writes of June:

She does not reach the same sexual center of my being that man reaches; she does not touch that. What, then, has she moved in me? I have wanted to possess her as if I were a man, but I have also wanted her to love me with the eyes, the hands, the senses that only women have. It is a soft and subtle penetration. (18)

To write as another woman

From what we have seen so far, we are tempted to say that Anaïs Nin as "a man's woman" is one of her masks or tactics for sexual passing, in the same manner that the Louveciennes house, which Nin called "a beautiful prison" (*D1* 7) and in which she lived as the beautiful wife of a banker, was also a radical "laboratory of body and soul." If we are to call her "a man's woman," we should hasten to add that she was "a woman's woman" at the same time.

Let us go back to Nin's motto "[t]o write as a woman" and the context in which it was spoken. In tackling the problem of June in alliance with Miller, she finds herself emptied out, yielding most of her thoughts on June to him, including sharing parts of her diary. She asks herself what is left for her to do, and the answer is presented: "To write as a woman and as a woman only" (233). In *Diary 1*, a phrase is intervened between the question and the answer, making the logic clearer: "To go where Henry cannot go, into the Myth, into June's dream, fantasies, into the poetry of June" (128). We are familiar with male writers appropriating private writings of women, often their wife or lover, to their work—in American literature, Scott Fitzgerald, Williams Carlos Williams, to name just a few. However, it is a rare case where appropriation is done in complicity and the pain is spoken out, written down, and textualized on the part of a woman. With Nin, anyway, the phrase "[t]o write as a woman" should be followed in our mind "about June/woman/woman-loving."

When Anaïs Nin, who used to be regarded as a tenacious heterosexist, oversteps the border into the region of homo/bisexuality, her discourse on women and femininity needs to be reconsidered.

Djuna-Anaïs talks to Johanna-June:

> Everything which composed the external Johanna was a concealment of her, not an expression... A thousand times I will unmask you, Johanna, because it is only you and I who know the inexhaustibility of woman's masks. And the last will fall only when we are dust. ("Djuna" 77-78)

It was Butler who declared that there is no gender identity behind gender expressions, and Joan Riviere who, in her monumental essay which has repercussions on contemporary gender studies, mentioned the inexhaustibility of women's masks, masks that are women. To put it otherwise, they share a standpoint that doesn't expect "true woman-(hood)" or "essence of femininity." (Though here I would not go into further analysis, it needs recognizing that underneath numerous masks, Riviere, as an analyst, hypothesizes "masculinity" while Nin hypothesizes "a child" ["Djuna" 78].)[7]

"Woman" is fiction, a socially and historically constructed concept which requires constant redefinition in the process of perpetual becoming. Butler amplifies Beauvoir's well-known statement and writes:

If there is something right in Beauvoir's claim that one is not born, but rather becomes a woman, it follows that woman itself is a term in process, a becoming, a constructing that cannot rightfully be said to originate or to end. As an ongoing discursive practice, it is open to intervention and resignification. (*Gender Trouble* 33)

Standing on this premise, we cannot assume to "become woman" is the final goal; *Henry and June* inevitably loses its frame of reference as bildungsroman, apparently set by the male editor. We seem to be standing on the point where we could reread, via Butler, both Beauvoir and Nin as a palimpsest. The publication of the unexpurgated diaries and contemporary gender studies have made it possible to bring into question "Anaïs Nin's concept of femininity" (153), which reportedly infuriated Beauvoir, as well as the concept of femininity itself. In fact, the Japanese translator of *The Diary of Anaïs Nin* volume one, Masako Hara (a.k.a. novelist Masako Meio) insightfully analyzed as early as 1974 that "For Nin, being a woman is not nature, it is an idea by all means… Her dictum '[t]o write as a woman' would be more precisely paraphrased as 'to write to become a woman'" (Hara 382).

There is no doubt that Anaïs Nin was infinitely fascinated by the story that is woman. The classically womanly woman Nin herself called "the 1830 type" (*ED4* 414) and the feminist icon who mothered not only Millet but Judy Chicago, etc. are but two faces/phases of her metamorphoses. She has kept betraying her image and her readers, until she became a woman nobody knows, "another woman not in the novels" (*D4* 176). In her fluctuation between the Victorian lady and the pioneering thus controversial feminist, or the radical experimenter of gender/sexuality leaving the twentieth century behind and reaching for the twenty-first, in her monstrous visage with "a thousand faces" (*D3* 166) lies Anaïs Nin's center of possibility.

Works Cited

Beauvoir, Simone de. *All Said and Done.* Trans. Patrick O'Brian. New York: Paragon House. 1993.

Butler, Judith. *Bodies That Matter.* New York: Routledge, 1993.

----. *Gender Trouble.* New York: Routledge, 1990.

Cixous, Hélène. *The Hélène Cixous Reader.* Ed. Susan Sellers. London:

Routledge, 1994.

Cornell, Drucilla. *Beyond Accommodation*. Lanbam: Rowman & Littlefield Publishers. 1999.

Freud, Sigmund. "Femininity." Vol. 22 of *The Standard Edition of the Complete Psychological Works*. Ed. and trans. James Strachy. 23 vols. London: Hogarth Press, 1964-66. 112-35.

Girard, René. *Deceit, Desire, and the Novel*. Trans. Yvonne Freccero. London: Johns Hopkins University Press, 1965.

Irigaray, Luce. *This Sex Which Is Not One*. Trans. Catherine Porter. Ithaca: Cornell University Press, 1985.

Klein, Fritz. "The Bisexual Option," *Bisexuality: A Critical Reader*. Ed. Merl Storr. London: Routledge, 1999. 38-48.

Kristeva, Julia. *Powers of Horror*. Trans. Leon S. Roudiez. New York: Columbia University Press, 1982.

Lacan, Jacques. *On Feminine Sexuality (Encore, The Seminar of Jacques Lacan, Book XX)*. Ed. Jacques-Alain Miller. Trans. Bruce Fink. New York: Norton, 1998.

Masako Hara, trans. *The Diary of Anaïs Nin*, vol. 1. By Anaïs Nin. Tokyo: Kawadeshobo-shinsha, 1974.

Miller, Henry. "Un Être Étoilique." *A Casebook on Anaïs Nin*. Ed. Robert Zaller. New York: New American Library, 1974. 5-22.

Millet, Kate. "Anaïs—A Mother to Us All." Vol. 9 of *ANAIS: An International Journal*. Ed. Gunther Stuhlmann. 3-8.

Nin, Anaïs. *The Diary of Anaïs Nin*. Ed. Gunther Stuhlmann. 7 vols. New York: Harcourt: 1966-80.

----. "Djuna." *The Winter of Artifice*. Paris: Obelisk Press, 1939. 9-108.

----. *The Early Diary of Anaïs Nin*. 4 vols. New York: Harcourt. 1978-1985.

----. *Fire*. New York: Harcourt, 1995.

----. *Henry and June*. 1986. London: Penguin Books, 1990.

----. *Incest*. New York: Harcourt, 1992.

----. "Je suis le plus malade des surrealists." *Under a Glass Bell*. London: Peter Owen Ltd., 1944. 57-69.

----. *A Spy in the House of Love*. Toronto: Bantam Books, 1959.

Riviere, Joan. "Womanliness as a Masquerade." *Psychoanalysis and Female Sexuality*. Ed. Hendrik M. Tuitenbeek. Hew Haven: College and University Press, 1966. 209-20.

Sedgwick, Eve Kosofsky. *Between Men*. New York: Columbia University Press, 1985.

Stuhlmann, Gunther. Ed. *ANAIS: An International Journal*. 19 vols. California: The Anaïs Nin Foundation, 1983-2001.

Woolf, Virginia. *A Room of One's Own*. 1929. London: Grafton Books, 1988.

Notes

[1] Since this article appeared, three more unexpurgated diaries have been published: *Mirages* (1939-1947); *Trapeze* (1947-1955); *The Diary of Others* (1955-1966); *A Joyous Transformation* (1966-1977) is forthcoming.

[2] The phrase was used by an interviewer to Wendy Becket who wrote and directed a play *Anaïs Nin: One of Her Lives*, which ran at Becket Theatre in New York from August 3 to 26, 2006. http://www.unitedstages.com. It is an interesting coincidence that the back cover of *Artists and Models* in Pocket Penguin 15 says: "Anaïs Nin became notorious following the publication of sensual journals."

[3] Rupert Pole is named as editor. However, the "real" editor is reported to be John Ferrone who used to work for Harcourt Brace Jovanovich. It is mentioned in an e-mail by Paul Herron, editor of *A Café in Space* to the Café in Space Discussion Group on October 3, 2005.

[4] It may be because Masako Hara stated clearly in her Translator's Note that Nin's *Diary* is idiosyncratic in that it leaves out everything about the diarist's married life, since in Japan, at least, the fact of her marriage has been known to readers since the translation of the *Diary*, volume one, was published in 1974.

[5] In a unique biography by Stephen Starck entitled *June Scattered in Fragments*, whose title itself cannot but remind us of Anaïs, we find passages as follows: "Any reader of Anaïs's diaries will be struck by similarities between the two women, both in their lives and their assessments of Henry" (26).

[6] As already mentioned by not a few critics, there is a striking similarity between Nin's description of female (homo)sexuality and what so-called

French feminists named *écriture feminine*. We may admire Nin's foresight or criticize her "essentialist" and "ontological" approach. What I find the most subversive and hyper-contemporary about Nin, however, is the way both Irigaray and Butler burgeon up in her.

[7] Drucilla Cornell criticizes the notion of the masquerade as only the masks a woman puts on to please her lover. I will point out briefly here that Nin's masquerade covers far wider a range than Cornell's definition, wide enough for Nin to be "a monster" with "a thousand faces."

Japanese edition of *The Diary of Anaïs Nin*

Satoshi Kanazawa

Multiplying Women
Reflection, repetition and multiplication in the works of Maya Deren and Anaïs Nin

The encounter of two women

I n the summer of 1944, when she and her friends were taking a walk on the beach of Amagansett, New York, Anaïs Nin encountered a strange scene. A woman was lying on the shore, letting herself be pummeled by the waves while two people filmed it.[1] Later, Nin found out the woman was Maya Deren, an avant-garde filmmaker, who was filming the opening scene of *At Land* (1945). After this meeting, the two female artists, both of whom were struggling underground figures, forged an enduring relationship, which one Nin biographer would later describe as a "rivalry" (Fitch 279).

In terms of age, at least, the word "rivalry" seems somewhat inappropriate because at forty-one, Nin was fourteen years older than Deren. In 1945, Nin saw Deren's first works, *Meshes of the Afternoon* (1944) and the finished version of *At Land*, and admired her talent, comparing her to Jean Cocteau. Because of Deren's youthful, incendiary energy, it was inevitable that Nin would get involved with her film-making.

Although she released only a handful of short silent films, Maya Deren is now hailed as a pioneer in American avant-garde filmmaking. Few books on film history fail to note her name. But, in a sense, Deren was an amateur director. Before she became a filmmaker, she was a poet. When she was younger, she wanted to be a dancer, or a singer, and it was the Czech filmmaker Alexander (Sasha) Hammid who introduced her to the world of film. They married in 1943, and then they shot *Meshes of the Afternoon* at their new place on Kings Road in Hollywood. The film, in which the two were both cast and crew, was shot exclusively by themselves. Although the film was only made for private use, it became as highly regarded as the surrealistic works of Cocteau, Salvador Dalí, or Luis Buñuel, and was awarded the 1947 Cannes Film Festival's "Grand Prix International for 16mm Film, Experimental Class."

Deren's work sheds light on the advantage amateurs have over professionals. An amateur is, in its Latin meaning, a "lover" of some-thing. While the professional artist is fettered by economic realities and marketability, the amateur takes action purely on the grounds of love for the object. Therefore, amateurs are free (Deren 17). It seems quite natural that Nin, who formed an anti-commercial literary circle with Henry Miller and other writers in Paris in 1930s, had an affinity for Deren's amateurism.

In a June 1945 entry in her diary, Nin made a remark on Deren's works: "Truly unconscious dream material, better in some ways than the early surrealist movies because there are no artificial effects, just a simple following of the threads of fantasy... I see the influence of Cocteau, except that she will not resort to any symbolism or artifice to present the dream. The dream resembles realism. The objects are not altered, there is no mystery. There is nothing to indicate that one is dreaming or free-associating. A curious prosaic quality imposed upon the imagination" (*Diary 4* 67-68).

Although these remarks were first published some twenty years later, they are among the earliest referring to Deren's work. Nin's insight was accurate, for she pointed out that Deren's works were prosaic, not poetic, and realistic. Generally speaking, one would expect quite the reverse to be expressed. Just as realism is supposed to represent reality as it is, Deren's works represent the dream as it is, according to Nin, without any artificial distortion.

With all this appreciation from the very beginning, why did Nin become displeased with Deren? One could conclude, in a prosaic, biographic manner, that it was simply because Nin was dissatisfied with her screen appearance in Deren's *Rituals in Transfigured Time* (1946). However, their relationship was so intricate that we do it disservice with such a dismissal. Mirrors, above all, will be the key to this study—I will examine how the two female artists respectively represented the role of mirrors and the reflection of self-image.

Multiplying women

The three most outstanding of Deren's short films, *Meshes of the Afternoon, At Land*, and *Rituals in Transfigured Time*, remind us of Buñuel's 1930s surrealism. With only these three 15-minute silent movies, she paved the way for new expression by younger filmmakers such as Jonas Mekas, John Cassavetes, Martin Scorsese, and David Lynch. The consistent theme of these works is the splitting and multiplication of the Self. How the Self, which is essentially supposed to be "one," is transformed into "many" is superbly documented through dreamlike images. Here we will see the process of repetition/splitting/multiplication by exploring the structure of the most suspenseful of the three, *Meshes of the Afternoon.*

Meshes of the Afternoon consists of 161 shots, according to Deren's own count (Clark 85-94). These shots are, on the whole, divided into five sequences.

The first sequence, from shot number 1 to 27, which we call here "sequence A," goes like this: At the walkway of a house with a Mediterranean look, someone deposits a flower. A shadow of a girl picks up the flower. The girl runs after the other figure but cannot catch up with it. She gives up pursuing, takes the stairway and steps into the room. In the empty room, there is a hint that someone has been there just before. After going upstairs, the girl sits in a chair by the window. There is a close-up of an eye, which eventually closes.

What is characteristic of sequence A is that the girl does not appear on the screen, and what the audience sees is composed from the first-person viewpoint of the girl. Her eye is shot in a close-up in shot 27, but her whole figure has never been introduced. When the sleepy eye is closed, one might expect that the whole thing would happen in her dream.

The next sequence, from shot 28 to 60, is the repetition and variation of sequence A. The camera captures the outside view, where the figure is walking. The figure is clothed in black, whose face is nothing but a mirror. Even though the "mirror" is walking very slowly, the running girl cannot catch up with it. She gives up pursuing and takes the stairway. At this moment (shot 37), the full visage of the girl, played by Maya Deren, appears for the first time. The act of opening the door and going upstairs is performed for a variation. The girl sees her double sleeping in the chair. She approaches the window, looking out onto the road. Up to this point, the second sequence has repeated the course of time in sequence A, so we can call the shots from 28 to 60 "sequence A'."

In terms of repetitions and variations, the structure of *Meshes of the Afternoon* is analyzable into the following five sequences:

A - A' - A'' - A''' - B

Until the final sequence B, time does not progress, and the exploration of the dream world is repeated. And, as is shown in the first repetition, the girl played by Deren is not one person. She is continually multiplying.

In sequence A'' (from shot 61 to 97), the double stands beside the sleeping girl, looking out onto the road, where we can see another girl running after the "mirror." In her shot list, Deren counts the second girl as "dream girl no. 1" and the third girl "dream girl no. 2." When the "mirror" has gone away and the third girl gives up pursuing, she repeats the act of opening the door. In the room, the "mirror" is carrying a flower. The third girl is perplexed. The "mirror" deposits the flower on the bed, and then disappears. The flower is replaced by a knife. The first girl is still sleeping beside the bed. "Dream girl no. 2" looks out of the window.

In Sequence A''', the last repetitive sequence (from shot 98 to 154), the tension rises to its highest level. "Dream girl no. 3" is pursuing the "mirror" on the road outside. She gives up pursuing, climbs up the stairway, and enters the house. At last, the three dream girls confront each other. "Dream girl no. 3" is slightly aggressive. The three girls start a "conference" concerning the key and the knife. "Dream girl no. 1" and "dream girl no. 2" are so suspicious that they throw a hostile, languorous glance at "dream girl no. 3" (Shot 112, Fig. 1). The sleeping girl is still in the chair, stirring as if in a nightmare. "Dream girl no. 3" holds the knife, wears strange glasses (which Deren describes as "mirror eyes"), and then, in a determined manner, strides toward the sleeping girl. "Dream girl no. 3" is ready to plunge the knife into the sleeping girl. And then, "dream girl no. 3" is replaced by a man. The man, played by Hammid, displays a lover's intimacy and deposits a flower on the bed, just as the "mirror" has done. He reaches out his hand to caress her. The flower changes into a knife, the girl opens her eyes and takes the knife to resist him. The man's face, which turns out to be a mirrored reflection, is shattered. The pieces of the shattered mirror fall into the sands on the seashore.

Fig. 1. "Shot 112" from *Meshes of the Afternoon*

Sequence B (from Shot 155 to 161) depicts the events after the varied A sequences. Walking up from the road and through the stairway is filmed again, but this time it is the man who climbs up the stairway. When he enters the room, he finds the girl sitting in the chair, bleeding to death.

With all this analysis of the shots, we cannot come close to the mysteriousness of *Meshes of the Afternoon*. What we ascertained here is not the mystery, but the clarity of the work. It is quite clear that each repetition multiplies the Self. Sequence A, which adopted the first-person viewpoint, is not mysterious enough to dispel its reality. In this sequence, the black-clad figure does not reveal its mirrored face, and the mysteriousness of the mirrored figure's inapproachability is restrained. Only in the dream sequences from A' to A''' do the surrealistic and mysterious qualities develop. Between the realistic sequences A and B, the repetitions of the dream are inserted.

As for the later works, *At Land* and *Rituals in Transfigured Time*, it will be sufficient to say, in order to avoid a prolonged discussion, that these are to some extent the repetitions and variations of the theme and technique of *Meshes of the Afternoon*. In these works, each woman played by Deren continues multiplying.

Against the mirror

Why does the Self multiply in the works of Maya Deren? To answer this question, it is quite clear, especially in *Meshes of the Afternoon*, that the mirror plays a crucial role. Who is the "mirror," and why does the destruction of the "mirror" cause the death of the Self? One might expect to find a psychoanalytic implication in the symbolic items placed in this work: a flower, a key, and a knife. Beginning with an interpretation of these items and referring to the mirror stage may seem to point toward a plausible explanation, but the fact is, however, that Deren denied that there were any psychoanalytic implications in her work. "A flower...is a flower, a mirror is a mirror, a knife is a knife" (*Diary 6* 351). Some critics, including Nin, pointed out that Deren's denial was actually a revolt against her father, Solomon Deren, who, while not a Freudian psychiatrist, was nonetheless involved with the treatment of "mentally defective" children (Clark 108). It is quite fair to say that Deren's revolt against psychoanalysis anticipates Susan Sontag's 1960s essay "Against Interpretation," in which Sontag challenges the modern style of inter-pretation, saying that by "reducing art to its content, and then interpreting *that*, one tames the work of art. Interpretation makes art manageable, comfortable" (Sontag 7-8), thus degrading art into the bourgeois collection of knowledge.[2]

Anaïs Nin was also an artist who persistently stuck to the mirror concept. She called her lifelong diary her mirror, and she confessed to Otto Rank that she "felt like a shattered mirror" (*Diary 1* 273). Henry Miller reflected on what the mirror meant for Nin in "Un Être Étoilique" (1939), which also would shed light on Deren's mirror. Miller compares the artist who delves into his/her consciousness in order to realize the world to "Jonah in the belly of the whale." His assertion on the characteristic of Nin's diary is as follows:

> The person who is doing this [Nin] is really an innocent little creature tucked away in the lining of the belly of the whale. In nullifying herself she really becomes this great leviathan which swims the deep and devours everything in sight. It is a strange *dédoublement* of the personality in which the crime is related back to the whale by a sort of self-induced amnesia. There, tucked away in a pocket of the great intestinal tract of the whale, she dreams away throughout whole volumes of something which is not the whale, of something greater, something beyond which is nameless and unseizable. She has a little pocket mirror which she tacks up on the wall of the whale's intestinal gut and into which she gazes for hours on end. The whole drama of her life is played out before the mirror. If she is sad the mirror reflects her sadness; if she is gay the mirror reflects her gayety. But everything the mirror reflects is false, because the moment she realizes that her image is sad or gay she is no longer sad or gay. Always there is another self which is hidden from the mirror and which enables her to look at herself in the mirror. This other self tells her that it is only her image which is sad, only her image which is gay. By looking at herself steadily in the mirror she really accomplishes the miracle of not looking at herself. The mirror enables her to fall into a trance in which the image is completely lost. The eyes close and she falls backward into the deep. The whale too falls backward and is lost into the deep. (Miller 287-88)

The mirror mentioned here is quite different than the mirror in Jacques Lacan's "mirror stage." For Lacan, the mirror is any reflective surface (a mother's face, for example), in which a child recognizes his/her image and identifies with it (and the Other). The mirror which

Miller imagines, however, does not involve a direct reflection or confrontation with the Self. It is, rather, the device which reflects the Other. Behind the mirror of the whale's bowels lies the world of the Other, but no one can break out of the whale. According to Miller, who was against psychoanalysis, one does not see the mirror of the Other to see oneself, but sees in the mirror of one's own consciousness the world of the Other.

Lacan's mirror stage presupposes the symmetry between the subject that sees and the object that is seen. And, as Luce Irigaray points out, the subject that sees and speaks has always been male, and the female is required to be the mirror/other/mother on which the male builds his ego. Irigaray denounces this notion of symmetry as a "phallocratic model":

> As for the priority of symmetry, it co-relates with that of the flat mirror—which may be used for the self-reflection of the masculine subject in language, for its constitution as subject of discourse. Now woman, starting with this flat mirror alone, can only come into being as the inverted other of the masculine subject (his *alter ego*), or as the place of emergence and veiling of the cause of his (phallic) desire, or again as lack, since her sex for the most part—and the only historically valorized part—is not subject to specularization. Thus in the advent of a "feminine" desire, this flat mirror cannot be privileged and symmetry cannot function as it does in the logic and discourse of a masculine subject. (Irigaray 129)

We should bring Jean Cocteau's *The Blood of a Poet* (1930) to mind, in which the protagonist is only able to enter into the mirror world "vertically." On the contrary, the protagonist in *Meshes of the Afternoon* never faces the mirror vertically. In Deren's works, the mirror is always slanted. The "dream girls" multiplied by repetition are never in accord with the self-portrait that might be reflected on the mirror when seen vertically. As shown in shot 112, they cast a languorous glance of the others, no matter how they look like each other.

The photographic works performed by Deren and shot by her husband Hammid quite often depend on the deforming effect of a mirror or glass (Fig. 2). It looks as if Deren never puts confidence in what the mirror shows. According to the shooting script of *At Land*, the film was supposed to have a sequence which relied on mirrors, but the scenes were finally omitted.[3] In Sequence E, the protagonist enters a bedroom, which is found to be a multi-faceted mirror. The mirror multiplies her image to such a degree that the images are never face-to-face with each other, and the image that is seen does not meet the eye of the woman who sees. Although her face is reflected from different angles, she will never acquire the front image (Fig. 3).

Fig. 2. From "Experimental Portraiture"

Fig. 3. An outtake from *At Land*

Now that we have seen how defiant Deren is of the symmetry of the mirror, it is no doubt that, for Deren, the mirror is not the device which reflects the Self, but the one that splits and multiplies the Self. Irigaray maintains that the revolt against the domination of the "flat mirror" over history "presupposes *a curved mirror*, but also one that is *folded back on itself*, with its impossible reappropriation 'on the inside' of the mind, of thought, of subjectivity" (Irigaray 155). This is exactly what Deren experimented on during the 1940s.

Let us return to the original question. Why does the destruction of the "mirror" cause the death of the Self? We have already reached the point where, because vertical symmetry is thoroughly challenged, the relation between question and answer is no longer considered as a one-to-one correspondence. We have also seen that Deren's mirror splits and multiplies. One possible answer to the question is: Even when she breaks the "mirror" in order to revolt against man, the very act of breaking the mirror reversely leads her to death as a woman, because in the real world it is always upon woman that society imposes the role of the mirror. Another answer is: At first she seems to have broken the "mirror" in order to repel the Other, but the destruction of the mirror only leads her to the destruction of her own mind because, as Henry Miller asserts, the mirror is something else than the Other, something which is attached inside and essential to the subject. All of these multiple interpretations we make are attributed to the traps that Deren elaborately set for us; a single, conclusive interpretation is impossible.

Anaïs and Maya before the glass

The shooting of *Rituals in Transfigured Time* started in August 1945. In Nin's diary, the first description of the shooting is in the entry of October 1945, in which she and her friends were asked to act in Deren's film. At first Nin's role was just to appear. Once the shooting started, however, Deren gave her "more and more to do," such as dancing (*Diary 4* 92).

While in *Meshes of the Afternoon* and *At Land* the girls who multiply are performed by Deren, she took a different approach in *Rituals in Transfigured Time*. This time the woman who splits is not performed by Deren alone, but played by multiple performers. Always interested in the sensuality of dancing, Deren designated Rita Christiani, a young dancer from Trinidad, as her double. In the original scenario, the roles of Deren and Christiani are interchangeable and signify the double aspects of one woman. The original scenario did not have the slightest mention of Nin's role (Clark 472). The role of another woman played by Nin was added as the shooting went on.

When their friendship began in 1944, Nin appreciated Deren's talent and vitality for filmmaking, admitting that Deren is "stronger than I am" (*Diary 4* 90) and described Deren's beauty in a scene from *Meshes of the Afternoon* as "a truly Botticelli effect" (76). Once she joined the film-making, however, Nin found Deren's strength to be merely the arbitrary power of the director. The shooting went on until the next year, and, in the entries of March and May of 1946, Nin harshly criticized Deren's work in progress.

There is no doubt that Nin and Deren had mutual sympathy for their common theme of woman's subjectivity, no matter what creative media they used. In April 1946, Nin wrote in her diary:

> All the various women may converge into one because down deep, in the unconscious, there are resemblances.
>
> Also in life women become other women, interchange. identify, and project. Parts of themselves in the other, through the other. There are exchanges, interchanges, and convergences, and parts of our-selves pass into others. (140)

It is quite probable that Nin wrote this passage under the influence of Deren, as we can find the word "interchange" in Deren's original scenario called "Ritual and Ordeal." While Nin truly understood that the theme of the film was interchangeability, she determined that the theme was lost and the film was a failure (149).

Rituals in Transfigured Time has a party scene in which several of Nin's friends appear. Rita strays into the party room. After the repetitive exchanges of useless greetings, Rita finally meets the man of fate, played by the dancer Frank Westbrook. Then the scene changes suddenly from interior to exterior. In the exterior scene, men and women dance, and Rita has ambivalent emotions towards Frank, such as fear and yearning, and runs away. She runs and runs from Frank until she reaches the museum court, where she finds Frank frozen as a statue. She is extremely frightened and runs again. Maya takes over the running and does not hesitate to dive into the water. The protagonist switches to Rita diving underwater, and the screen image is inverted into the negative. The negative close-up of Rita's face from the last scene refuses to give us any clue to a single, fixed meaning (Fig. 4). Is it fear and agony, or peace and relief that she expresses? In terms of an inverted image, this close-up also has a mirror effect. In the works of Maya Deren, the mirror always subverts and displaces the meaning.

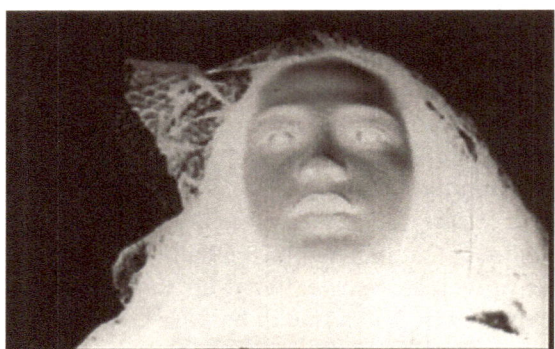

Fig. 4. The last shot of *Rituals in Transfigured Time*

To criticize *Rituals in Transfigured Time*, Nin used the word "empty" or "emptiness" several times. After the twelve hours of filming the party scene, Nin was exhausted, realizing that what they had acted out was emptiness (*Diary 4* 135-36). This criticism sounds strange because it is quite obvious that the aim of this prolonged scene in the 15-minute short film is to visualize emptiness. What really irritated Nin was presumably her feeling that she was treated like a pawn for Maya's caricature. Furthermore, Nin denounced the film for having "no sensual connection" between the men and women (136). Most of the cast are, according to Nin, homosexuals. This again is a strange attack, for, as is pointed out, the film was apparently intended to question heterosexuality (Pramaggiore 252).

We can presume that Deren and Nin had heated discussions, but most of the surviving material is written exclusively by Nin. One of the few things that Deren left behind is a poem dedicated to Nin. Written in August, 1945, when the shooting had just started, the poem sounds like a predictive objection to the criticism Nin would make the next year:

For Anaïs Before the Glass
By Maya Deren

The mirror, like a cannibal, consumed,
carnivorous, blood-silvered, all the life fed it.

156

You too have known this merciless transfusion
along the arm by which we each have held it.
In the illusion was pursued the vision
through the reflection to the revelation.
The miracle has come to pass.
Your pale face, Anaïs, before the glass
at last is not returned to you reversed.

This is no longer mirrors, but an open wound
through which we face each other framed in blood.

August 19, 1945 (Clark 537)

Once you stand before the mirror, you have to resign yourself to the carnivorous consumption. These sound like overly audacious words to address the writer, fourteen years older. It can be read as a declaration requiring self-sacrifice to the artwork. Nin's pale face is not simply returned to her as a reversed image. For Deren, to stand before the mirror is to look into an open wound and see the bloody figure Always facing her mirror-diary, Nin should have recognized "this merciless trans-fusion."

Nin and her friends, however, completely changed their attitude towards Deren, according to the diary entry of May 1946 It was Nin who had introduced her to Frank Westbrook, who played the important role of driving Rita, the protagonist, to change. According to the diary, Nin became more nervous than Westbrook himself when Deren required him to leap from one rock to another in naked feet. Westbrook did jump, but the filmed footage was found to be unsatisfying to Deren, so that the scene was finally cut. This kind of perfectionism seemed inhuman to Nin (*Diary 4* 146-47).

The day she saw the finished film, Nin became filled with anger. She had confessed previously that she was the oldest and feared close-ups, but Hammid had assured her that the editing would respect her concerns. Seeing herself in the finished film, however, Nin was quite shocked to find that her close-up (Fig. 5) was "shiny-skinned and distorted by magnification," while Deren had always been made beautiful by the editing (156). It is more likely that Nin was discontented with Deren's arbitrariness than with her lines of age revealed, for some thought "Maya made Anaïs look quite wonderful" (Fitch 279).

Fig. 5. Anaïs Nin in *Rituals in Transfigured Time*

"The camera can be a lover, or a hater, or a sadist, or a defamer... It lies" (*Diary 4* 351). Nin went on: "The quest for ugliness is one I never understood. Was it because Americans were for the most part born in ugliness, familiar with it, and had grown to love it, or because they associated beauty with the undemocratic upper class, art, the past, Europe, and repudiated it? The American definition of realism was ugliness. To avoid being accused of creating illusion, they always showed the same ugly view of everything. Maya magnified the skin blemishes, the knotted nerves, the large ears; she stressed the oily surfaces, the thyroid white of the eyes, the baldness or the pimple. Maya's actors happened to be beautiful. She uglified them. I had never seen as clearly as in Maya, the power to uglify in the eye behind the camera" (353).

This kind of challenge to American naturalist realism is quite familiar to the readers of Anaïs Nin. We remember, for example, how conflicted Nin was with Henry Miller's grotesque portrayal of Paris during the 1930s, how his wife June resented being portrayed as ugly in his writings. Nin asked him why he wrote more about June's defects and less about her magnificence. The answer is: "...I take goodness for granted. I expect everybody to be good. It is evil which fascinates me" (*Henry and June* 135).

Involving her friends with her filmmaking, paying no fees or transportation costs, and, according to Nin, concentrating on her filmmaking so inhumanly, Deren could be compared with Miller, who, in the 1930s, wrote *Tropic of Cancer* and other writings while living off his friends. In the climax scene of *Henry and June*, where June accuses Miller of making a monster out of her by distortion, Nin shows her sympathy for both of them: "I am not vacillating between Henry and June, between their contradictory versions of themselves, but between two truths I see with clarity. I believe in Henry's humanness, although I am fully aware of the literary monster. I believe in June, although I am aware of her innocent destructive power and her comedies" (270-71).

Her diary tells us how, in the chaos of her muses Henry and June, Nin developed into a writer, which seems to imply that she should also have understood Maya was a filmmaking "monster." *The Diary of Anaïs Nin, Volume 4* came out in 1971, when Deren was already gone. The "feud" between them was, therefore, a story which was concocted long after Deren's passing. In 1975, when asked about Deren ignoring the promises to not to use close-ups, Nin answered: "[T]oday I wouldn't blame her for that. Because I've watched films being made. And I realize that the film was more important than ourselves. We just wanted to see ourselves a certain way. We were not professional" (*A Woman Speaks* 254). In spite of this realization, Nin published her diary, written thirty years previously, without apparent modification, which shows that Nin herself was possibly a literary "monster."

Concerning the quarrel between the two artists, Ute Holl gives us the following observation: Whereas Nin trusts in the mirror as a registering device, Deren believes in the mirror as a highly creative instrument (Holl 153). This picture is quite useful, but their relationship seems more complicated. To read the story of their "feud," we can depend only on Nin's diary.[4] This is the trap that the diary, "the document of the truth," sets for us. Whereas Nin's diary account is that she was made ugly by Deren's filmmaking, the same charge could be made in reverse: that it was Deren who was made ugly in the diary. Although Nin presented Deren as a "monster" in her diary, the fact is that Nin truly appreciated Deren's talent. And perhaps Deren, who wrote "Your pale face, Anaïs, before the glass / at last is not returned to you reversed," would accept that her face was not simply returned to her from the mirror of Nin's diary. Their mirrors were indeed the ones through which they faced each other "framed in blood."

Is it that possible that we cannot simply accept that Nin expressed anger for Deren in her diary because she was trying to honestly expose her own immature feelings, one of which is anger? It was very daring for a female writer to express anger in 1971, let alone 1946, because, in a male-centric society, in which the woman's role is supposed to be "mirror-mother," her anger is not expected. Anger was a privileged territory for male writers. Deviation from the role of "mirror-mother" is where Nin and Deren come together. For the two artists, to stand before the mirror is to revolt against the traditional domination of the "flat mirror," the "vertical" domination of the subject who oversees the object who is seen. Anaïs before Maya, Maya before Anaïs, standing before the curved mirror, the two women split, multiply, interchange, and finally converge into one. In doing so, they became accomplices—that is, being woman—in the revolt against the traditional subject of discourse.

Works Cited

DVDs

Maya Deren: Experimental Films. New York: Mystic Fire Video, 2002.

In the Mirror of Maya Deren. Dir. Martina Kudláček. New York: Zeitgeist Films, 2004.

Books

Clark, VèVè A., Millicent Hodson and Catrina Neiman, eds. *The Legend of Maya Deren: A Documentary Biography and Collected Works, vol. I, pt. II: Chambers (1942-1947).* New York: Anthology Film Archives, 1988.

Deren, Maya. "Amateur versus Professional." *Essential Deren: Collected Writings on Film.* Ed. Bruce R. McPherson. Kingston, New York: Documentext, 2005.

Fitch, Noël Riley. *Anaïs: The Erotic Life of Anaïs Nin.* Boston: Little, Brown, 1993.

Holl, Ute. "Moving the Dancers' Souls." *Maya Deren and the American Avant-Garde.* Ed. Bill Nichols. Los Angeles: University of California Press, 2001.

Irigaray, Luce. *This Sex Which Is Not One.* Trans. Catherine Porter and Caroline Burke. Ithaca, NY: Cornell University Press, 1985.

Miller Henry. "Un Être Étoilique." *The Cosmological Eye.* New York: New Directions, 1939.

Nin, Anaïs. *The Diary of Anaïs Nin, Vol. 1, 1931-1934.* Ed. Gunther Stuhlmann. New York: Harcourt Brace Jovanovich, 1966.

----. *The Diary of Anaïs Nin, Vol. 4, 1944-1947.* Ed. Gunther Stuhlmann. New York: Harcourt Brace Jovanovich, 1971.

----. *The Diary of Anaïs Nin, Vol. 6, 1955-1966.* Ed. Gunther Stuhlmann. New York: Harcourt Brace Jovanovich, 1977.

----. *Henry and June.* New York: Harcourt Brace Jovanovich, 1986.

----. *A Woman Speaks: The Lectures, Seminars and Interviews of Anaïs Nin.* Ed. Evelyn Hinz. Athens, Ohio: Swallow Press, 1975.

Pramaggiore, Maria. "Seeing Double(s): Reading Deren Bisexually." *Maya Deren and the American Avant-Garde.* Ed. Bill Nichols. Los Angeles: University of California Press, 2001.

Sontag, Susan. *Against Interpretation and Other Essays.* New York: Picador, 2001.

Notes

[1] Anaïs Nin noted in her diary "[t]wo men" (*Diary 4* 75). Actually, those who were shooting were Alexander Hammid and a female assistant Hella Heyman. After Deren and Hammid divorced, he married Heyman.

[2] In Martina Kudlácek's documentary film *In the Mirror of Maya Deren*, Marcia Vogel, a co-director of Cinema 16 Film Society, where the films of Maya Deren were screened, speaks of Deren: "She [Maya] was just a woman ahead of her time... So à la the '60s, with flower children and stuff."

[3] Clark 181. Published in 1988, the book is annotated, saying sequence E was "never filmed" (175). Later, the footage was found, and the outtake is fragmentarily inserted into *In the Mirror of Maya Deren*.

[4] In the interview in 1975, Maya's ex-husband Hammid reemphasized the feud between Nin and Deren, saying "She [Anaïs] hates me and Maya because we didn't make her beautiful in the film" (Clark 538). On the other hand, Noël Riley Fitch writes in her biography of Nin: "Contrary to the impression left by the diary, Nin and Deren remain outwardly friendly... In the mid-1950s Anaïs and Maya are even planning a film together about labyrinths, using Wall Street as a setting" (Fitch 342).

Toyoko Yamamoto

Interview with Lady Nobuko Albery
The "Collages" character today

One can easily conclude that Anaïs Nin was a *Japonisante* upon analyzing her writing and her personal interest in Japan. Anaïs liked the delicacy of Japanese things and the inventive way Japanese culture links beauty and nature. In her final novel, *Collages*, Anaïs featured a Japanese woman, Nobuko, on the "stage" of her story. Now, I would like to take the liberty of pulling Nobuko off the stage, or out of the book, and introduce her as her real self. Additionally, I would like to mention how my alma mater, Kobe College, connected me to Lady Nobuko Albery—the real Nobuko on whom the character of the book was based.

Personally, my journey with Nobuko Albery began when I saw her name on the list of overseas directors in the alumnae bulletin; she was the one in London. Nobuko and I both attended Kobe College Junior and Senior High School in Nishinomiya, Japan. We attended at different times, but the connection among the alumnae of this women's school is strong. Kobe College was founded by two American missionary women, Eliza Talcott and Julia Dudley, in 1875, and the campus was designed by the architect William Merrell Vories. In addition to Nobuko, Kobe College has other connections with Anaïs Nin, most notably lectures on her by professor emerita Catherine (Broderick) Vreeland. Emiko Tsuji, another Kobe college alumna, was so impressed by Catherine's extension class and Anaïs's diaries and novels, that she was instrumental in inviting and sponsoring Anaïs's brother Joaquín Nin-Culmell's lectures and visits to Japan in 1989. In the Alumnae Hall on campus, Joaquín also played his composition, *Tonadas*, on the piano. During this visit, I was thrilled to meet him for the first time and so fortunate to listen to his music. These kinds of connections enhanced my own fascination with Anaïs's work.

Because of these personal ties, I was able to meet, chat with and correspond, both in letters and emails, with Nobuko. I was honored to establish a friendship with her, and her down-to-earth ways and sensitive, warm personality impressed me. She had no air of celebrity. I am grateful for her consent to have formal interviews for this article with the words: "Yes, let's meet in letters." Accordingly, what follows is the result of our correspondence between Nobuko in Monte Carlo, Monaco, and me in Tokyo, Japan.

TY: Anaïs wrote your name firstly in the *Diary*, in the winter of 1962-1963, in the list of a group of friends with Sylvia Spencer, Daisy Aldan and Caresse Crosby, who gathered at Marguerite Young's apartment in Greenwich Village, New York. During this occasion, Marguerite introduced Anaïs to her friends, Elizabeth Bowen and Ruth Stephan. Shortly after this meeting, in the *Diary*, Anaïs described the salon visit at Ruth Stephan's gorgeous house in Greenwich, Connecticut in the spring of 1963. For this gathering, Anaïs and Hugo, her husband, drove to Ruth's house taking you with them, and Anaïs described you as "A Japanese dream. An exquisite being. Small, dainty," and she adored your "balance of child, woman, sprite, wit, poetry and exoticism" (*Diary 6* 324).

Certainly you made a strong impression on Anaïs by dressing in a kimono besides your charming personality. Both of you, Nobuko and Anaïs, are fabulous women, and I would like to know how you two came to know each other in New York in the early 1960s. When and where was your first encounter with Anaïs Nin, and what was your impression of her then?

NA: Strangely, I came to know Anaïs after I had met her husband, Hugo Guiler, first at a reception somewhere near where I lived, Judson Hall, the female students' dormitory of New York University, located rather incongruously inside the tower of Judson Church overlooking Washington Square. He introduced himself as an experimental filmmaker and said when his wife, who spent much time in Los Angeles, returned to New York, he would like her to meet me, as she loved Japan and its culture.

Before actually meeting her, I learned from Isamu Noguchi, the Irish-American-Japanese sculptor, whom I often met in the apartment of Mr. and Mrs. Genichiro Inokuma, then the most attractive Japanese couple, adored by every member of the city's cosmopolitan artistic community, that Anaïs had had an outrageously "liberated" life in Paris. (Later I heard from an American artist, who had known both Isamu and Anaïs during the 1920s in Paris, that Isamu had been one of her numerous lovers.) At the time, being ridiculously naïve and unsophisticated, I was rather shocked by such a revelation; therefore, when I did actually meet her, I was joyfully surprised to find her so utterly untouched or soiled by the scabrous legends of her former years. She was an impeccably well-mannered lady, demure and kindly, and such an exquisite listener too. She must have been over 60 by then, but her Madonna-like beauty was still quite impressive, and so were her ballerina-like, sliding, serene movements and her velvet-soft voice. The Guilers took me to see a French film, *The Forbidden Games*, and later to a small French restaurant for supper. She spoke English with a French accent, which was particularly attractive and suited her voice and personality, and helped to keep alive the kind of exotic, slightly mystic image of herself, which she most likely wished to cultivate.

Nobuko, 1960s

TY: You are the pioneer who introduced the American writer, Anaïs Nin, to Japanese readers since you handed Nin's novel, *A Spy in the House of Love*, to Tomohisa Kawade, who was 28 years old then, the son of the great publisher, Kawade Shobo. Then Kawade found the noted translator, Koji Nakada, whose translation brought the first of Nin's books to the Japanese, *Ai no Ie no Supai*. Anaïs wrote in the *Diary*, in the fall of 1964: "When Nobuko went to Japan she aroused the interest of a Japanese publisher, Kawade, in my work. When I was in New York, they both came to see me. Nobuko acted as translator. Kawade came with a basket full of the delicate, small gifts that I love. The result of the visit is that he will publish [*A*] *Spy in the House of Love*" (*Diary 6* 368).

Anaïs also reported, "My Japanese publisher invited me to Japan to celebrate the publication of *A Spy in the House of Love*" (*Diary 7* 4). While she was traveling in Japan from Tokyo to Ibusuki, the most southern peninsula of Kyushu in 1966, Tomohisa Kawade set up a round-table discussion with Anaïs Nin, Kenzaburō Ōe (1935-2023) then a young writer and now a Nobel Prize winner, and Jun Eto (1932-1999), then a young critic whose symposium was printed in *Bungei*, February, volume six, the 2nd number, in 1967. In this literary article, at the start of the conversation, Ōe mentions to Nin that he knows "Nobuko Uenishi," using your maiden name, and both Ōe and Nin acknowledged knowing Nobuko.

In the *Diary*, Anaïs wrote: "At lunch Nobuko translated a beautiful letter from a Japanese translator, Mr. Nakada, and part of the long interview I had with Kenzaburō Ōe, which was published in its entirety" (*Diary 7* 38). Koji Nakada is in his mid-eighties now and still a striking translator and critic who came to our Anaïs Nin Society in Japan. I serve as the head of the group, and he gave us a lecture on his perspective of Anaïs Nin at the International House in Roppongi, Tokyo. Tomohisa Kawade inherited the Kawade Shobo publishing company. Tomohisa Kawade is a tanka poet from whom I once received an elegant letter written in calligraphy mentioning your name, Nobuko Uenishi, as a friend-acquaintance of Anaïs Nin.

So, without your literary sense to choose *Spy* out of Nin's other novels and to take action, the book would never have been in the spotlight in 1960s Japan at all. Moreover, such connective lines were spinning around you, your wonderful influence created the result of bringing Anaïs Nin's work into the Japanese public's awareness and conversation. Could you tell us the background of all these developments? Was there a salon culture among the scholars who were studying

Japanese literature in New York in the 1960s?

NA: Goodness me, I have forgotten that I met Kenzaburō Ōe in New York in the early 1960s! At that time, many young prominent Japanese artists were drawn to the culturally vibrant city: if I remember correctly, only a few days before I went to see Mr. Ōe at the Waldorf Astoria hotel, I had been meeting Shintaro Ishihara, Keita Asari and Seiji Ozawa (at the time Bernstein's assistant at the New York Philharmonic) on account of the soon-to-open Nissei Theatre. If one can rely on the memory of my first husband, Ivan Morris, I believe Yukio Mishima was in New York or rather on the East Coast just then. In any event, Mr. Ōe seemed to be obsessed about the fact that both Mr. Ishihara and Mr. Mishima were in the area and seemed extremely anxious not to bump into either of them.

As for Tomohisa Kawade, whom I found more an artist than a businessman, I cherish a highly romanticized souvenir. I remember him talking longingly about a young lady in the North East (Tohoku), whom, I guessed, he wished to marry. Illogical perhaps, but I fancied this young girl like a small unripe apple and due to this image, I found Mr. Kawade refreshing and sympathetic.

You ask me if there was a sort of salon of so-called Japanophiles and Japanologists, and at once I think of the modest two-roomed apartment in the 95th street between Lexington and Park Avenues, where Mr. and Mrs. Inokuma received practically every Japanese artist and friend who either worked or studied in New York, together with many travelers who passed through the city: architects, painters, diplomats, industrialists, and so on. Later, when I married Ivan Morris, as he was then the Chairman of the Columbia University's Oriental Studies department, we entertained regularly such scholars, critics and writers as Donald Keene, Edward Seidensticker, Ronald Dore, and visiting Japanese authors, but I don't think I can call it a salon, it was more a place to exchange scholarly opinions and ideas. Amongst Ivan's friends outside his university circle, the famous writers like Norman Mailer, Frank Conroy, Anthony West, Brendan Gil, V. S. Naipaul, often came to dine or stayed in our apartment. Most of them had a disparaging opinion of Anaïs as a writer. Their hostility seemed to stem from the fact that, thanks to her generous banker husband, she had begun her career by self-publishing, while they themselves had had to struggle to find publishers. Also, they judged her diary-writing, unlike Proust's grand opus, narcissistic and confessional, a psychoanalytic meandering. Writers, or all artists, are insecure and jealous; even so, I found their attitude quite misogynous and ungenerous and was often angry and sad.

TY: You and Anaïs seemed to share a close friendship and you used to lunch together and enjoy women's talk. Anaïs wrote in the *Diary* in the winter of 1966-67, about warning you that only a marriage with a "*grande passion* is pleasurable and bearable" (*Diary* 739); otherwise, it will just make you feel claustrophobic, and she showed her understanding of your difficult marriage to Ivan Morris because of his possessiveness: "[He] wants her to give up her job with Toho, give up entertaining producers (part of her job is to effect interchange of plays and films with Japan), lecturing and teaching" (*Diary* 739).

Could you tell us how you came to know Kazuo Kikuta, a notable playwright, producer and manager of the Toho-Takarazuka company? You are a pioneer here again by introducing the Japanese to see Broadway musicals in Japan. Could you tell us which musicals, or plays and films you worked for as an agent in New York besides *My Fair Lady*?

As you wrote in your autobiographical novel, *Japanese Pride and Prejudice*, Kazuo Kikuta had extended his business to London with a sincere interest in Charles Dickens and asked you to negotiate the production of *Oliver!* to bring it to Tokyo. This project offered you a fateful encounter with Donald Albery, who was a distinguished theater impresario destined to be your next husband. Do you think Anaïs's suggestion for a marriage with a "*grande passion*" influenced you in some way to keep your career and make yourself freer to live?

NA: Kazuo Kikuta gave me the job of being his New York representative soon after I graduated from the Dramatic Arts Department of New York University. A year before he interviewed me, he had taken a great risk and won an immense success with *My Fair Lady*, the first Broadway musical he produced and directed for Japanese theatre-goers; therefore he was favorably inclined to accept me as his agent in New York to watch out for plays and musicals suitable for Japan. His ambition was to one day write and produce his own musical which could gain a world-wide acclaim. Starting with *Kiss Me Kate*, I negotiated and obtained the rights to most Rogers and Hammerstein classics like *The King and I*, *Oklahoma*, *South Pacific*, *The Sound of Music*, *Fiddler on the Roof*, *Hello Dolly*, then later *Les Misérables* and *Miss Saigon*, which I also translated. When Kikuta sensei had the brilliant inspiration to put *Gone with the Wind* on stage, the negotiation with the agents and lawyers representing both the Margaret Mitchell Estate in Atlanta and MGM Films took no less than two years. Then came *Oliver!* with the London cast in English which, against all the pessimistic forecasts, had a historical long run at the Teikoku Gekijo (Imperial Theatre) in 1968. I worshipped Kikuta sensei, who, little known to today's younger generations, had been the hero who had saved a hundred million Japanese from harrowing despair and violence and anarchy during the catastrophic immediately-after-the-war years with his legendary radio-drama, *Kane no naru Oka* (*The Hills of the Ringing Bells*), by nightly offering some hope, laughter and a sense of solidarity. His love of Dickens led me to meet my future husband; therefore he was not only my adored hero but a matchmaker as well.

As for Anaïs, freedom was of supreme importance and necessity. A woman, she believed, must live her own life freely, unfettered by social mores and male approval. We did talk about "*un grand amour,*" which I myself believe as a "once-in-a-lifetime thing" but I suspect that, for Anaïs, a great passion had a less durable hold, of which a woman could fall in and out as she, and no one else, chose. I knew both of her two husbands: I had great sympathy and affection for Hugo, a gentleman, sober and reserved, not exciting or seductive. I could not help a sense of guilt and betrayal when on some occasions Anaïs asked me to lie to Hugo and say she had just left or was on the way somewhere, when in fact she was with Rupert in Los Angeles or god-knows-where. To this day I wonder if either man had been truly her 100% *grand amour...*

TY: In Anaïs's final novel, *Collages*, Anaïs used you as a model and described you as a Japanese woman whose letters show exquisite aestheticism: "From New York she wrote on purple tissue paper because the sun was absent... Another letter came in orange tissue paper, because the sun was out... Nobuko wrote: 'I could not write you yesterday because it was raining and I did not find any pearl grey paper to match'" (*Collages* 81-82). You have a similar attention to detail when choosing your delicate kimono patterns, which Anaïs wrote favorably about in the *Diary*. "[S]he excused herself for wearing in March a kimono embroidered with a flower which only blooms in June. So that they literally were a design corresponding to a seasonal design in nature. Chrysanthemums in the ninth month" (*Diary 6* 324-25).

Even though Anaïs may have wanted to create a woman who is bound by her traditional culture, I feel she loved your aesthetic sense and your concern to articulate the importance of weather and seasonal matching of paper, textiles, designs and colors of the letters you sent. You certainly showed this thoughtfulness for the season and the design on the kimono as well.

How did you cultivate such an aesthetic sense and express its representations (even though such sensible culture does exist in Japan)? How did you feel about your correspondence with Anaïs then?

NA: My first husband, Professor Ivan Morris, who translated Sei Shonagon's *Makura no Soshi*, (*The Pillow Book*) into exquisite, pure and concise English, was a hard teacher to me in language; he detested any sentimentality and what the French call *sensiblerie*—an excessive show of sensitivity and aestheticism—and told me to follow George Orwell's draconian six rules in writing English, which led me to lose much of my youthful fun of showing off my *sensiblerie*! I regret this, but at the same time, when I read what I used to write to Anaïs and other friends, I no longer find it my cup of tea…

TY: While you were studying drama for your Master's at NYU, I assume you were living near Washington Square. I wonder if you went to the apartment where Hugo and Anaïs lived, and whether Hugo lived there long after Anaïs died. Could you tell me anything about your memories there, or if you recall anything about the interior or Hugo's personality? Where was their apartment in New York in the 1960s?

Once you told me in our email letters that you were reading Henry James' *Washington Square*, do you have any special likeness or feelings to the atmosphere in those areas around Soho or the Village?

NA: About Hugo's apartment in the modern block of high-rise apartments just behind Washington Square, it was unquestionably the home and domain of Hugo, where his lifestyle and personality dominated. He was a dependable gentleman banker who aspired to be something of an artist with his experimental films. The apartment I often visited, therefore, had his well-to-do New York banker's imprint and style: sober, functional, with the walls and carpet in subdued beige, nothing ultra-fancy or trendy. Anaïs, with her beautiful, good manners, was superb in adjusting to Hugo-land; she floated gracefully and silently inside it, making tea for me or serving drinks to the bourgeois-bohemian guests who came to view Hugo's films projected on the beige wall. But a leopard cannot change its spots: Anaïs tried, but remained a foreigner in the surroundings, neither American nor European and yet both, not exactly the mistress of the house, almost a mysterious, exotic guest.

TY: Your later pursuits in the field of drama and theater came to fruition in your outstanding novel, *The House of Kanze*, published in 1985. Graham Greene reviewed this book as a remarkable novel that entices readers into the theatre world of 14th century Japan and the experiences of the masters of Kanze, Noh players. In Iris Murdoch's review, she admired your perspective of the artists' passion, the Noh theater history and your keen sense of humor. How much I wish that Anaïs could have read this novel of yours because she was a fervent Japanophile, and she wrote that she reread *The Tale of Genji* many times, and she read all the Japanese literature and history she could obtain. Could you tell us what your motivation and inspiration was for writing such a grand Noh player, Zeami and the Kanze family?

When you and I had tea at the Imperial Hotel in Tokyo some years ago, you told me that you knew Akiyo Tomoeda, the contemporary Noh player of the Kita school, who is a living national treasure. What kind of impact does knowing a top Noh player in Japan of the present period have on you after *The House of Kanze* was published?

NA: Had I not had the fluke chance of meeting Sadayo Kita sensei, the second son of the 15th head of Kita Noh School, most likely I would not have been inspired to write *The House of Kanze*. He was engaged by the State Department of America, as part of the Japan-U.S. cultural exchange program, to teach Broadway professional actors in a Noh play, *Ikkaku Sen-nin*. He came to New York, assisted by the young Akiyo Tomoeda sensei, and I had been engaged by the State Department's protocol agency to be their interpreter/stage assistant for more than three months. I learned so much from this experience, and thereafter my curiosity into the life and person of the great Zeami grew exponentially. It came out in English in both Great Britain and America, later in French and in German. I still cannot quite believe that I had it in me to write this; Graham Greene recommended it as one of the best two novels he read in the *Observer* newspaper; Iris Murdoch wrote me an insightful, glowing critique for the book's blurb. To my incredulous joy, the first female writer to become the so-called "immortal" member of the Académie Française, Madame Marguerite Yourcenar, read it in English and told her publisher, Gallimard, to publish it. As it is in the Gallimard's very special edition, called Edition Blanc, it enjoys the supreme privilege of never going out of print. I owe this privilege to Zeami himself and both

Sadayo Kita and Tomoeda sensei.

TY: After Sir Donald Albery, your husband, died, you went through a devastating experience both physically and mentally; nevertheless, your inner strength enabled you to found the Japan Amarant Society in 1990. You must have realized that many Japanese women, as you did, suffered from menopause, and you made them aware of HRT, or hormone replacement therapy. In *Japanese Pride and Prejudice*, you illustrated the ordeals you had to face with realistic, but humorous wit so that the readers are deeply absorbed in the protagonist's agitations. It reminds me of the difficulty of the women's movement in the late '60s and the early '70s that Anaïs pointed out. As far as Anaïs thought then, any social enlightenment or movement in the public had to be dealt with as individuals, that it was personal revelations that enforced the women's collective voice.

What do you think today about this social project of personal concept that you founded in Japan? How do you feel about identity in one's motherland and feelings of re-displacement? In your case, how was your homecoming, and how did you deal with the undertaking of your project? How did your ideas about noblesse oblige, or philanthropic charity, or business, or the combination of these frustrate you in the sense of social norms or culture between the West and the East?

NA: When I founded Japan Amarant Society to help middle-aged women cope with their *heikei* (menopause), in order to save the cost of hiring a professional designer, I created the Society's logo myself: "My Body, My Life, My Choice." I wanted our members to take a hard, honest look at their lives and take control of not only their bodies but the long future ahead of their menopause, especially when the life expectancy is growing longer and longer, and the traditional dependence on children and society was no longer viable. The last phrase of the Amarant logo, "My Choice," caused some resistance; it was considered too militant, too aggressive, too egotistic. But, I persisted; for, after having lived half a century, a woman must take control of her own body and life and choose how to live the rest of her adult life, even how to die. I knew I was asking a lot: once you make any decision or choice, inevitably, you have a heavy responsibility to enact it. You not only need courage, but immense discipline.

By the time our Society observed its 13th anniversary, having published as many as 37 Amarant News Letters, sadly, I realized that middle-aged Japanese women still would not, or could not, choose and bear the responsibility of their own choices: they seemed to find it more comfortable and socially acceptable to let others decide for them: their elders, families, doctors, social conventions and mores or, worse, the media and trends.

In my last message to the members, I wrote about my ex-housekeeper, aged 72, whom I once invited to stay in the country house. Before going to bed, she handed me a piece of paper. "Madame, if something happens during the night and you find me dead tomorrow, please ring this number." She had not much confidence in her delinquent son and had taken out funeral insurance; she had chosen all the details of her own funeral, even the music to be played and the passage from the Bible to be read and had paid for all such services. She is French from St. Malo in Brittany: the Bretons are known to be stubborn, hard-working, independent-minded people. I admire her. If only my Amarant members had had such foresight and courage of her "My Choice"!

TY: In *Collages*, Anaïs writes that Renate wonders whether Nobuko, who is bound in her enveloping kimono, seeks to shake off the rituals of the past and emerge from centuries of confinement (*Collages* 82). Through a vast life and cross-cultural experiences, the real Nobuko has beautifully attained the highest, distinct and free life. You have been writing your memoirs, and you mentioned that you have found an ending for them. Could you share with us the sense of achievement from writing the memoirs and some of your mottoes in your *vade mecum* that you believe in now?

NA: People tell me: You're too old to ski, stop! I will not stop, and when there is no snow, I trek and walk. I have arthrosis in my fingers, rather painful, but I go on playing the piano. I have been devouring the books for which I have never had enough time: Proust's *A la Recherche du Temps Perdu* on Kindle and in French. I just finished reading Homer's *The Iliad* and *The Odyssey*. And, loyal to "My Body, My Life, My Choice," I have *not* stopped my estrogen hormone treatment, even though so many incompetent doctors and inconclusive statistics warn me of all sorts of health risks. I have been on estrogen now for over 20 years and find it perfectly suited for me, mentally and physically and it insures me the highest quality of life I can hope for. So, why should I stop? If all goes wrong and I die three or five years earlier, at least I have lived fully without losing my own personality and becoming gaga. It would be worth forfeiting some years of my life. Madness? Maybe, but it is my choice.

Nobuko Albery

Yuko Yaguchi

The Text that Is the Writer
On reading "The Diary of Anaïs Nin"

In her first published article in a literary magazine, the October 1930 issue of *The Canadian Forum*, Anaïs Nin—albeit pseudonymously—wrote that D. H. Lawrence "has been difficult to measure because he is the kind of writer who rouses either enthusiasm or hate."[1] This sounds like a prediction of what would happen to her as a writer later on, that "syndrome of attack and adoration."[2]

It is a mystery why one has a difficult time keeping cool before her. Those who adore her do so naïvely, as if they regarded her as a living goddess, while those who attack her sound moralistic, their criticism more like condemnation. It seems ironical that one of the main criticisms of her, the lack of a sense of humor, which itself is not unreasonable (Nin admits "I am guilty of too serious, too grave living"),[3] can be applied to those very same critics.

The Japanese translator of *A Spy in the House of Love,* Koji Nakata, after confessing that he had regrettably failed to write a book or an extended essay on her, made an interesting point:

> I feel that in discussing her I cannot use the same approach I use in assessing other writers. I would have to invent a new mode of criticism to do justice to her. It will be difficult, but then Anaïs Nin is a difficulty.[4]

I do not think Nakata means that Anaïs Nin is difficult as Joyce, Proust, Kafka are difficult. It would be another difficulty which frustrated his attempt to write about her critically. There is something elusive about this artist, something that digresses from what defines a "genuine" writer.

First, there is the problem of how to appraise her major work, the *Diary,* as a literary form. In my mind, *The Diary of Anaïs Nin* has some particular features of its own. After having been ignored as a novelist for decades, it was the *Diary* that gained Anaïs Nin recognition as a writer. In that it is the opposite, for instance, of Virginia Woolf's *Diary.* While Woolf's *Diary* was accepted as written by a celebrated writer, perhaps because of its "biographical" interest in the artist, Nin's *Diary,* on the other hand, could be called "the making of Anaïs Nin." As Anaïs

Nin often admitted, her fictions, with few exceptions, might well be called the byproducts, the "outcroppings," of the diary. Most importantly, she presented the diary as a work of art, after elaborate editing and preparations until it reads like an "autobiographical fantasy" (Edmund Wilson)[5] or a "journal-novel" (Franklin and Schneider),[6] in which Anaïs Nin plays a narrator-persona. Thus, we can understand that *The Diary of Anaïs Nin* occupies a unique, even exceptional position in the rich, yet subterranean tradition of diary writing.

Secondly, Anaïs Nin is a chain of contradictions: for every statement she makes, we are likely to find another that will clash with the former. It is not easy to form an "objective" estimate of someone who keeps changing and moving, without missing her fluidity.

Finally, it was one of her (quixotic?) ambitions to contrive a fusion between life and art, to turn herself into a work of art:

> There is no separation between my life and my craft, my work. The form of art is the form of art of my life, and my life is the form of art. (*D* 4 142)
>
> I am more interested in human beings than in writing, more interested in lovemaking than in writing, more interested in living than in writing. More interested in becoming a work of art than in creating one. (*D* 4 177)

Anaïs Nin seems to reject contemporary literary theories, which urge a "divorce" between an artist and her text. Or rather, she poses herself as a living irony, as it were, against such critical trends. Whoever wants to read and/or discuss Anaïs Nin is forced to face her as a total entity.

At the same time, we sense a tragic undertone beneath those bold assertions. A writer is doomed to live a double life, living and then writing, which is always "a delayed reaction, the second tasting of life" (*D* 1 73). Duality was one tyrant Anaïs Nin could hardly appease or control.

In a short autobiographical note, written at the request of an editor at *Harper's Bazaar*, Anaïs Nin concluded: "I am a writer. I would rather have been a courtesan. The rest is in the diary" (*D* 4 178). Although she has often been chided for being narcissistic—and perhaps she was, indeed, a narcissist—her vision was always "painfully clear,"[7] clear enough to realize that everyone carries in their mind a "deforming mirror" (*D* 1 105). Her mirror, in its double function, can also be flawless and reflect the slightest flaw on the part of the gazer. "The process of creation," she wrote, "*is* criticism of yourself,"[8] and in her autobiographical note she described her flaws or sorrows as though reciting a poem. Because of this painful clarity she wished for a blind existence, which is the life of the courtesan, or the life of June, Henry Miller's second wife. "What are we?" she asked, "Only the creators. She IS" (*D* 1 48).

Anaïs Nin often expressed her love-hatred toward writing. If we are to believe her claim that there is no separation between her life and her art, we cannot blame those critics who either attack or adore her personally rather than her work. The confusion, or the identification of the two, in fact, is found in both the artist and in her critics. Yet the point should be clearly made: If the life and the work of Anaïs Nin are deeply interwoven, or helplessly entangled, we should try to "read" both of them, instead of passing moral judgments. In other words, Anaïs Nin, her life or her art, contradictory or harmonious, exists in her text alone.

Indeed, in reading Anaïs Nin's text, we realize that we are dealing with a text named Anaïs Nin. It gives us a strange feeling, as if we were looking at Siamese twins. This must be what Nakata felt when he met Anaïs Nin: "An astounding unity and a strange chaos in her personality" (*A* 4 135).

The text named Anaïs Nin, moreover, is a multiplying text. The original series of *The Diary of Anaïs Nin* ended with Volume Seven, published posthumously, three years after her death in 1977. This was followed by the four volumes of *The Early Diary of Anaïs Nin,* beginning with the "childhood" diary, in 1914, and ending with the "Diary of a Wife," in 1931. Now we have the ongoing, "unexpurgated" volumes of the "Journal of Love," which started in 1986 with *Henry and June,* as well as *A Literate Passion: Letters of Anaïs Nin and Henry Miller, 1931-1953,* first published in 1987.

Each time a new volume comes out, an unknown Anaïs appears, and we have to change our view of her, slightly or dramatically. The publication of *Henry and June* and subsequent volumes of the unexpurgated diary, must have been a shock to those who favored the classical, authentic Anaïs who had once called herself "the 1830 type."[9]

This multiplying of the text, and the changing of the image, inevitably shakes the validity of early criticism. It is as if Anaïs Nin did it on purpose, to knock the critics who wrote those "puritanical, tight-lipped reviews" (*D* 5 157). She once gave us a hint as to what she was made of: "We know now that *we are composites* in reality, collages of our fathers and mothers, of what we read, of TV influences and films, of friends and associates."[10]

Anaïs Nin, then, is a collage, always in the making, of constant inconsistency. It is useless—in fact, impossible—to grasp her totally from any fixed point of view. To cope with such a "difficult" writer we must create our own collage out of the text named Anaïs Nin, our own version of Anaïs Nin.

The first volume of *The Diary of Anaïs Nin, 1931-1934,* which covers her from the age of twenty-eight to the age of thirty-one, deserves to be called *the* diary of the *Diaries,* a text of extremely exquisite texture. It coincides with the highlights of the diarist's early life. A number of monumental encounters—with Henry and June Miller, Antonin Artaud, psychoanalysts René Allendy and Otto Rank, along with the re-encounter with her own father, Joaquin Nin—make it a volume with an all-star cast. And it was during this period that Anaïs Nin was experiencing the most dramatic and drastic phase of her life: the birth of the young woman as an artist.

The opening pages are embroidered with literary as well as historical figures from the past, and with images which would haunt her throughout her life: Water separating two worlds; living on the periphery, or somewhere between; the motif of life and death—a fountain emerges "like the headstone of a tomb." The large gate at the rented house in Louveciennes takes on "an air of a prison gate." She is aware of being in a "beautiful prison," with no guards (?), and with a gate "being always half open." She realizes this "hibernating" is more like death than life, and various sounds—the rheumatic creaking of the gate, cars driving up the gravel path with a crackling sound, the barking of a dog—all entice her to "a full, open life."

She paints every room in the house in a different color "with a sense of preparation for a love to come," as if waiting for someone to wake her, some "guest of honor" to release or kidnap her. She compares her home, her life, herself, to an "alchemist's workshop," a "laboratory of the soul," which can also be used as a metaphor for the diary. Her life, in a sense, was a long effort to prepare herself to be a laboratory of the soul, where she made various experiments, using herself as a guinea pig.

Unlike Madame Bovary, she is not going to take poison. Instead, she decides to be a writer, for she knows that she can escape from this beautiful yet suffocating prison only through writing. Here starts the story of death and rebirth, "an odyssey from the inner to the outer world" (*D* 1 107). "To be inside or outside," she writes, "was my nightmare" (*D* 2 240). Her life was constant correspondence between the two, like the whistle of the train that went "from and to Paris." Her multivalent diary, at its utmost possibility, is to serve as a sort of membrane through which "osmosis" (her favorite term) takes place.

In his essay, "Beyond the Pleasure Principle," Sigmund Freud describes an infant who, in his mother's absence, invented a game: He threw out a reel to which a piece of string is tied and uttered the word "*fort*" (gone), then pulls back the string, welcoming it with "*dā*" (there). This incident is considered to account for how one obtains the ability to speak: one is led to speak in/out of the absence of a loved one; the initial severance gives one the ability to symbolize, to speak.[11] It is exactly what happened to the eleven-year-old Anaïs.

Anaïs Nin started her diary originally as a letter to her father—who had left the family and caused her an incurable trauma—on a ship which took her from Spain to America, to a strange New World. It was her desperate attempt to hurdle two worlds, to heal the wound of separation through her own words. This is a significant fact to be remembered: The diary, which later played a thousand roles in its protean versatility—as shelter, mirror, window, as her "shadow," as an adventurer's log, and also as her vice, drug, and prison—was born as a letter, a love letter. It was written to someone else, to charm him, entice him. It was her first tool of "communication by seduction."[12] "It was monologue, or dialogue, dedicated to him, inspired by the superabundance of thought and feelings caused by the pain of leaving him."[13]

The border between a diary and a letter, speaking to oneself and speaking to someone else, is believed to be obscure. So is the distinction between monologue and dialogue, inside and out. Is it possible, in the first place, to draw a clear line between the two? Or, to put it another way, the diary is a place in which the two meet, cross, and interfere with each other.

Another point worth noting is that the diary started on a journey. Anaïs was uprooted and exiled into a new country, a new culture. This "exile" served as another urge for Anaïs to speak, to speak a foreign language:

I immediately developed a passion for the English language—

a passionate curiosity, a passionate interest which usually only a foreigner will experience. Because I did not take English for granted, I felt like an explorer, discovering it had an infinite variety of words.[14]

The experience made Anaïs Nin—who was a hybrid at birth of Spanish/Cuban, French, and Danish ancestry, who had spent her infancy on tours of various European cities with her father—even more cosmopolitan, or *déraciné*. Her life, in fact, was spent in oscillation between two worlds: Europe and America, Latin and Anglo-Saxon, Catholicism and Puritanism. At the age of twenty-one, she wrote: "Neither in reality nor feeling do I belong to any nation" (*ED* 3 78). It is an irony that America long called her "the Paris-born" Anaïs Nin, while her first novel published in France in 1962 bore the subtitle: *roman américain*. This "foreignness" is one of the clues, perhaps, to an understanding of Anaïs Nin, as well as to understand the lack of understanding about her. Reading some of the moralistic, puritanical criticism of her, one might wonder whether perhaps she was "too French" in American eyes.

Belonging nowhere, being an outsider everywhere, taught Anaïs Nin a particular style of living. Like one of her characters, Djuna, she adopted "the basic structure of the nomads."[15] She speaks of a plant called "the plant of life," which can exist without roots. "Its leaves throw off foamy hairs. Wherever a piece of this plant falls it flowers richly" (*D* 3 11). Just like the plant, she was a woman with "transportable roots" (*WS* 17).

Through such magic words Anaïs Nin learned how to digest reality, and the separation between living and dreaming, living and writing, became increasingly blurred. Two years after she began her diary she wrote: "I imagine a little spirit who is always near me and whispers in my ear, 'To dream is to live, to live is to dream.'" She was then thirteen years old. A few years later, she talked almost euphorically to her diary, "to melt into one book—my life!" (*ED* 2 54)

It is surprising that even at an early age Anaïs Nin had a clear-cut self-consciousness as a "writer"—"I have ink in my blood" (*ED* 2 208). The fusion of life and art was not merely a romantic catch phrase, it was how she existed. "I write as I breathe, naturally, flowingly, spontaneously, out of an overflow, not as a substitute for life" (*D* 4 177). She needed to write in order to live: It was, literally, her art of life.

Yet the *Diary* is a double-edged sword: fusion could lead to confusion. The deeper the diarist goes into the writing of the diary, the more it begins to resemble a prison:

> Dear Diary, you have hampered me as an artist. But at the same time you have kept me alive as a human being. I created you because I needed a friend. And talking to the friend I have, perhaps, wasted my life. (*D* 1 260)

The diary had been created to transform unbearable reality, to acquire another way of breathing. But in its metamorphosis it became the only reality, or an opium pipe to inhale reality:

> The diary is my kief, my hashish, and opium pipe. This is my drug and vice. Instead of writing a novel, I lie back with this book and a pen, and dream, and indulge in refractions and diffractions. I can turn away from reality into the refractions and dreams it projects, and this driving, impelling fever which keeps me tense and wide-awake during the day is dissolved in improvisations, in contemplations. I must relive my life in the dream. The dream is my only life. (*D* 1 333-34)

What was supposed to be a remedy turned into a malady. More strictly speaking, the diary was both, ambiguity itself. Anaïs Nin's life can be considered a prolonged "affair" with her diary and, at the same time, a constant struggle to break away from it.

Anaïs Nin's attitude toward the diary was ambiguous, but so were the attitudes of the people around her. Hugh Guiler, her husband, was "a little jealous" of her diary, as she reports, and he teased her that she could not spend all her life writing in the diary. But he acknowledged that it was her "life's work" in which she reached her perfection (*ED* 3 5). Otto Rank, her psychoanalyst, tried to free her of the compulsion to write down everything in the diary. He asked her to live without it for a while, which made her feel "deprived of opium." Yet she also noted: "When I showed [Rank] what I wrote about him he was pleased. As was Henry. Kill the diary, they say; write novels; but when they look at their portrait, they say: 'That is wonderful'" (*D* 1 301). And Henry Miller, who in 1937 applauded her diary as "a monumental confession," had also aimed at its destruction at an earlier stage.

Are all these men illogical and self-contradictory, or is it the diary's quality itself that makes them so? Something about the diary, Anaïs Nin feels, makes them afraid of it: "I ask myself is it fear on the part of man, fear of a woman unveiling her own truth? Is there any other reason for everybody's being against it?" (*D* 2 253) A diarist constructs a kind of fortress into which even the one closest is not allowed; in which observations of the world are made in which no one can share; it creates a world of one's own. Nobody, Anaïs Nin asserts, "has the last word for me, whoever he may be" (*ED* 4 417). It was the diary which guaranteed and created her intellectual and spiritual independence. Otto Rank was very well aware of this and sought to deprive her of her diary for, otherwise, she would never "surrender" to him. For Miller, the issue was more delicate, since it was deeply connected to Anaïs Nin's position as a writer. In a letter to her, in 1933, he wrote:

> I almost wish to implore you to stop writing anymore in your journal and concentrate all your energies on the task ahead of you. The hours that go to the journal are an evasion, fundamentally, of the imminent, the ever-impeding problem—that of mastering your medium, of becoming the artist you are. (*LP* 217-18)

At the time, Anaïs Nin had published *D. H. Lawrence: An Unprofessional Study* but had not yet emerged as a novelist. Miller earnestly tried to be her "teacher," to make an artist out of her, just as Anaïs Nin played midwife to the birth of Henry Miller, the writer. Yet, in spite of all the advice and warnings from her "teachers" and her own struggles to become a recognized writer, she was unable to give up her "vice." Even at the age of fifty-six she was forced to note: "I am imprisoned in the diary. Wherever I begin, it leads me back to characters already painted... Where am I?" (*D* 6 191) She remained a bad student of "Literature"; she dropped out of the formal school of Literature, as she had at the age of sixteen dropped out of formal education. She admitted that she was a "failure as a writer" (*D* 5 106). In his excellent essay on Nin's diary, "Un Être Étoilique," Henry Miller touches upon an interesting point. "In a profound sense," he writes, "this *is* the work of art which never gets written—because the artist whose task it is to create it never gets born" (Être 13).

Anaïs Nin seems like a stubborn child, resisting to be born. She remains in the matrix, a cradle of creation, perpetually in the process of becoming. Perhaps she knows that "the Law of the Father" rules, as Jacques Lacan puts it, and that she will be forced to speak His language.

In the end, in her usual manner, she declines to be anything but Anaïs Nin. She may not deserve to be called a "genuine" writer; she certainly is non-standard. Yet the difference between a "major" and a "minor" poet should not be a matter of "greatness," between "great" and "less great." A minor poet may have a field of her own, a network of inner streets too intricate for a "major" poet to follow. The original meaning of the word "baroque" is a "flawed pearl." Should we call Anaïs Nin a "baroque" artist, with all her possibilities and limitations?

In his pioneering critical study of Anaïs Nin in 1968, Oliver Evans assumed that in her *Diary* Anaïs Nin had been completely honest. "If a diary has any value, it is that, for on any other basis it simply could not justify itself."[16] On the other hand, Nancy Scholar repeatedly casts doubts on the *Diary*'s truthfulness, sincerity, and authenticity.[17] In my opinion, neither attitude seems adequate as literary criticism. It is obvious that written words, diaries or documentaries should acquire some of the attributes of fiction, but I do not assume that this threatens the work's authenticity or the author's sincerity. After all, we are not checking facts, we are reading a work of art.

Anaïs Nin, it is *true,* stresses her "excessive need of truth" (*D* 1 290), her "devouring passion for reality" (*D* 1 332), yet the truth she sought so excessively and devouringly must be differentiated from mere factuality. We can easily imagine, moreover, that a person craving truth so exorbitantly is suffering from its absence, from uncertainty, or perhaps because the world of her imagination is so immense that she needs to balance it with a sense of "truth." Anaïs Nin calls the work of a diarist "the second tasting of life" (*D* 1 73).

But in her case, it happens more than twice. There is, first, the original, handwritten text; then comes the typed manuscript; finally, the edited and published version. In this process she relived and recreated her life, like a ruminant. To rewrite her life, to fill in and reconsider, obsessionally, was an effort perhaps to "realize" her life. The diary was both a disease and a cure.

Anaïs Nin also is quite aware of the fictionalism of the diary. She has a sense of what she leaves out and embellishes. When she rereads her childhood diary and finds out how little Anaïs was idolizing her parents, she decided that "it was fiction" (*WS* 151), and she tells Henry Miller "the journal is therefore a lie" (*H&J* 113).

Even early on, Anaïs Nin treated her diary as a work of art. At seventeen, she writes that she loves the diary "because a creator always loves his creation, like a mother her children" (*ED* 2 55). At twenty-eight she asserts: "Perhaps I do not exist except as a fantastic character in this story" (*ED* 4 480).

Many years later, when she was searching for a publisher for the *Diary,* she received a letter of polite rejection from a New York publisher stating that the manuscript "reads almost like a loosely constructed novel," that he expected more forthrightness, the "real" feeling, and that he was not certain that it was commercial enough (*D* 6 383).

I believe that the fictional, or novel-like, quality of the *Diary* does not impair what Anaïs Nin regarded as "the naked truth." There is a phase in which one undresses oneself in elaborate dressing. In that sense, *The Diary of Anaïs Nin* might well be regarded as a literary striptease. Her husband, her lovers, are implied but not clearly identified (and, according to her last will and testament, these issues are being unveiled in the posthumous publication of the previously "unpublishable" parts).

When Anaïs Nin, in the 1950s, launched her project of a "continuous novel—which eventually became *Cities of the Interior*—her intention, immensely influenced by Proust, was ambitious and experimental. But the idea of a "continuous novel" might be more properly applied to the *Diary.*

Anaïs Nin is the name of a strenuous will, or of a megalomaniacal desire, to transform a self, a life, into a story, a fiction, even a myth.

In her book, *Le Journal Intime,* Beatrice Didier maintains that the publication of the diary is not a threat to distort the quality of the writing but is its own logical inevitability. "The impasse of the diary's maternal universe," she writes, "can be solved through its birth... The psychoanalytical therapy that diary-writing can achieve is completed on the day of its publication."[18] Anaïs Nin's case seems to prove the correctness of this assertion.

Nearly three decades passed between Henry Miller's first public applause for the diary in T. S. Eliot's magazine, *The Criterion,* in 1937, and the first publication of *The Diary of Anaïs Nin* in 1966. During that time, Anaïs Nin, the diarist, became a legendary figure, while Anaïs Nin, the novelist, remained unaccepted, was given, as she wrote, the "solitary cell treatment" (*D* 5 214). We do not hesitate today to affirm that the *Diary* is her major work, but quite a few malicious reviews of her novels during this period undoubtedly were out of balance. (At the same time, her hypersensitivity to criticism might be considered her weakness as a writer.)

During all these years, the publication of the *Diary,* nevertheless, had been an ongoing issue. The "self-contradictory" Henry Miller, who once had tried to destroy the diary, had become one of its most enthusiastic promoters. To Anaïs Nin he wrote in 1941:

> You will be accepted all right, and royally, when your magnum opus appears. That is the Diary... Don't put up a fight for your minor efforts. Concentrate all your efforts on the big thing... You've made the most difficult sacrifice one can make—to squelch your own work. It's like trying to hide a natural child. (*LP* 339-40)

In 1933, he had urged William Bradley, a literary agent in Paris:

> Can you be certain what you find uninteresting will not appeal to thousands, perhaps millions of others?... I am thinking of the work as if it were actually launched. I am thinking of the Japanese reader, the Hindu reader, the Spanish reader, the Scandinavian reader... I am thinking of the reader to come in the year 2000 A.D. (*LP* 201)

For Anaïs Nin, these thirty years were years of inner conflict. Though she admits that her novels have emerged from siftings of the diary, that her fictions were "outcroppings" from her "magnum opus," her original ambition had been to be recognized as a novelist. It is unlikely that she planned to be a renowned diarist as she has been, from the start. Publication of any part of the lifelong diary involved many problems, "many human, ethical constrictions" (*D* 7 187). She was afraid, too, of being exposed to the world, to leave the comforting shelter of the diary-womb. Just before the impending publication of *The Diary of Anaïs Nin,* she dreamed she was struck by lethal radiation (*D* 6 378). She feared being hurt by the malicious eyes of the world, and of hurting others by her revelations. There was also her own sense of guilt about various aspects of her life. The taboo-breaking Anaïs was still a woman haunted by feelings of guilt. But the need to emerge was stronger, "as the snake pushing out of its old skin" (*D* 6 380). If she had failed her second birth as a novelist, she had to try it again as a diarist. The too-long-postponed birth of an artist was to be achieved with the diary.

"I am like a new woman," she wrote, "born with the publication of the diary" (*D* 7 35). Suddenly, the newborn Anaïs, who had been suffering from the "solitary cell treatment," was meeting the world. Originally begun as a letter, publication of the diary once again made it a letter, not to the lost father but to the world. "The journalists ask me if I am still writing in the *Diary*. I answered yes automatically, but one day I realized that it was not true. The *Diary* has become a correspondence with the world" (*D* 7 228).

The final decade of Anaïs Nin's life was filled with letters and lectures, which prompted some people to call her a "cult" figure. Yet for Anaïs Nin it was not only her own discovering of the world, it also was her being discovered by other women. She received letters from women in all walks of life who identified with her, who wrote "it is *my* journal," who confessed their own problems, their loneliness and lack of confidence. Her diary, Anaïs believed, had made them "eloquent" (*WS* 163).

The publication of *The Diary of Anaïs Nin* certainly was timely: the women's movement was on the rise (though, from a feminist point of view, Anaïs Nin turned out to be a controversial figure). Those who had never spoken before began to feel a voice within, yearning to be articulated. If it was achieved through the *Diary,* it should be applauded as a real feat that would validate Anaïs Nin's own words: "I write like a medium" (*D* 4 93). An artist, of course, can serve as a medium, a catalyst—which had been Anaïs Nin's ambition as well. But when we remember that she used to be (and still is?) criticized and sometimes attacked for being personal, subjective, and narcissistic, it seems rather ironic.

The *Diary*'s publication and its consequences convinced Anaïs Nin that an artist can go "through and beyond the self," and that she had done it (*D* 7 288). It seems an inordinately happy denouement, even if her saying that she had reached "a collective emotional identity" may be somewhat optimistic (*WS* 163). It is understandable that after decades of isolation—"America tried to kill me as a writer, with indifference, with insults" (*D* 5 157)—Anaïs Nin became euphoric. But it is certain, at least, that the publication of the *Diary* brought her a reconciliation with the world which was inevitable, since her diary therapy was completed on the very day of its publication.

Notes

1 Reprinted in *The Mystic of Sex and other Writings*. Edited and with a Preface by Gunther Stuhlmann (Santa Barbara, CA: Capra Press, 1995), p. 13.

2 Harriet Zinnes, "The Fiction of Anaïs Nin," in *A Casebook on Anaïs Nin*. Edited by Robert Zaller (New York: New American Library, 1974), p. 35.

3 *The Diary of Anaïs Nin, Volume Four, 1944-1947*. Edited and with a Preface by Gunther Stuhlmann (New York: Harcourt Brace Jovanovich, 1974), p. 178. All subsequent citations from the seven *Diary* volumes are given in the text as (*D*).

4 Koji Nakata, "Letter from Japan: Unity and Chaos," in *ANAIS: An International Journal*, Volume 4, 1986, p. 135. Subsequent citations are given in the text as (*A*).

5 Edmund Wilson, Review of *Under a Glass Bell, The New Yorker*, April 1, 1944, cited in *Casebook, op. cit.*, p. 3.

6 Benjamin Franklin V and Duane Schneider, *Anaïs Nin—An Introduction*. (Athens, OH: Ohio University Press, 1979, p. 76).

7 Henry Miller, "Un Être Êtoilique," in *The Criterion* (London, #17, 1937), cited in *Casebook, op. cit.*, p. 8. Subsequent citations are given in the text as (Être).

8 Anaïs Nin, *A Woman Speaks: The Lectures, Seminars, and Interviews of Anaïs Nin*. Edited by Evelyn J. Hinz (Athens, OH: The Swallow Press, 1975), p. 168. Subsequent citations are given in the text as (*WS*).

9 *The Early Diary of Anaïs Nin*. Four volumes, 1914-1931 (New York: Harcourt Brace Jovanovich, 1978-1985), Volume 4, p. 414. All subsequent citations from the four volumes are given in the text as (*ED*).

10 *The Novel of the Future*. (Athens, OH: The Swallow Press, 1968, 1986), pp. 84-85.

11 Sigmund Freud, "Beyond the Pleasure Principle," in Volume 18 of *The Standard Edition of the Complete Psychological Works*. Edited by James Strachey (London: Hogarth Press, 23 Volumes, 1964-1966), p. 15.

12 Anaïs Nin, *Children of the Albatross*, in *Cities of the Interior*. (Athens, OH: The Swallow Press, 1959), p. 203.

[13] Anaïs Nin, *Winter of Artifice.* (Athens, OH: Swallow Press, 1974), p. 60.

[14] *Anaïs Nin Observed: From a Film Portrait of a Woman as Artist.* Edited by Robert Snyder (Chicago, IL: The Swallow Press, 1976), p 98.

[15] *The Four-Chambered Heart,* in *Cities in the Interior, op. cit.,* p. 335.

[16] Oliver Evans, *Anaïs Nin.* (Carbondale, IL: Southern Illinois UP, 1968), p. 4.

[17] Nancy Scholar, *Anaïs Nin.* (Boston: Twayne Publishers, 1984), pp. 26-30.

[18] Beatrice Didier, *Le Journal Intime.* (Paris: Presse Universitaire, 1976), p. 136.

Mako Idemitsu

The Diary of Anaïs Nin
Excerpts from the book "What a Woman Made"

In the fall of 1967, the writer Anaïs Nin invited me to lunch with her at her home in Silver Lake, east of Hollywood. In her published diary, this event is described under the title "Lunch with Mako." *The Diary of Anaïs Nin*, first published in English in 1966, is a voluminous work that she began writing at the age of 11 in 1914 and continued to write for more than 70 years of her life. Since its first publication in English in 1966, the volume of the diary has been enormous. But only three years of the decades-long work of the diary, during the period of 1931-34, have been published in Japanese.

I understood what Anaïs was thinking on that lunch day as follows. Japanese women, including myself, who were married to Americans at the time made such decisions in the hope that they would be liberated. But they cannot be liberated. True liberation, she said, must come from their inner world. She only uses the English word "liberate" and does not tell what we need to be liberated from. But I believe, based on the content of the conversation I had with her, that it is liberation from the traditional values toward women of the society in which we were born and raised. I, too, wrote about the same day in my journal.

> Anaïs and I had lunch together. She was wearing a black and white dress and earrings. She was elegantly dressed, free from preconceived notions of day or night. Her figure and the view of Silver Lake from the living room. And the cloudy sky. The sun was shining slightly. The white and gray sky blended together so beautifully that I felt as if I had left California and arrived in a foreign country.
>
> My conversation with her was about Spanish women, Japanese women, the difficulty for women to be independent in society, and my autocratic father. We also talked about my surroundings. It was nothing special, but it was the first spiritual exchange I had had in a long time, and the atmosphere was like a refreshing autumn breeze. I was nervously smoking my cigarette, though.

I feel embarrassed. We had a discussion about women's independence. While I foolishly thought it was nothing so special, Anaïs uncovered the problems of Japanese women out of the same conversation. She was right. I escaped from the patriarchal home in which I was born and raised and the Japanese society that seeks to bind women to traditional values. I was not particularly conscious that marrying an American would liberate me, but I cannot deny that somewhere in my heart I had that desire.

I first heard about Anaïs Nin when I overheard the writer Henry Miller say at a dinner table that of her many works, the *Diary* was the best. I immediately bought its English edition and read it, neck and neck with a dictionary. I was deeply moved, as if my soul resonated with it. I asked my friend Bernard Forrest to introduce me to Anaïs when I found out that she was one of his close friends. He immediately invited me to dinner with her. In the hills above Beverly Hills, Bernard lived alone in a mountain house nestled in nature, looking forward to treating his guests to homemade English cuisine.

Anaïs was graceful as she walked down the high-ceilinged cobblestone corridor with the sound of rustling robes, which reminded me of the elegance of European aristocracy in the English atmosphere of the house. She stared at me with her big, shiny eyes and held out her hand gently. I had no idea at the time that she was in her sixties, the same generation as my mother, who was a grandmother in both name and reality. It is shocking to think about it now. Her presence transcended her age. Anaïs, her partner Rupert Pole, Sam [Francis] and I were the only guests. We sat facing each other in a quiet living room surrounded by tropical plants and flowers. At such dinners, there is usually a lot of empty banter, as if we were afraid of awkwardness or interruption, but the five of us, including Bernard as host, did not like that. There was a pleasant tension in the air, even though silence tended to dominate the room. It was as if each of us had a fishing line in front of us. Through that line, there was communication beyond words.

After that, Anaïs and I invited and were invited by each other. One evening when I invited Anaïs and Rupert over for dinner, something happened. Apart from Anaïs and Rupert, I invited only two couples whom I had carefully selected from among my acquaintances after much thought and consideration on my own, hoping that they would get along well with one other. But I was wrong. They were mean and aggressive toward Anaïs. I could not understand what they were talking about volubly, but when Anaïs, who seemed to have a different opinion, tried to open her mouth, they interrupted her. I could tell that what they were saying made her uncomfortable, even if I didn't understand what exactly they were saying. In such a situation, the host should be the one to try to create a positive atmosphere in the place, but Sam did not seem to be interested in playing that kind of role. He kept his arms folded and looked like he was just going to leave it at that. I was perplexed. Anaïs stopped dealing with people who made no attempt to hide their hostility toward her. They all fell silent.

She picked up a child's sandal left on the couch and stared at it. She seemed to be in deep thought. I wondered what she was thinking, and I thought of the small sandal in her hand and the young child she might have given birth to. I thought of the stillborn girl she had given birth to in Paris decades earlier. I recall a chapter from her work of diary in which she was talking to a baby in her belly.

"You should not be thrust into this black world, in which even the greatest joys are tainted with pain, in which we are slaves to material forces." He kicked and stirred. (*The Diary of Anaïs Nin*, Vol. 1: 1931-1934)

I saw a vision of the child on her lap, a transparent figure illuminated by the pale purple sunset. At that moment, she beckoned me over. Come here, she gestured. I sat down beside her and placed my hand on her knee. Her soft hands wrapped around mine. I apologized in my heart for inviting such terrible people, but her warmth seemed as if to speak to me, that it was not my fault and that I should not have to go through the pain.

On another occasion, I witnessed Anaïs being attacked again. It was when I went to a gathering to listen to her talk with my friends from a women's consciousness-raising group. Many women were gathered in a large living room of a luxurious house in an upscale residential area. In the center of the room, she was sitting elegantly and gracefully in a dress that hung softly at her feet, and she smiled when she saw me enter the room with my friends. Usually on such occasions, I knew that I should greet her personally, but my shyness prevented me from doing so. I don't remember the details, but she began to talk about women expressing themselves, creating, being an artist, etc. The soft, lovely voice was like a beautiful melody. Everyone listened quietly.

Suddenly, a harsh, malicious female voice rang out. She probably said something like this while shouting, "What do you think of those women who have to engage in physical labor for a living?" I looked toward the voice. A young woman in a white blouse and jeans, her blonde hair tied back in a loose bun, her back straight, was looking at

Anaïs with a confident look in her eyes that said, "I am right and you are wrong." She looked like a member of the Christian women's organizations. When Anaïs tried to open her mouth, the woman interrupted her in a sharp voice, asking a similar question in different words. And so it went again and again. It was strange that no one, including the owner of the house, said anything. Finally, Anaïs gave the appearance that she no longer had anything to say and walked away. No one followed her, and the sound of the door slamming violently shut is still ringing in my ears nearly thirty years later. The people gathered there began chatting amongst themselves, and the young woman who had been relentlessly questioning them had somehow disappeared.

Later, after returning to Japan, I learned that Anaïs had entered a period of fighting against illness. When I returned to California for summer vacations, I contacted Anaïs, because I wanted her to show my first 16mm film *Woman's House*. But her illness was serious and the time went by without being able to see her. She passed away in 1977.

A few years later, I came up with the idea of placing a monitor inside a screen and projecting what was going on in the character's mind. With this technique, I began to produce works on the theme of archetypes, one of the concepts of Jungian psychology. In the creative process, the subject matter changed to family and women's issues. In my most recent work, I depict the process of imprinting women's roles as they are born and raised, and how this imprinting becomes the reason for their self-sacrifice. I have tried to visualize the inner world of human beings.

I wonder what Anaïs, who had been exploring the inner world and pointing out that the duties and roles of womanhood are embedded throughout the generations, would feel and think if she were alive and saw my work. I fondly recall when she found out that I had started filmmaking, she took the trouble to find me at a party and encouraged me, saying, "This is what I wanted to do, too."

—Translated by Asami Watanabe

Masako Hara (Meio)

The Last Visit with Anaïs Nin

When I arrived in Los Angeles last December to visit Anaïs Nin, I was informed that her condition had worsened drastically. In addition to the pain caused by her tumor, which was no longer curable, she was experiencing all kinds of suffering due to the malfunctioning of her internal organs. Also, she suffered from repeated attacks of depression. After several months of this condition, Anaïs Nin gave up on hospital treatment and returned home.

"This will be Anaïs's last fight. If she had been a person of normal will, she would have given up on living, but Anaïs's strong fighting spirit has kept her alive this long. It's a tragic sight," Rupert, her husband, said in the car.

I had just lost my father to a cerebral hemorrhage two months earlier. He was seventy-three years old, the same age as Anaïs. When I learned that I would soon lose Anaïs as well, I began to feel a sense of destiny. I had found in Anaïs Nin's literature the theme of the psychological conflict between father and daughter, and it had an immeasurable influence on my thinking about my own problems. The overlap and conflict between my father's dying face, wrought in agony, as he drew his last breath only three hours after the seizure, and the white face of Anaïs Nin, who continued to struggle with unending pain, began to take on a symbolic meaning that was more than a mere coincidence.

Now with her very thin body Anaïs's final struggle seemed so appropriate for her. She had struggled all her life with various obstacles in order to live and mature, and now she was facing a pain she could share with no one. The *Diary of Anaïs Nin* is nothing less than a record of her lifelong struggle with an indominable will. The loss of her father, which motivated the *Diary*, unrequited love, long and patient training and disappointment as a writer, and the severe aftereffects of a neurological disorder. I had just been moved to read in her *Diary*, Volume Six that she had to suffer from the unexplainable anxiety of the psychiatric problems she thought she had conquered in her twenties but actually they had taken her almost to old age. However, she boldly faced each obstacle one by one.

People expected a "womanly" gentleness, grace, and softness from visibly sensitive Anaïs Nin, who always insisted on writing "as a woman, and only as a woman."

She never failed them. However, if asked to name only one "womanly" quality about her, I would answer "strength" without hesitation. The style of her *Diary* is surprisingly powerful, as she herself defined it as "a long study of the psychological obstacles which have prevented woman from her fullest evolution and flowering" ("Notes on Feminism" 25). In her writing style, she pursued "womanhood" and writing to overcome all the obstacles to it. I know of no other example in which "womanhood" and "strength" are so synonymous as in hers.

"I hope you won't be shocked to see Anaïs. She's become so weak that she doesn't really want to see anyone," Rupert said. Anaïs herself could barely speak anymore, but she could listen, so a fifteen-minute visit was arranged. I knew that this would be my last visit with Anaïs, so I had a lot that I wanted to talk about with her. I wanted to talk about the just-released sixth volume of her *Diary* and her essay collection, *In Favor of the Sensitive Man*, about the parts of her personal life, especially those that were not written in her *Diary*, and about my recent views on her literature.

But what Anaïs Nin wanted most from me was to know if the first volume of her *Diary* was selling well in Japan. More than any other country, she hoped that her *Diary* would be well received in Japan because Japan is the country that gave birth to diaries as literature, and especially women's diaries, a thousand years ago; she had deep faith in the sensitivity of Japanese readers who still have that tradition. It was a natural expectation, given the enthusiasm with which she is now read and studied by young American men and women. I could not bring myself to tell her honestly that her works, including the *Diary*, have been translated into Japanese, but only a few people have read them. As the translator of the *Diary*, I doubt that Anaïs Nin will ever find the same readership in Japan as she did in the United States. This is because book sales are not a literary evaluation but a sociological phenomenon. I am more interested in what supports Anaïs Nin's popularity in the U.S.

Anaïs Nin's greatest achievement as an American writer was to bring the feminine principle to America and American literature, where the masculine principle of power dominated. Her career as an American writer spanned three decades, but it did not truly begin until 1966, when she published the first volume of her *Diary*. The reason is that her main theme is always the strength of a woman, which is not only different from, but can even compete with, the strength of a man. In no other society is the strength of women so misunderstood and so unjustly undermined as in the United States. Men have feared it as an unexpected counterattack from the very nature they have conquered. But for this reason, as the feminist movement swept America, the *Diary* quickly began to be read like a scripture for women.

"Unjustly" associated with the feminist movement, Anaïs Nin wrote that for young women searching for their value as women, "To become man, or like man, is no solution. There is far too much imitation of man in the Women's Movement. That is merely the displacement of power. Woman's definitions of power should be different" ("Notes" 28). It has even come to serve as an ideologue calling for the establishment of feminine principles. But it was the inner confession of a daughter struggling to regain her father's lost love and to become a woman that truly captured the hearts of American women. Anaïs Nin's lengthy *Diary* is a constant questioning of how maturity is possible for the daughter in search of her lost father as in the myth of Pericles. The amplitude of Nin's soul attracted the anxious souls of women floating at the bottom of the feminist movement of the 1960s.

A sociologist theorizes that the feminist movement was triggered by the decline of male authority represented by the U.S. president. To borrow from Hideo Ohki's observation in his *Puritanism: The Psychological Structure of Modernization* that American democracy has its roots in Puritanism, "searching for the true father," and that the presidential election is a national "search for the father," the feminist movement is a "search for the true father by the daughters." The revolt of American daughters, like King Lear's daughters, which arose with the fall of their fathers' authority, has the structure of the myth of Pericles. Anaïs Nin and the feminist movement are thus united in their psychological motivation.

As Anaïs Nin says, "Each woman has to know herself, her problems, her obstacles… I want woman to realize she can be master of her own destiny" ("Notes" 27). She is a writer who has thus completed the myth of Pericles within herself, and for her, maturity means completing her internal destiny with her own hands. But to base one's problems and destiny on one's trauma of the loss of the father is to limit the relationship of love to that of father and daughter. In other words, that way, a woman cannot leave the daughter's position. If the father loses his authority or disappears, and the daughter is exposed to the insecurity of love, she can only rebel or become neurotic. And if she seeks her value and love only as a daughter, she will forever remain a wandering, anxious soul.

Daughter logic may liberate women from male authority, but it will not liberate them from anxiety, for it is rather the rationalization of anxiety itself.

The American feminist movement eventually faded away, exposing lesbianism, but interestingly, Freud pointed out that women's homo-sexuality reproduces the mother-daughter relationship. In other words, in Freudian terms, the daughter's rebellion conceals a craving for the mother's authority that is rooted in the so-called pre-Oedipus stage of maternal bondage, which is even lower than the stage of the search for the father. If the American women's movement cannot transcend the logic of the daughter, it is because America historically lacks the maternal principle, the tradition of women passed down from grand-mother to mother and from mother to daughter. There is no mother's authority over father's authority, no mother's logic over daughter's logic. America is essentially a father-daughter society. It matures men, but it fails to mature women. Anaïs Nin was the first writer to attempt to play the role of mother for wandering American daughters. But Nin herself, as her life symbolizes, could not transcend the logic of the daughter in her pursuit of femininity. If Anaïs Nin's literature, which shares the soul and breadth of American women, is to achieve the same fervor in Japan, it will be when the Japanese women rise in a daughters' revolt. Japan is still a society firmly supported in the logic of the mother. The path that leads women toward maturity is clear in the mother principle.

Anaïs Nin's *Diary* and her entire quest for "femininity" began with the failure of the love between father and daughter, according to her own self-interpretation. However, Freud points out in a chapter titled "The Feminine" that this extraordinary fixation on the lost father, the Oedipus complex that formed relatively late in life, was an escape from the failures of earlier relationships. Anaïs Nin's Periclesian psychodrama, then, is merely a form of escape from anxiety and its rational resolution, and the roots of her anxiety and fixation lie in another relationship. We should consider that the deepest trauma for Anaïs Nin is that of her original relationship with her mother. And all the problems related to "femininity" may stem not from her relationship with her father, but from her relationship with her mother. For identification with the mother is the beginning of femininity, and the rejection of the mother's authority causes the woman to flee to the father's construct. And when the father's love is rejected, the pain reminds her of that original sin of "mother-killer." The true drama of Anaïs Nin's soul may be the Puritan dialectic of the craving for the father's authority or the craving to be a "daughter of pleasure" (*A Spy in the House of Love* 99) worthy of the father's love, and thereby the guilt of rejecting the mother. Is true liberation from that possible only by rethinking the relationship not between father and daughter, but between mother and daughter?

I wanted to say all these things to Anaïs Nin at the end of my visit. How would she answer my questions? But when I began to ask Anaïs Nin about the relationship of her mother and her Puritanism, she, who had been listening with her eyes closed, suddenly raised one hand, interrupted me, and called for Rupert.

"Did you hear what she just said?"

"No, I didn't hear it. What was she talking about?"

Anaïs tried to say something, but shook her head, mumbled, "I'm tired, I'm so tired," and never spoke again. She was very old. Rupert told me, "Anaïs has suffered more than she should because she is a Puritan."

—*Translated by Atsuko Miyake*

Works Cited

Nin, Anaïs. "Notes on Feminism," *The Massachusetts Review.* vol. 13, no. 1/2, *Woman: An Issue* (Winter-Spring, 1972), pp. 25-28.

----. *A Spy in the House of Love.* Peter Owen, 1971.

Ohki, Hideo. *Puritanism: Kindaika no Seishinkouzo* (*Puritanism: The Psychological Structure of Modernization*). Chukoshinsho, 1968.

Shigeru Kashima

Imagination That Is Impure, Strange, and Demonic
A review of The Diary of Anaïs Nin, ed. and trans. Yuko Yaguchi

A naïs Nin is well-known for her *Diary* of forty thousand pages written from the age of eleven to seventy-three. When *The Diary of Anaïs Nin* was first translated into Japanese in 1974, however, we had no idea that it was a "created diary" rewritten by the diarist, which is now called the "Edited Diary." For instance, readers get the impression that Anaïs was single when she met Henry Miller. In reality, however, she lived in a suburban village near Paris as the young wife of a banker, Hugh Guiler. Her relations with psychoanalysts René Allendy and Otto Rank were disguised as well.

These facts came to light when the *Unexpurgated Diary of Anaïs Nin, from a "Journal of Love,"* covering the years 1931 to 1939, was published posthumously in accordance with the wishes of the diarist. (Its first volume, *Henry and June,* was adapted to film by Philip and Rose Kaufman). In it, Anaïs Nin described with no reserve fiery sex with Miller and intimate relations with Allendy and Rank. As a written record of sexuality penned by a female author, nothing so far has come close to the *Unexpurgated Diary of Anaïs Nin.* (In Japanese we can read *Henry & June* and *Incest* from the series.)

What is this new translation of Nin's *Diary,* then? It consists of selections from three volumes of the *Early Diary*, which were published between the "Edited" and the "Unexpurgated" series, and all seven volumes of the "Edited Diary." Does this imply that it is the same as the already-translated "Edited Diary" except for the "Early Diary" part? It is exactly this point where the complexity of *The Diary of Anaïs Nin* stands out. Because of the enormous quantity of the English titles, great craft was required in the editing, and the result is this new *Diary of Anaïs Nin,* which is remarkably distinct from the old translation. The editor [Yuko Yaguchi] adeptly included an entry from February 3, 1928:

> I have been living through queer days...feeling myself split into two women—one, kind, loyal, pure, thoughtful; the other, restless and impure, acting strangely, loosened, wandering, seeking life and tasting all of it without fear, without convictions, without restraint, without principle, a demon whom I will call "Imagy," after the origin of its curse, imagination.

Hence Anaïs Nin kept the "Diary of Imagy," while living a happy and comfortable life with her husband. But then appeared Henry Miller and his wife June, whom Miller called a "great liar."

As June walked towards me from the darkness of the garden into the light of the door, I saw for the first time the most beautiful woman on earth... I had never seen her until last night. Yet I knew long ago the phosphorescent color of her skin, her huntress profile, the evenness of her teeth.

In a word, Anaïs found "Imagy" in June, and vice versa. As a result, Henry was excluded from the female bond. "What is this powerful magic we create together and indulge in? ... What do June and I seek together that Henry does not believe in? Wonder wonder wonder."

When we read through the "Edited Diary" in this new translation, we come to realize that Nin rewrote her Diary not so much to deal with the privacy issue but to analyze her relationship with June more thoroughly. In this sense, the "Edited Diary," the first volume to be more specific, was the masterpiece by Anaïs Nin.

—*Translated by Yuko Yaguchi*

"Anaïs Nin's *Diary* and the Japanese Literary Diary Tradition" first appeared in *Mosaic* 11.2, 1978.

"Twittering Machine of Paradise" first appeared in *A Café in Space: The Anaïs Nin Literary Journal*, Vol. 1, 2003.

"Examining *Anaïs Nin no Shôjo Jidai*" first appeared in *A Café in Space: The Anaïs Nin Literary Journal*, Vol. 1, 2003.

"Glimpses of Present-Day Japanese Women," written in 1992, first appeared in *A Café in Space: The Anaïs Nin Literary Journal*, Vol. 2, 2004.

"Anaïs Nin as Father's Daughter" first appeared in *Mari Mori and Anaïs Nin*, Shincho-sha, 1997.

"Translating Anaïs Nin's *Incest* into Japanese" first appeared in *A Café in Space: The Anaïs Nin Literary Journal*, Vol. 1, 2003.

"Body Image in *House of Incest*" first appeared in *A Café in Space: The Anaïs Nin Literary Journal*, Vol. 2, 2004.

"A Woman of the Diary: Anaïs Nin" first appeared as Chapter IX of *Meikyu no Onnatachi* (*The Women of the Labyrinth*), 1981, Tokyo, TBS Britannica.

"A Spy in the House of Sexuality" first appeared in *A Café in Space: The Anaïs Nin Literary Journal*, Vol. 4, 2007.

This version of "Multiplying Women" first appeared in *A Café in Space: The Anaïs Nin Literary Journal*, Vol. 8, 2011.

"Interview with Lady Nobuko Albery" first appeared in *A Café in Space: The Anaïs Nin Literary Journal*, Vol. 15, 2018.

"The Text that Is the Writer" first appeared in *ANAIS: An International Journal*, Vol. 16, 1998.

"The Diary of Anaïs Nin" first appeared in *What a Woman Made: An Autobiography of a Film Artist*, Iwanami Shoten, 2003.

"The Last Visit with Anaïs Nin" first appeared in *Gakuto*, vol. 74, no. 3 in 1977.

"Book Review: Imagination That Is Impure, Strange, and Demonic" first appeared in the June 11, 2017 issue of *Mainichi Shinbun*, one of the three major national newspapers in Japan. Now it can be read in Kashima's book review site "All Reviews" https://allreviews.jp/review/33

NOTES ON CONTRIBUTORS

Catherine Vreeland (Broderick), Professor Emeritus of Kobe College, happily keeps up with Anaïs Nin in Japan news while editing and writing in the Pacific Northwest.

Mako Idemitsu is a renowned film artist, whose works are held at Museum of Modern Art and the Pompidou Center. Daughter of a Japanese oil titan, she moved to the U.S. in 1965 and started working as a film artist (with the encouragement from Anaïs Nin) while she was married to an established artist, Sam Francis.

Satoshi Kanazawa is Professor of Comparative Culture at Takasaki University of Commerce. He has translated some of Henry Miller's works into Japanese, including *The Colossus of Maroussi, The Air-Conditioned Nightmare*, and "Un Être Étoilique." His contribution here is a translated and revised version of an article that first appeared in the literary magazine *Suisei Tsushin* featuring Anaïs Nin, and later appeared in *A Café in Space*, Vol. 8. His books on popular culture include *American Films across the Color Line* and *Hip Hop Chronicle*.

Shigeru Kashima is a distinguished critic and translator of French literature. His copious titles of works include *I Want to Buy Horse Carriages!* (Suntory Literary Award), *I'd Rather Think Used Books More Important than Your Own Children* (Kodansha Essay Award), *Paris Manners by Occupation* (Yomiuri Literary Award), *On Passage*, *Strangers in Paris*. The last title, depicting expatriate writers in Paris, has chapters on Miller and Nin.

Masako Meio (Hara-Karatani) (1939-1995) was a Japanese writer and translator who wrote novels under the name of Masako Meio. She translated *The Diary of Anaïs Nin*, Vol. I and *The Novel of the Future*.

Atsuko Miyake is an adjunct lecturer at Kyoto University, translator of *Ladders to Fire*, co-translator of *Conversations with Anaïs Nin*, and author of several papers on Nin, including "Anaïs Nin's Words of Power and the Japanese Sybil Tradition" in *Anaïs Nin: Literary Perspectives*. She lives in Osaka, Japan.

Toru Nakamura is professor in the Faculty of Commerce at Chuo University, Japan. He is the translator of Henry Miller's *Book of Friends* and Michael North's *Reading 1922: A Return to the Scene of the Modern* (Oxford University Press, 1999).

Hidekatsu Nojima (1930-2009) was born in Tokyo, Japan, and was a literary critic and a scholar of English and American Literature. He was a professor of English Literature at Ochanomizu Women's University. One of his groundbreaking achievements was his translation into Japanese of *Nightwood* by Djuna Barnes as *Yoru no Mori*, which was published in 1982 and dedicated to Yukio Mishima.

Yoshiho Satake is Associate Professor at Aoyama Gakuin University, Japan. Her research interests include corpus linguistics and English language teaching.

Kazuko Sugisaki is Professor Emeritus of Gifu Seitoku Gakuen University, Japan, and a former trustee of The Anaïs Nin Trust. She is the translator of *Henry and June*, *Incest*, and *Linotte*, and a co-translator of *Delta of Venus*. She also authored *California Bound: A Wagon Train's Journey of Two Thousand Miles*.

Asami Watanabe (translator) is a professor in the Department of English and Cultures at Hokkai-Gakuen University.

Sumiko Yagawa (1931-2002), author of *Anaïs Nin no Shôjo Jidai* (*Anaïs Nin as a Young Girl*), was known as a translator of foreign literature for children (such as *Little Women* by Louisa May Alcott, *Alice's Adventures in Wonderland and Through the Looking-Glass* by Lewis Carroll, *The Happy Prince* and *Lord Arthur Savile's Crime* by Oscar Wilde, *The Snow Goose* and *Snowflake* by Paul Gallico, and *Juggler's Tale* by Michael Ende) and as an essayist. Her book on Nin helped Japanese readers become familiar with the diarist.

Yuko Yaguchi is a professor of English and Gender Studies at Niigata University of International and Information Studies. She has translated the Paris edition of *The Winter of Artifice* and *The Diary of Anaïs Nin* into Japanese. Her latest book, *Anaïs Nin's Paris Revisited: The English-*

French Bilingual Edition is now available on Kindle at Amazon. She is currently working on a monograph on Nin.

Toyoko Yamamoto is the head of the Anaïs Nin Society in Japan, founded by Kazuko Sugisaki. Toyoko has an M. A. in English and American Literature from Boston College and is a lecturer at Tokyo Woman's Christian University, teaching American literary works and culture. She attended the first Anaïs Nin International Conference in 1994 where she presented "Anaïs Nin's Femininity and the Banana Yoshimoto Phenomenon." She has written several articles on Nin, including "Anaïs Nin's Mobility: Traveling and Other Cultures" for *Essays and Studies in British & American Literature*, Vol. 60, 2014. She participated in the Japanese book *Anaïs Nin's Life and Works: A Comprehensive Guide* and collaborated in the Japanese translation of *Conversations with Anaïs Nin*. She has translated *In Favor of the Sensitive Man and other essays*, *Children of the Albatross*, and William Claire's poem, "Thinking of Anaïs Nin" in "Rendezvous with Two Languages," *A Café in Space*, Vol. 3, 2005. Her translation of *The Four-Chambered Heart* is to be published in the spring of 2023.

ALSO AVAILABLE FROM SKY BLUE PRESS

A Joyous Transformation: The Unexpurgated Diary of Anaïs Nin, 1966-1977 by Anaïs Nin (forthcoming)

The Diary of Others: The Unexpurgated Diary of Anaïs Nin, 1955-1966 by Anaïs Nin (print, ebook)

Trapeze: The Unexpurgated Diary of Anaïs Nin, 1947-1955 by Anaïs Nin (print, ebook)

Mirages: The Unexpurgated Diary of Anaïs Nin, 1939-1947 by Anaïs Nin (print, ebook)

Reunited: The Correspondence of Anaïs and Joaquín Nin 1933-1940 by Anaïs Nin and Joaquín Nin (print, ebook)

Auletris: Erotica by Anaïs Nin (print, ebook, audiobook)

The Quotable Anaïs Nin by Anaïs Nin (two volumes; print, ebook)

The Portable Anaïs Nin by Anaïs Nin, ed. Benjamin Franklin V (print, ebook)

Letters to Lawrence Durrell 1937-1977 by Anaïs Nin (print, ebook)

D. H. Lawrence: An Unprofessional Study by Anaïs Nin (ebook)

House of Incest by Anaïs Nin (ebook)

The Winter of Artifice: 1939 Paris Edition by Anaïs Nin (print, ebook)

Winter of Artifice: American Edition by Anaïs Nin (ebook)

Under a Glass Bell by Anaïs Nin (ebook)

Stella by Anaïs Nin (ebook)

Ladders to Fire by Anaïs Nin (ebook)

Children of the Albatross by Anaïs Nin (ebook)

The Four-Chambered Heart by Anaïs Nin (ebook)

A Spy in the House of Love by Anaïs Nin (ebook)

Seduction of the Minotaur by Anaïs Nin (ebook)

Cities of the Interior by Anaïs Nin (ebook)

Collages by Anaïs Nin (ebook)

The Novel of the Future by Anaïs Nin (ebook)

Anaïs Nin: The Last Days, a Memoir by Barbara Kraft (ebook)

Henry Miller: The Last Days, a Memoir by Barbara Kraft (print, ebook)

Anaïs Nin's Lost World: Paris in Words and Pictures 1924-1939 by Britt Arenander (print, ebook)

Facts Matter: Essays on Issues Regarding Anaïs Nin by Benjamin Franklin V (print, ebook)

Anaïs Nin Character Dictionary and Index to Diary Excerpts by Benjamin Franklin V (print, ebook)

A Café in Space: The Anaïs Nin Literary Journal, Vol. 1 by Anaïs Nin, Janet Fitch, Lynette Felber… (print, ebook)

A Café in Space: The Anaïs Nin Literary Journal, Vol. 2 by Anaïs Nin, Benjamin Franklin V, Masako Meio… (print, ebook)

A Café in Space: The Anaïs Nin Literary Journal, Vol. 3 by Anaïs Nin, Gunther Stuhlmann, Richard Pine, James Clawson… (print, ebook)

A Café in Space: The Anaïs Nin Literary Journal, Vol. 4 by Anaïs Nin, Alan Swallow, John Ferrone, Yuko Yaguchi… (print, ebook)

A Café in Space: The Anaïs Nin Literary Journal, Vol. 5 by Anaïs Nin, Duane Schneider, Sarah Burghauser… (print, ebook)

A Café in Space: The Anaïs Nin Literary Journal, Vol. 6 by Anaïs Nin, Joaquín Nin, Tristine Rainer, Christie Logan… (print, ebook)

A Café in Space: The Anaïs Nin Literary Journal, Vol. 7 by Anaïs Nin, John Ferrone, Kim Krizan, Tristine Rainer…

A Café in Space: The Anaïs Nin Literary Journal, Vol. 8 by Anaïs Nin, Benjamin Franklin V, Anita Jarczok, Kim Krizan… (print, ebook)

A Café in Space: The Anaïs Nin Literary Journal, Vol. 9 by Anaïs Nin, Anita Jarczok, Joel Enos… (print, ebook)

A Café in Space: The Anaïs Nin Literary Journal, Vol. 10 by Anaïs Nin, Benjamin Franklin V, Kim Krizan, William Claire, Erin Dunbar… (print, ebook)

A Café in Space: The Anaïs Nin Literary Journal, Vol. 11 by Anaïs Nin, Henry Miller, Alfred Perlès, John Tytell… (print, ebook)

A Café in Space: The Anaïs Nin Literary Journal, Vol. 12 by Anaïs Nin, Kim Krizan, Benjamin Franklin V… (print, ebook)

A Café in Space: The Anaïs Nin Literary Journal, Vol. 13 by Anaïs Nin, Barbara Kraft, Danica Davidson… (print, ebook)

A Café in Space: The Anaïs Nin Literary Journal, Vol. 14 by Anaïs Nin, Jessica Gilbey, Joaquín Nin-Culmell… (print, ebook)

A Café in Space: The Anaïs Nin Literary Journal, Vol. 15 by Anaïs Nin, Rupert Pole, Steven Reigns… (print, ebook)

A Café in Space: The Anaïs Nin Literary Journal, Anthology 2003-2018 (print, ebook)

ANAIS: An International Journal, Anthology 1983-2001 (print, ebook)

www.ingramcontent.com/pod-product-compliance
Lightning Source LLC
Chambersburg PA
CBHW030322020726
47493CB00004B/1127